Topics in Judaica Librarianship

Topics in Judaica Librarianship

David B. Levy
2019

Dedicated to my beloved daughter Ruth, may you be zoche l'gadol l'torah, l'chuppah ul' maasim tovim.

יְשִׂמֵךְ אֱלֹהִים כְּשָׂרָה רִבְקָה רָחֵל וְלֵאָה

יְבָרֶךְ אֲדֹנָי וְיִשְׁמְרֶךָ

יָאֵר אֲדֹנָי פָּנָיו אֵלֶיךָ וִיחֻנֶּךָּ

יִשָּׂא אֲדֹנָי פָּנָיו אֵלֶיךָ וְיָשֵׂם לְךָ שָׁלוֹם

License Notes

Educational institutions may reproduce, copy and distribute portions of this book for non-commercial purposes without charge, provided appropriate citation of the source, in accordance with the Talmudic *dictum* of Rabbi Elazar in the name of Rabbi Hanina (*Megilah* 15a): "anyone who cites a teaching in the name of its author brings redemption to the world."

Copyright 2019 David B. Levy

ISBN: 978-0-359-87980-9

Table of Contents

1   Preface

6   Chapter 1 The importance of Judaica Genealogical Research as a subdiscipline of Judaica Librarianship: Methods, Strategies, and ancient genealogical archives to serve in the Ma'amadot

23   Chapter 2 Censorship of Rambam's *Sefer HaMadah and Moreh Nevukhim* (for external censorship for instance of Talmudim see chapter 4)

33   Chapter 3 The Making of the JE (1901=1906) and EJ (1972)

61   Chapter 4 Rabbinic Reverence, Love, and Cherishing of Texts: People of the Books

97   Chapter 5 Ethics, Politics, Hermeneutics, and Theology of Hebraica Translations: Is the Library of Tower of Babel?

124 Chapter 6 Reel Librarians: The Image and stereotype of the librarian and Jewish librarian in Film, TV, and literature

190 List of Selected Publications

Preface

Overview Summary

The essays published in this set on Judaica Librarianship stem largely from papers delivered at the Association of Jewish libraries annual conferences. The volumes are organized within the rubric of: (1) History of Judaica libraries (Jewish Textual Collections), (2) Ethical/Halakhic concerns of Judaica Librarianship in the online environment, (3) Topics in Judaica Librarianship, (4) Long versions of book reviews in field of Judaica Librarianship, and (5) Genealogical research as a subfield of Judaica Librarianship: Researching the origins of the Rav Menachem Mendel Gluskin (ztsl) family back 13 generations in Eastern Europe.

The history section includes a scope from (a), antiquity, (b) to second temple, (c) dead sea scroll scriptorium, (d) medieval textual collections, (e) Renaissance, (f) on modern libraries via the prism of fourteen outstanding scholar librarians, and (g) the post-modern library that employs database construction, digitization, and web development, etc.

The second volume of essays under the category of: *Ethical and halakhiic concerns of the online environment* contains essays on (a) Topics of opening email and privacy, the question of erasing Hashem's name on a computer screen, issues of plagarism, etc. (b) women and the ethical use of the internet, (c) application of the Chofetz Chaim's *Isurei Loshon Ha-rah* ve Motzi shem rah, to the online environment, (d) The Ethics of Care- Reference Services at LCW, and (e) ethical use of technology and its risks.

The third volume of essays under the rubric of: *Topics in Judaica Librarianship,* includes chapters on (a) The image and stereotype of the librarian in general and Jewish librarian in particular, in film, literature, and TV, (b) Questions concerning translation of Jewish languages, as interpretation: Is the library a tower of Babel?, (c) why is Genealogical research as a sub discipline of Judaica librarianship so important, (d) Internal Censorship of Rambam's *Moreh haNevukhim and Sefer Mada* and external censorship of works such as the Talmudim, (e) The Making of the Jewish Encyclopedia (1901-1904) and the Encyclopedia Judaica (1972).

The fourth volume are long versions of various Judaica librarianship book reviews with a rif on what makes a good book review

The fifth volume is a study in genealogical research as a subdiscipline of Judaica librararianship on the Rav Menachem Mendel Gluskin family's roots 13 generations prior in Eastern Europe.

Acknowledgements

We would like to thank the Association of Jewish Libraries for permission to republish the contents of this volume. Chapter 1, titled "on the importance of Judaica Genealogical Research" awaits to be published at the upcoming AJL Chicago conference in 2020 as part of a longer study on methods, strategies, and techniques of genealogical research. Chapter 2 on Censorship of Rambam's Sefer Madah and Moreh HaNevukhim (the Maimonidean Controversy) was published in the 2000 AJL Proceedings for a conference that took place in Washington DC. [© 2000 AJL. Reprinted with permission]. Chapter 3 on "the Making of the Jewish Encyclopedia (JE) and Encyclopedia Judaica (EJ) " was previously published in the AJL 2002 Denver Proceedings [© 2002 AJL. Reprinted with permission]/ Chapter four titled, "Rabbinic Reverence, Love, and Cherishing of Texts" appeared in a section at the Charleston South Carolina AJL 2016 Proceedings [© 2016 AJL. Reprinted with permission]. Chapter 5 titled, "Ethics, Politics, Hermeneutics, and Theology of Hebraica Translations" appeared previously in the 2007 Scottsdale, Arizona AJL Proceedings [© 2007 AJL. Reprinted with permission]. Chapter 6 titled, "Reel Librarians appeared previously in the Boston AJL Proceedings from 2018 [© 2018 AJL. Reprinted with permission].

Chapter One

Why Judaica Genealogical Research Matters

A subfield of Judaica Librarianship

Interest in researching the ancestors of the Gluskin family is a personal quest not merely a genealogical project, but for historical clarity about the life of our previous family members in previous generations, in Eastern Europe, and their scholarly activities as part of a journey for MEMORY, as the Besht, notes, "Bizikranot yesh ha-geulah". We cannot do justice to the present unless we remember and learn from the noble deeds of our ancestors. Further we cannot know where we are going unless we know where once we have walked in generations before us. This teaches us to trust the future, remember the past, and live the present informed and guided by the light of the holy soul sparks that shine as glistening "names" in Gan Eden. My book is not so much one in search only of Yichus. It is a journey to uncover the misrat nefesh of our ancestors, for we are mere dwarfs in ruchnius, intellectual virtue, and moral and spiritual middot compared to our forefathers in Eastern Europe. We can only know where we are going if we walk by the light of their inspiring examples. I am not writing Hagagraphy.

Personally the academic example of research librarian Dr. Aryeh Vilsker who suffered greatly from persecution of Jews in Russia by the Communists1, is a role model I can only hope to emulate a tincture of, as Dr. Vilsker was a great research librarian beyond any measure of Judaica research librarians today and recent times. see AJL Charletesville, SC. Proceeedings at http://databases.jewishlibraries.org/node/51186   Dr. Vilsker orbits with great Jewish librarians such as Drs. Moritz Steinschneider, Alexander Marx, Umberto Cassutto, Gershom Scholem, Menachem Schmelzer, and Malachi Beit Ari, etc . Yet the models of rabbis in our ancestry the likes of Rav Menachem Mendel Gluskin who also suffered under the Communists (imprisoned 2x with his father in law Rabbi Eliezer Rabinowitz) and great Av bet dayanim such as Rabbi Aaron Gluskin of Paritch after Rabbi Hillel of Paritch, Rabbi Yehoshua Gluskin of Lviv, and Rabbi Moshe Zev Gluskin (a companion of the GRA) provide spiritual and moral/ethical examples as well as magnanimous greatness in the realm of intellect from which we have so much to learn from. We learn from parasha HaZinu:

זְכֹר יְמוֹת עוֹלָם, בִּינוּ שְׁנוֹת דֹּר-וָדֹר; {ס} שְׁאַל אָבִיךָ וְיַגֵּדְךָ, זְקֵנֶיךָ וְיֹאמְרוּ לָךְ

The importance of Genealogical Research

Thus the question arises why research Jewish genealogical roots? What is ultimately at stake? As per research of Dr. Rabbi Moshe Shualy (dissertation Dropsie College) Kohanide and Levitical families kept great care in preserving genealogical documentation of ancestry in order to serve in the beit HaMikdash as part of the process of the Mamadot, or the going up to Jerusalem from the outskirts and villages described in the mishnah as a ceremony whereby Kohanim and Leveim were rounded up with the accompaniment of music and procession, to go up to serve in the Jerusalem Temple in 24 rotations during the year. Each rotation (mamad) involved the elevation of 12 hallot from a marble table to a gold table to illustrate the process of elevating in kedushah.

The Beit HaMikdash archive of yichusin was finally destroyed by fire in 70 C.E. by the Romans (Jos.Wars 6:354). The Sanhedrin examined the purity of priestly descent, on the basis of genealogical tables (Megillat or Sefer Yuhasin) which are known to have been preserved in the Beit HaMikdash. In Yevamot 5:4 we read,

רבי שמעון בן עזאי אומר מצ א תי מגילת יוח סין בירושלים.

Further reference to genealogical documents is found in Tosefta Haggigah 2:9, 235; Yevamot 4:13, 49a-b. These documents of Yichus in the Beit HaMikdash at this time were guarded with great care. Josephus writes, "A member of the priestly order must, to have a family, marry a woman of his own race... he must investigate her pedigree, obtaining the genealogy from the archives (the genealogy of his own family taken from the public registers)" (Josephus, Apion 1:31).

Meseket Kiddushin2 Mishnah 4:43 attests to this emphasis on genealogical purity as noted when we read,

הנושא אשה כהנת צרי ך לבדוק אחרי ה ארבע אמהו ת שהן שמנה א מה ואם אמה ו אם אב י אמה ואמה ואם אביה ואמה ואם אבי אביה וא מה ל ויה וישראלית מוסיפין עלי ה ן עוד אחת

(One who weds a woman who is a priestess, must investigate after her for four mothers, which are eight; her mother, and the mother of her mother, and the mother of her mother's father and her mother, and the mother of her father and her mother, and the mother of her father's father and her mother. A Levite woman and Israelite woman- they add to them one more.). While Josephus mentions Tiberia (the last place for the relocation of the Sanhedrin from the Lishkat ha-Gazit of the Beit HaMikdash, to Yavne, Shefaram, Bet She'arim , and Sepphoris), the capital of Galilee being the seat of the royal bank and archives (Life, 38), rabbinic texts mention Sepphoris (Kiddushin 4:5) and Gadera (Esther Rabba 1:3) as other locations for Jewish archives. For more on genealogical archives in antiquity see http://databases.jewishlibraries.org/sites/default/files/proceedings/proceedings2001/levydavidshort1.pdf

Dr. Benjamin Sax whose Yahrzeit is 5 Av (yahrzeit of HaAri HaKodesh of Safed) was killed in a tragic car crash when my mother (zl) was very young and my grandmother Miriam (was driving the car) and subsequently miraculously survived only after a hip , knee, shoulder, teeth, replacements. As the bionic women my grandmother always was an optimist and positive seeing the glass half full, and my mother (zl) took great care of my grandmother even like Rabbi Tarfon putting his hands on the cold floor so his mother's feet not become cold in the winter, and putting on her slippers and making sure all her needs were met etc

Mikorot on Jewish Genology from Bible[4],[5] to Rabbinic texts

In Genesis6, 7 , 8 , 9genealogy is named by the word toldot,10 , 11, 12 which also means history, which is given in Genesis13 , 14 in subsequent waves or rythms.15 Tribes have genealogies that were remembered and transmitted through generations.16 There are many types of genealogical lists.17 In the biblical period historical ethnographic genealogies (Gen 4:2318; Gen 5:119,20,21, 22, 23 , 24, 25; 6:926, 27; Gen 9:1028, 29; 10:130,31, 32 , Gen 11:2733, 34), Lamach,35 Abraham the patriarch,36, 37,38 tribal genealogies39 (census lists in Numbers), and individual genealogies were kept. Examples of individual genealogies are (1) the house of David40 , 41(I Chron. 2:10-1542; 3:1-2443), (2) the House of the Zadokite priesthood44 (I Chron 5:28-4145; 5:14) and individuals (II Kgs 22:346; Jer 36:1447), Not just kings have genealogies recorded but so do hand maids. 48The house of Saul is given in I Chron 8:3. Sometimes artisans, hokhamim, poets whose professions were hereditary were linked with some ancient ancestor (I Chron 2:55; 4:21, 23). Such later types of lists were used for national census, military service, or tax purposes. In Ezra 2:62 a list of priestly families returning to Zion sought proof of their pedigree but could not find it. Nehemiah (7:5) mentions "the book of genealogy of those who came up first."49 The existence of genealogies is etymologically correlated to certain idiomatic expressions linguistically (Ex 32:32; Ezek 13:9; Ps 139:16). The list of Aaron's genealogy50 may go back to a text in which there existed generation skipping data (I Chron 5-6).51 In Megillos Esther written in the Persian period the lineage of Mordekhai is given (Esth 2:552; genealogies in Sefer Shmuel,53 I Sam 9:154, 55). In I Chron 2:55 the names of families such as the Tirathites is given.56 Caleb, the husband of Miriam is also given in I Chron 2:42-49.57 Sometimes the given name of a tribe or family occurs in different contexts or compound lists. Aram is listed in Gen 10:23 as the father of Uz whereas in Gen 22:20-21 Uz is the son of Nahor and an uncleof Aram. In Gen 36:5, 14 Korah is a son of Esau, but in Gen 36:16 the clan of Korah is descended from Esau's son Eliphaz. In Chron 2:9 Ram is the son of Hezron and the brother of Jerahmeel, yet in the same chapter verse 27 Ram is the eldest son of Jerahmeel. A name can also be included in several genealogical lists Fr example Zerah , Korah, Kenaz are included in Edomite lists in Gen 36, are also found on the list o the families of the tribe of Judah in I Chron 2 and 4. Beriah appears as one of the sons listed as the sons of Reuben (Gen 46:9) and also as one of the sons of Perez son of Judah (Gen 46:12).

In Second Temple Period

Purity of descent is most emphasized in the Beit Sheni Tekufah with regards to Kohanim and those Israelite families who lay claims to eligibility of the daughters to marry Kohanim. Families who had no record of their descent but were not suspected of impure lineage were referred to as issah (good dough). The kohanim in order to preserve their pure status were restricted to marital ties with families whose purity of descent was not in doubt and were therefore required to know their genealogy in detail and that of families whose daughters married kohanim. Families claiming purity of blood kept ancestral lists. According to Josephus (Jos Apion 1:7) in the Beit HaMikdash Kohanide genealogies on all priestly families even in the diaspora was required for deposit in Jerusalem. According to Kiddushin Kohanim who performed avodah from the altar upward and from the dukhan upward and members of the Sanhedrin (1/2 of which were Kohanim) were usually not suspected of impure genealogy (Kid 4:4-5). We read:

משנה מסכת קידושין פרק ד

משנה ד

הנושא אשה כהנת צריך לבדוק אחריה ארבע אמהות שהן [*] שמנה אמה ואם אמה ואם אבי אמה ואמה ואם אביה ואמה ואם אבי אביה ואמה לויה וישראלית מוסיפין עליהן עוד אחת:

משנה ה

אין בודקין לא מן המזבח ולמעלה ולא מן הדוכן ולמעלה ולא [*] מן סנהדרין ולמעלה וכל שהוחזקו אבותיו משוטרי הרבים וגבאי צדקה משיאין לכהונה ואין צריך לבדוק אחריהן ר' יוסי אומר אף מי שהיה חתום בערכי הישנה של צפורי רבי חנינא בן אנטיגנוס אומר אף מי שהיה מוכתב באסטרטיא של מלך:

Likewise in Sahedrin 4:2 we learn:

משנה מסכת סנהדרין פרק ד

משנה ב

דיני הטומאות והטהרות מתחילין מן הגדול דיני נפשות [*] מתחילין מן הצד הכל כשרין לדון דיני ממונות ואין הכל כשרין לדון דיני נפשות אלא כהנים לוים וישראלים המשיאין לכהונה

Further in Aruchin 2:4 performance of avodah lessened doubt, sufek, the gematria of satan:

משנה מסכת ערכין פרק ב

משנה ד

ועבדי הכהנים היו דברי רבי מאיר רבי יוסי אומר משפחות [*] בית הפגרים ובית צפריה ומאמאום היו משיאין לכהונה רבי חנניא בן אנטיגנוס אומר לוים היו

Chapter One 12

Certain sages were of noble birth such as Rabbi Yehudah HaNasi who lived in Beit Sharim in the winter and Tzipori in the summer, where the breeze provides relief from the summer heat since Tzipori as the name means is like a bird pirched on a hill. Yet the crown of torah trumped genealogy as Rabbi Akiva Resh Lakish, and Rabbi Meir learned later in life as baalei teshuvah. Al pi Kabbalah some of Hazal were said to descend in gilgulim from evil roots such as Sisera, Sennacherib, Haman, Nero, and a tikkun is made by their descendants becoming rabbinic scholars as it says the late descendents of Haman are in Bnai Brak learning torah.

The Hasmonians area special case who sought to defend themselves against the contention that only Davidic descendants could lay claim to kingship . The Talmud recounts how they shed doubt on King davids blood line from Ruth ,[58] back to Perez,[59] which the Biblical text makes clear is pristine and fit for the mashiach to come from:

רות פרק ד

וִיהִי בֵיתְךָ כְּבֵית פֶּרֶץ אֲשֶׁר יָלְדָה תָמָר לִיהוּדָה מִן הַזֶּרַע אֲשֶׁר יִתֵּן יְקֹוָק לְךָ מִן הַנַּעֲרָה הַזֹּאת:

(יג) וַיִּקַּח בֹּעַז אֶת רוּת וַתְּהִי לוֹ לְאִשָּׁה וַיָּבֹא אֵלֶיהָ וַיִּתֵּן יְקֹוָק לָהּ הֵרָיוֹן וַתֵּלֶד בֵּן:

(יד) וַתֹּאמַרְנָה הַנָּשִׁים אֶל נָעֳמִי בָּרוּךְ יְקֹוָק אֲשֶׁר לֹא הִשְׁבִּית לָךְ גֹּאֵל הַיּוֹם וְיִקָּרֵא שְׁמוֹ בְּיִשְׂרָאֵל:

(טו) וְהָיָה לָךְ לְמֵשִׁיב נֶפֶשׁ וּלְכַלְכֵּל אֶת שֵׂיבָתֵךְ כִּי כַלָּתֵךְ אֲשֶׁר אֲהֵבַתֶךְ יְלָדַתּוּ אֲשֶׁר הִיא טוֹבָה לָךְ מִשִּׁבְעָה בָּנִים:

(טז) וַתִּקַּח נָעֳמִי אֶת הַיֶּלֶד וַתְּשִׁתֵהוּ בְחֵיקָהּ וַתְּהִי לוֹ לְאֹמֶנֶת:

(יז) וַתִּקְרֶאנָה לוֹ הַשְּׁכֵנוֹת שֵׁם לֵאמֹר יֻלַּד בֵּן לְנָעֳמִי וַתִּקְרֶאנָה שְׁמוֹ עוֹבֵד הוּא אֲבִי יִשַׁי אֲבִי דָוִד: פ

(יח): וְאֵלֶּה תּוֹלְדוֹת פָּרֶץ פֶּרֶץ הוֹלִיד אֶת חֶצְרוֹן

(יט): וְחֶצְרוֹן הוֹלִיד אֶת רָם וְרָם הוֹלִיד אֶת עַמִּינָדָב

(כ): וְעַמִּינָדָב הוֹלִיד אֶת נַחְשׁוֹן וְנַחְשׁוֹן הוֹלִיד אֶת שַׂלְמָה

(כא): וְשַׂלְמוֹן הוֹלִיד אֶת בֹּעַז וּבֹעַז הוֹלִיד אֶת עוֹבֵד

(כב): וְעֹבֵד הוֹלִיד אֶת יִשָׁי וְיִשַׁי הוֹלִיד אֶת דָּוִד

The mashiach must come from Ruth as a righteous *giuret* who is linked to Peretz the son of Judah and Tamar. The image of Eliyahu riding on a humble donkey signifies the humility of the messiah as does the lowly thorn bush (rather than a large tree) from which Moshe hears the call of *the gatung* to redeem the Jewish people from bondage.

On the eve of the Hurban by the Romans Rabbi Yochanan ben Zakai who was smuggled out in a coffin from the sieged Jerusalme (See Avot De Rabbi Natan) and asked Vespacian for (1) a Yeshivah in Yavne, and (2) a physician to cure Rabbi Tzadok who was starving hmself on fruit juice as mourning for the Beit HaMikdash, that no subsequent rabbinical court would deal with matters concerning genealogy (Eduy 8:3) as we read:

משנה מסכת עדויות פרק ח

משנה ג

[*] העיד רבי יהושע ורבי יהודה בן בתירא על אלמנת עיסה שהיא כשרה לכהונה שהעיסה כשרה לטמא ולטהר לרחק ולקרב אמר רבן שמעון בן גמליאל קבלנו עדותכם אבל מה נעשה שגזר רבן יוחנן בן זכאי שלא להושיב בתי דינין על כך הכהנים שומעים לכם לרחק אבל לא לקרב:

Chapter One 14

Such a consideration led to a rejection previously in time of Sefer Yuhasin which was a Midrash on Chronicles[60] (see Pes 62b).

During the period of the Amoraim[61] in Pumberditha, Suria, and Nehardia we find the Talmuds recording of many families that sought to maintain genealogical purity engaging in the practice of an uncle marrying a niece to ensure the purity of the blood line (Yev 62b). During the Amoraim and Geonic periods many families in Babylonia are mentioned in the Talmud and Mishnah in placing importance on tracing back. Thus in Tosefta Peah 4:11 we read:

תוספתא מסכת פאה (ליברמן) פרק ד

הלכה יא

היה משתמש בכלי זהב מוכרן ומשתמש בכלי כסף בכלי כסף מוכרן ומשתמש בכלי נחשת בכלי נחשת מוכרן ומשתמש בכלי זכוכית אמרו משפחת בית נבטלה היתה בירושלם והיתה מתיחסת עם בני ארנון היבוסי העלו להם חכמים שלש מאות שקלי זהב ולא רצו להוציאן חוץ מירושלם

הלכה יב

Likewise in Ta'anit 4:5 such emphasis is made:

משנה מסכת תענית פרק ד

משנה ה

זמן עצי כהנים והעם תשעה באחד בניסן בני ארח בן יהודה [*] בעשרים בתמוז בני דוד בן יהודה בחמשה באב בני פרעוש בן יהודה בשבעה בו בני יונדב בן רכב בעשרה בו בני סנאה בן בנימין בחמשה עשר בו בני זתוא בן יהודה ועמהם כהנים ולוים וכל מי שטעה בשבטו ובני גונבי עלי בני קוצעי קציעות בעשרים בו בני פחת מואב בן יהודה בעשרים באלול בני עדין בן יהודה

Chapter One 15

באחד בטבת שבו בני פרעוש שניה באחד בטבת לא היה בו
מעמד שהיה בו הלל וקרבן מוסף וקרבן עצים:

משנה ו

The list in Taanit 4:5 originates from the Persian period. This concern is again voiced in the gemarah in Yevamot 16b.

While a Jew is Jewish law is defined as someone whose mother is Jewish,[62] A well known Mishnah of every ten year old in Yeshivah learning Mishnah lists ten social groups who returned from Babylonian exile in 486 BCE in genealogical purity:

(1) Kohnanim

(2) Leveim

(3) Israelite

(4) Halalim (sons of marriages of disqualified kohanim

(5) Gerim (convets)

(6) Harurim (manumitted slaves)

(7) Mamzerim (bastards, children of a Jewish father and non-Jewish mother[63]

(8) Nethinim (descendants of the Gibeonites who had brit milah at time of Yehoshua but not regarded as full Jews because their ancestors conversion was incomplete

(9) Shetukim (silent ones, who do not know the identity of their father

(10) Asufim (foundlings, who know neither their mother or father

Chapter One   16

We read in Kidushin 4:1

משנה מסכת קידושין פרק ד
משנה א
עשרה יוחסין עלו מבבל כהני לויי ישראלי חללי גירי וחרורי [*]
ממזרי נתיני שתוקי ואסופי כהני לויי וישראלי מותרים לבא זה
בזה לויי ישראלי חללי גירי וחרורי מותרים לבא זה בזה גירי
וחרורי ממזרי ונתיני שתוקי ואסופי כולם מותרין לבא זה בזה:

The Mishnah chapter 4 of Kiddushin is devoted to the relationships between these groups i.e. rules applying to intermarriage between one group and another. Yet the Mishnah perplexingly states that a learned mamzer takes precedence over an uneducated Kohen Gadol as we read in Horayot 3:8:

משנה מסכת הוריות פרק ג

משנה ח

כהן קודם ללוי לוי לישראל ישראל לממזר וממזר לנתין ונתין [*]
לגר וגר לעבד משוחרר אימתי בזמן שכולן שוין אבל אם היה
ממזר תלמיד חכם וכהן גדול עם הארץ ממזר תלמיד חכם קודם
לכהן גדול עם הארץ:

נשלמה מסכת הוריות

The Talmud makes frequent mention to families of honorable genealogy who quarreled over yichus, stating "when men quarrel among themselves they quarrel over birth (Kiddushin 76a). The amoraim proclaimed, "anyone with a family of stigma stigmatizes others and never praises anyone, " and Samuel adds, "he stigmatizes with his own stigma (Kiddushin 70b). Thus it takes on to know one. "The Holy one is reluctant to uproot a name or family

Chapter One 17

from its place in a genealogical tree (Genesis Rabbah 82:11; 11) Tus we read in Sukkah 5:8:

משנה מסכת סוכה פרק ה

משנה ח

חל להיות יום אחד להפסיק בינתיים משמר שזמנו קבוע [*] היה נוטל עשר חלות והמתעכב נוטל שתים ובשאר ימות השנה הנכנס נוטל שש והיוצא נוטל שש רבי יהודה אומר הנכנס נוטל שבע והיוצא נוטל חמש הנכנסין חולקין בצפון והיוצאין בדרום בילגה לעולם חולקת בדרום וטבעתה קבועה וחלונה סתומה:

סליק מסכת סוכה

The sages also protested against anyone who takes a wife not fit (Kid 70a) "because he disregards the importance of birth."

In the messianic era Hashem will purify the tribes to become distinct. As was clear in the parting of the Reed sea where each tribe walked through 12 walls of potable sweet water. The question arises in the gemarah what type of bracha does one say over the exotic fruits that sprung from the sea bed, as later commented on by the *Nodeh biYehudah*.

In the Geonic periods in Israel and Babylonian the Talmud takes great care to trace the Exilarchs back to the house of David as was made of the geonim suh as Hai Gaon. In the Middle ages Davidic lineage was claimed for some Gedolim such as Rashi and his grandsons Rabbi Jacob Meir (Rabbenu Tam) and Rabbi Shmuel ben Meir who descended from Rabbi Yonatan ha-Sandlar (Sandlar a tanna who was a shoe maker, from the root of sandal; related to angel Sandelphon who watches over a fetus when the size of a shoe), who in turn was regarded as being of Davidic descent.

Zekut avot continues into the modern period and particularly among Hasidic dynasties certain Tzadikim would marry their daughters to sons of other Hasidic dynasties. Thus Ger, Vishnetz, Burke, Chabad,[64] Bobov, etc. would engage in marriage the equivalent lihavdil(!) to the likes of the Kings of England, Frane, and other secular royal dynasties, in order to secure alliances amongst the Hasidic royal lines.

Some notes on Sources and Methods on Rabbinic Genealogy

A researcher will be lucky if they have rabbeim in the family if they are searching for genealogical documents. There are many facets and avenues of research.[65] This is because:

(1) Rabbinic culture[66] cares about yichus[67, 68, 69]

(2) Rabbinic biographical sketches can be found[70]

(3) Rabbinic manuscripts sometimes include a family tree that can link to other trees[71]

(4) Sheolot ve-teshuvot may refer to a rabbinic family as the Nodeh BiYehudah describes the halakhic issue of his niece who was a perpetual niddah due to a blood condition that posed a problem for the marriage night and consummating marital relations

(5) Yizkor books[72, 73] note Rabbinic leadership and their families. Yizkor books[74] are a treasure trove as they contain maps, photos, shtetl records, cemetery records, synagogue records, etc.[75]

(6) Pinkasim[76] of synagogue records include sometimes genealogical records including circumcisions[77] and marriage records[78] and death[79]

(7) Yahrzeits are often recorded for mystical reasons in Rabbinic documents. For example Fraidl Rabinowitz shares the 13 of Kislev with her husband Rav Menachem Mendel Gluskin because "there souls were so bound up with each other."

(8) Rashe tevot can be used to trace rabbinic dynasties

(9) Genizot[80]

(10) The books authored by rabbis are often named after family names in abbreviation such as Eked Sefarim.

(11) If a family maintains it is descended from Gedolim like the Besht, the GRA, or the Maharal of Prague their homework is done, once they trace back to these great scholars, because these rabbinic leaders themselves were able to produce and took pride in their genealogical roots. For instance the Maharal can be traced back to Dovid HaMelech and thus the 7 Chabad rebbes go through the Maharal.

(12) For non-rabbinic families today archives such as YIVO (for Yiddish speaking Jewry from Eastern Europe), Leo Baeck (for Geman Jewry), Yad Vashem[81] (for Shoah records), Holocaust Museum,[82] and Beit Tefusoth maintan Genealogical research libraries and records. There are a host of holocaust organiations that also maintain genealogical resources.[83] Genealogical databases for the kinder transports exist.[84] And refugees in general.[85] International tracing service is another avenue.[86] Research projects can be consulted. [87] For Shoah survivors databases that contain Holocaust testimony can be accessed at the Yale Fortunoff database, Yad Vashem database, and Shoah Visual History Foundation under the auspices of the

Chapter One 20

University of Southern California. For a list of the similarities and differenes of these 3 databases see paper by David B Levy on TC website. Sephardic genealogy during the Holocaust is another impotant avenue of research.[88] Sephardim some claim have taken a great pride in genealogy above and beyond ashkenaz.[89]

(13) Public Records[90,91] including US records[92] and records of organizations like the Joint[93], vital records,[94] central Zionist archives[95] archives of local eastern European locations like Kaunas[96], Lithuania,[97] and Zhitmir,[98] bank records[99]birth records of Tzarist Russia[100] and central archives for the Jewish people in Poland[101], business directory records[102]

(14) Historical Jewish press[103, 104]

(15) Library genealogical collections[105,106] i.e. LC,[107], JTSA,[108] and archives[109,110], [111] and genealogical institutes[112] finding aids and reference books,[113] general starter guides,[114] and knowledgeable librarian archivists[115]

(16) Local archives of specific places[116] such as Ukraine, [117],[118], [119], eastern Europe,[120] poland[121] and minsk[122], southern Russia, [123]Galicia[124], Spain[125], Hungary[126], [127]central Europe[128], Netherlands,[129] Germany[130], [131], Rhodes[132], Province France, [133], Alsace France,[134] Cheklosavakia,[135], southerin Germany, [136] Poland,[137] Italy,[138], [139],[140] Salonika,[141] New Zealand[142], Ottoman Turkey[143], transcarpathia[144], Lithuania[145], Scotland[146], Romania, [147] Byelrussia[148] [149], Israel[150]

Chapter One 21

(17) Genetics[151, 152, 153, 154] and genetic testing[155, 156], and DNA studies[157, 158, 159, 160, 161, 162, 163, 164, 165] and genes[166, 167, 168]

(18) Tombstone[169, 170] inscriptions[171] and epitaphs[172] and cemetery records[173, 174, 175, 176, 177, 178] burial books[179]

(19) New Technologies[180] such as database construction[181] and databases,[182, 183, 184, 185, 186, 187, 188] websites, internet,[189, 190] digitization[191], automated matching of family trees,[192] search engines,[193] CDROM.[194] and trends[195]

(20) Cartography and maps[196] and background on towns[197]

(21) Photos [198]

(22) Demographic studies and knowledge of Jewish geography[199]

From the above desiderata we see that Jewish genealogy has a long history from antiquity to the present although modern organized genealogical associations may be put in historical context.[200] Jewish genealogy has a long history of significance and meaning beyond the modern period[201] and even the modern Jewish library.[202] Yet Jewish genealogy is not only a sub field of Judaica librarianship but of Jewish studies itself.[203, 204] Within Jewish genealogy there is the practical research[205] side and the theoretical understanding of the importance of memory. As Baker has noted there should be a symbiotic relationship between Research Judaica librairans and genealogists to assist in the recollection of memory.[206] Jewish genealogy is a field that continues to evolve.[207]

Chapter One 22

Chapter Two

Censorship of Rambam's Sefer Ha-Madah and Moreh Nekuhim

זה הפרק אשר נזכרהו עתה אינו כולל תוספת ענין על מה
שכללו אותו פרקי זה המאמר ואינו רק כדמות חתימה עם באור
עבודת משיג האמיתיות המיוחדות באלוה ית' אחר השגתו אי
זה דבר הוא - והישירו להגיע אל העבודה ההיא אשר היא
התכלית אשר יגיע אליה האדם והודיעו איך תהיה ההשגחה בו
בעולם הזה עד שיעתק אל 'צרור החיים':

(part III, ch.1 Guide for the Perplexed)

Introduction
This essay investigates the reasons why Rambam's *Sefer HaMadah* and *Moreh Nevukhim* were censored. Thus it will not focus on external censorship of Jewish books such as the Church's persistent and periodic burning of the Talmud in France, Spain, and Italy, particularly during the period 1240-1600, or government burnings of Hebraica as early as that recounted in the book of Maccabees (1:50) by Antiochus IV, to climax during the Nazi period.

Yet further consideration on censorship recalls that the

Tanakh itself does not tolerate all things, for example idolatry, as when *Eliyahu HaNavi* in an act of censorship eliminates the *Baal* prophets, who cut themselves, in attempt to make it rain. Like Pinchas ben Elazar ben Aharon the Kohen, Eliyahu soul spark is zealous for haShem or embodies what in Yiddish is called zizirut.

Indeed the canonization of the *Tanakh*, represents acts of censorship, where disputes were held in Yavne by out sages, whether *Kohelet* was too skeptical, *Esther* too assimilationist, or *Shir HaShirim* too erotic. While the rabbis would include *Shir HaShirim* as an allegory of *HaShem's* love for the people Israel, and Rabbi Akiba could proclaim it the *Holy of Hollies*, the canonization of Hebrew scripture may have involved a process where many writings were considered, and only some incorporated. i.e. What happened to the *Book of the Wars of the Lord (BaMidbar 21 : 14)*, *Chronicles of the Kings of Israel and Judah*, *The Book of Jashar (Josh. 10: 13)*, and the *Midrash of Iddo (11 Chron. 13:22)*? These texts are cited in the Tanakh. Is Cassutto correct that they were ur-texts, or just oral forms of text with which the ancient Hebrew were familiar?

Philosophy Regarded by Some as a Dangerous Suspect Activity Leading to Heresy

In the Jewish tradition distrust of philosophy is illustrated by the *Hai Gaon of Pumbeditha* (998-1038) who asserted that the study of philosophy can lead to heresy. The dangerous threat viewed by Judaism as coming from philosophy is noted when the *Meshullam ben Solomon* writes, "Oh men cease from drawing waters from a well the father's neither bor nor dug. What have you to do with the philosophers..." In Spinoza's *Traetatus Theologieo Politicus*, Spinoza *ad captum vulgi*, bluntly says, "the Jews despise philosophy", and as late as 1765 Moses Mendelssohn felt it necessary to apologize for recommending the study of logic, and to show why the prohibition against the reading of extraneous profane books (*Sforim Hitzonim*) does not apply to works on logic. Even Rabbi Nahman of Bratzlov (1770-1811), cautioned against Maimonides *Millot Hahiggayon, Sefer HaMadah and Moreh Nevukhim*, while Rabbi Moses Leib of Sassov (1745-1807) reprimanded the young men in Cracow who studied these philosophic works, Rabbi S.R. Hirsch in Letter to ben Uzziel assumes a dialogue form to show the young interlocuter Benjamin why he should not be perplexed that living in the modern world is a contradiction to medieval Judaism as Hirsch formulated a neo-orthodoxy compatible with contemporary times.

Heschel conceives of the opposition towards Rambam's philosophic texts as a case whereby Jewish religious authorities feared that Talmudic study would be compromised at the expense of the increased interest in philosophy.[208]

R. Alfakar saw that there is an unbridged gulf between Greek philosophy and the Torah, as noted when Touati writes, "*D'apres Juda Alfakhar aucune conciliation s'est possible entre la philosophie greque et la religion juive qui s'opposent irreductiblement.*" While Rambam did embrace in part Aristotle's moral theory in the <u>Nicomachean Ethics</u> of the "mean" or *Derek haEmzain*[209], theories of the four causes[210], and Aristotle's deprecation of touch as the lowest sense, Rambam recognized the unassimilatibility into Judaism of Aristotle's view of the eternity of the Universe in favor of Biblical *creation ex nihilo*, (yesh mi-ayn) as well as rejection of Aristotle's view of Providence (*Hashgihah pratit*)[211] *not operativing sublunar*. Although philosophy is less of a suspect activity for Christianity[212], the Church also saw Aristotle's teachings as a threat and thus censored Aristotle's work!

Further if we agree with Leo Strauss that the conflict between philosophy and religion, *Athens and Jerusalem,* is the secret vitality of the west, the interpretation of the Maimonidean controversy as just a geographical or regional conflict becomes problematic. Weinberger writes, "The strife around *Sefer HaMadah* and the Guide entailed a clash between two worlds, that od the Sephardim with their Islamic Arabic culture of which Maimonides was a product, and that of the Ashkenazim of northern and southern France, who lived in a Christian civilization."[213] Although it may be the case the Rabbis of northern France, who devoted themselves mostly to Talmudic studies and frowned upon secular scholarly pursuits, sought to stop the spread of Maimonides1 philosophical teachings into the north of Spain (where scholars like ibn Tibbons and the Kimhis, in escaping the Provence from the Almohades brought with them works of Saadia Gaon, Bahya ibn Pakudah, and Yehudah Ha-Levi), we must recall the suspect (hashad) status of philosophy.

Why censorship of the Mishneh Torah?

In regards to fear that the MT would supplant study of the Talmud, Zeitlin writes, "There seemed at first to be grounds for this charge in the fact that he did not mention the name of any of the *Tannaim or Amorain.* Further he has stated in his introduction that anyone familiar with the Pentateuch would after reading the MT, have a knowledge of all the Oral laws without having recourse to any other book."[214] Rambam in his epistle to Pinhas, the Dayyan of Alexandria refuted these charges. Admiring rabbis such as Samuel HaKohen, Saadya ben Berakhya, R. Nissim, and R. Shemarya recognized the importance of the MT as a code.

However some of the rabbinic community objected to *Sefer HaMadah*, for Maimonides placed among the five categories of heretics. Those who believed that the creator was corporeal.[215] The *Midrashim* give accounts of great banquets in *Olam HaBah*, where the righteous will partake of the most delicious foods and wines, while the wicked gaze on with their hands tied, forbidden to partake. Rambam in *Hilkot Teshuvah* and elsewhere proclaims that there is no eating, drinking, or anything corporeal in *Olam HaBah* but the righteous sit with crowns on the heads enjoying the light of the *Shechinah*.[216] The crowns represent the wisdom, understanding, and knowledge gained in this world, including for the Rambam scientific learning such as philosophy and medicine. Rambam rejects a corporeal Creator espoused in works such as *Shi'ur Qomah*[217], as encapsulated by *Yigdal's* proclamation, "*Ain Lo Demut HaGuf VeAino Guf*"

Touati lists Rambam's negation of the corporeality of the Deity as the first criticism in the following list of attacks Rambam faced from anti-Maimonidists: (1) *l'enseignement de Mainonide sur l'absolue incorporalite de Dieu; (2) ses theories sur la prophetic ramenee a une vision; (3) sa tendance a restreindre le champ du miracle; (4) sa negation des demons; (5) sa reduction des anges au role de monteurs des Spheres celestes; (6) les interpretations spiritualistes qu'il avait donnees du Paradis et L'enfer; (7) les motifs qu'il avait ass ignes aux precepts religieux (mitsvot); (8) l'alegorization des recites bibliques a laquelle se livraient ses disciples; (9) le dedain qu'ils auraient affiche a l'egard des Sages du Talmud; (9) le relachement de la pratique religieuses qu'on croyait constater chez eux et don't on imputait la responsibilite a l'etude de la philosophie.*[218]

Why Censorship of the Moreh Nevukim?

One reason that the Guide was censored was because Maimonides offers an allegory on Part III, chapter 51, on the approximate remoteness and nearness of classified groups of people to the inner chamber of the seventh heavenly palace where Moshe Rabenu is located in dialogue with HaShem[219]. Those most far removed outside the city of God, are all human beings who have no doctrinal beleif neither one based on speculation nor one that accepts the authority of tradition. The second farthest group away from the palace are those "who have turned their backs upon the ruler's habitation", and "who have incorrect opinions." The third group farthest away from the palace are described when Rambam writes, "Those who see to reach the ruler's habitation to enter it, but never see the ruler's habitation, are the multitude of the adherents of the Law, I refer to the *ignoramuses who observe the commandments*". They serve the Creator out of blind mechanistic duty on the contingency of receiving a reward motivated out of fear and punishment, rather than serving out of love. Antigonos of Socho reciving the tradition from Simon the Just, says, *"al Tihiyu kaAvdem hamishmsheem et haRav as Minhat izKabal Piran, eleh heyo KaAvadem hamishmsheem et HaRav shelo al Minat li Kabail Piras."*

Although religious authorities feared that "la philosophie est responsible du retachement de la pratique religieuse"[220], the main fear of Jewish religious authorities appears to be direct revelation of secrets. Teaching in writing, to be differentiated from oral teaching, the secrets of the Tanakh (i.e. *ma'aseh merkavah16, ma;aseh bereshit*[221], *prophetology*[222], *angelology*[223], *Sitre Torah* as contradictions of th Torah 2, etc)[224] is forbidden by orah law. For example, Mishneh Hagigah 2: 1 reads, *"En doresin ba'arayot biselosah welo bema'aseh beresit bisenayim welo bammerkabah beyahid ella im ken haya hakham wehebin midda 'ato. Kol hammistakkel be'arba'ah debarim ratuy*[225] *ke'illu lo ba la olam mah lema'lan umah lemattan mah lefanim umah le'ahor. Kol sello has al kebod qono ratuy*[226] *ke'illu lo ba la'olam.*" The subject of the merkavah found in M.Hag 2:1 is found further in the corresponding section of the Tosefta (T.Hag.2:1-7), and in the *gemara* to this to this Mishneh in *Yerushalmz* (hag.77a-d) and *Bavli* (Hag. 1 1 b-16a),[227] These texts presume the dangers of this esoteric subject, for according to M. Hagigah 2: 1Merkavah may not be expounded (*en doresin bammerkabah*) except under special circumstantces, and according to Megilla 4: 10, it may not be used as a prophetic lection in the synagogue (*en maftirin hammerkabah*). Special knowledge of esoteric subjects, is reserved for a small group of initiates. Rabbinic anecdotes stress its secret and wondrous nature, and hazard for the pre-mature.

Strauss argues that Rambam had to break these rabbinic laws, in order to save the law[228], namely if the Rambam did not write down the secrets of the above esoteric subjects, they risked being lost depriving those who were perplexed of the Rambam's guidance. While Rambam promises to transmit the secrets of *ma'aseh bereshit* (Creation in Genesis 1) which the Rambam links with physical science (*hokmat Hatebah*), and *ma'aseh merkavah* (chariot vision in Ezekiel 1, 10; 43: 1-3) which the Rambam links to metaphysics *(Hokmat Elokut)2* Strauss cautions against these reductions, for Maimonides may intentionally contradict himself in order to keep the esoteric teachings of *the Guide* separate from exoteric teachings.[229] Strauss' differentiation between esoteric and exoteric becomes all the more interesting in the light of Halperin's thesis that there are two types of rabbinic *merkavah* exegesis, the exoteric exegesis recorded in Talmud, Midrashim, and Targumim; and an esoteric exegesis reserved orally on in secret books for an elite.[230]

Rambam recalls a tradition in the Talmud attributed to Rabbi Simeon ben Lakish that the Merkavah are the *Avot* and which is recaitilated in *Zohar* 262b *Vaethhanan* where we read. *"Only HaShem had a delight in thy fathers (Devarim 15). Commenting on this, R. Simeon said that the patriarchs are the holy chariot above. As there is a holy chariot below, so there is a holy chariot above. And what is this? As we have said, the holy chariot is the name given to the Whole, all being linked together and made one. But the fathers are only three, and the chariot has four wheels. Who is the fourth? It says, 'And chose their seed after them', this includes David HaMelech, who is the fourth to complete the holy chariot, as we learnt, 'The patriarchs are the consummation of the whole, and the Body was completed through them that made one. The Davis HaMelech came and perfected the whole and made firm the body and perfected it. Rabbi Yitzak said, 'As the patriarchs merited to be crowned with the holy chariot, so did David merit to be adorned with the fourth support of the chariot."* Philosophy is comprehension of the whole.

Anti-Maimonideans

Three anti-Maimunist Rabbis included R. Solomon ben Abraham of Montpellier and his two disciples, R. Jonah Gerundi and R. David ben Saul. Dubnov comments on these three rabbis placing a ban on Maimonides philosophical work when he writes, *"Das dreigliedrige Rabbinerkollegium entschloB sich nun zu einem folgenschweren Schritt: es Verhangte den cherum ueber alle diejenigen, die sich mit Philosophie und mit profanen Wissenschaften ueberhaupt, insbesondere aber mit den philosophischen Werken des Maimonides (More Nevuchim und Sefer HaMada) befaBten, wie auch ueber solche, Die Ueberlieferungen der Bibel und des Talmud in rationalistischem Geiste auszulegen wagten (zu Beginn des Jahres 1232).*[231] These anti-Maimondeans sought th support of the Dominicans to enforce the Cencorship od Main on ides work. Graetz, employing a technique of the

Thucydides, reconstructs a possible dialog between R. Solomon ben Abraham and R. Gerondi and the Dominicans by writing, *"Ihr Verbrennt eure Ketzer, verflogt auch unsere."*[232] As to the rabbis appealing to the Dominicans, Dubnov gives the following lelengthier reconstruction of the dialog that may have taken place, *"Wir wissen da Bes in unserer Stadt Viele Ketzer und Gottlose gibt, die sich durch die Lehre des Moses Aus Aegypten, des Verfassers ruchlosen philosophischen Buecher, verfuehren lieBen. Verilget ihr eure Ketzer, so vertilget mit ihnen auch die unseren und verbrenner die schaedlichen Buecher."*[233]

Motivation of the Friars to Carry out the Book Burnings?

The following three reasons are advanced by scholars as to the motivations for the friars to burn Rambam's philosophic works: (1) The friars, then recently forming, and wishing validation in the eyes of the established Catholic Church, welcomed the position of authority to serve the arbiters in a Jewish matter; (2) The friars confused Maimonides philosophical work with the Rambam's *halachic* writings, which the Church still regarded as containing matters dangerous to ecclesiastical power[234]; (3) The friars who had been given authority by the Church to root out the Albigensian heretics in France, were caught up in their zeal. Whatever the motivation of the friars, the rabbis who may have urged them to burn Rambam's writings, soon found that their strategy backfired, for a few years later the friears initiated a long history of censorship of the Talmud that involved over 300 years of Talmud burnings. According to Rabbi Hillel of Verona, the burning of Rambam's books toow place near the cathedral Notrc Dame, and the bonfire was lit with tapers from that alter. Rabbi Abraham Maimuni, according to some accounts, pictured the fire that burnt his father's books, *with the letter ascending to heaven,* as making them immortal, even as *Eliyah HaNavi* was translated alive to heaven in a fiery chariot.

Conclusion
While the question of censorship of *Hebraica* is an important question for Jewish librarians and archivists, this essay has focused on the internal censorship of Rambam's philosophical writings.

Chapter Three

The Making of the Encyclopedia Judaica and the Jewish Encyclopedia

Description:

The *Jewish Encyclopedia* and *Encyclopaedia Judaica* form a key place in most collections of Judaica. Both works state that they were brought into being to combat anti-Semitism. This presentation treats the reception history of both the JE and EJ by looking at the comments of their admirers and critics. It also assesses how both encyclopedias mark the application of social sciences and emphasis on Jewish history, as well as anthropology, archeology, and statistics. We will consider the differences between the JE and EJ, some of the controversies surrounding the making of the encyclopedias, and the particular political, ideological, and cultural perspectives of their contributing scholars.

Introduction:

The 1901-1906 *Jewish Encyclopedia* and 1972 *Encyclopaedia Judaica* form an important place in collections of Judaica. Both works were brought into being to combat anti-Semitism, to enlighten the public of new discoveries, and to disseminate Jewish scholarship. Both encyclopedias seek to counter-act the lack of knowledge of their generations and wide spread assimilation.

Both works have their admirers and detractors. The EJ has been called "a shining landmark,"[235] "a work of transcendent value,"[236] "an indispensable reference tool,"[237] and "an essential purchase for colleges, universities, seminaries, and all public libraries."[238] On the other hand the EJ has been called by Solomon Zeitlin a product of "public relations," "often inaccurate," and "inconsistent."[239] The JE has been praised for its thoroughness, beautiful illustrations, enrichment of Jewish cultural life, "monumental epoch making climax of Jewish progress in the 19th century,"[240] and "a peacemaker between different denominations of Judaism."[241] It has also been said of the JE that "it will teach the gentile to respect where he has despised; it will teach the Jew to respect himself."[242] However, the JE has been criticized for overstating its case with regards to the importance of the Jews , "placing overemphasis on individuals born Jews but whose association with the Jewish community was tenuous,"[243] and as " contradictory," and incorrect.[244] At first, Steinschneider claimed it was "dilettantish," and Ahad Ha-Am clamed it was "just another American work that is done with big noise and publicity."[245] However they came to appreciate its value later.

Right wing Jews sometimes find both encyclopedias as promoting a modern nontraditional, and at times irreverent approach to sacred traditions. Such traditionalists reject "Higher Biblical Criticism" which both encyclopedias incorporate. Higher Biblical criticism divides the Biblical text into various sources, each with its own author, origin, and dating thereby placing revelation in a precarious position. Many traditionalists find it impossible to reconcile the doctrine of divine revelation with the evidence of textual errors and duplication that suggest that the Torah was written by human beings, even if divinely inspired. In addition the application of the findings of the emerging fields of comparative religion, archeology, folklore, and linguistics often reinforce Biblical criticism by undermining the uniqueness of biblical stories and rituals. Finally, Darwinian evolutionism seemed to remove the concepts of divine creation and providence from the story of the origin and direction of the world. Likewise these encyclopedias tend to present the Talmud not necessarily as a divinely revealed work[246] but as a historical document seen "as a storehouse of archeology that serves as an important source of information on Jewish culture and on the history of science and civilization."[247] Hence they place modern and traditionalist approaches in tension.

Both encyclopedias also saw themselves as a way to combat anti-Semitism by increasing general non-Jewish knowledge about Jews and Judaism. The JE followed in the wake of the Dreyfus Affair while the EJ followed in the wake of raised Holocaust consciousness during the 60s and 70s. It can be argued that the resurgence of anti-Semitism provided increased external motivations to undertake comprehensive Encyclopedic works. The encyclopedias were seen to combat prejudice through presentation of accurate information about Jews and Judaism. The Anti-Semitism of the century, rather than discouraging encyclopedic work, renewed urgency for promoting an accurate understanding of Judaism and Jews. Both Isidore Singer and the editors of the EJ proposed their works in order to combat anti-Semitism by educating the non-Jewish world. However, Schwartz identifies the belief that the JE could end anti-Semitism as naïve. Schwartz writes, "Like many others of their time, the men involved in the encyclopedia project were naïve in their belief that knowledge could end prejudice. The JE increased Christian understanding of Jews at the time as the many articles and reviews indicated, but it hardly quashed anti-Semitism."[248] Schwartz further notes, "Some strove to combat anti-Semitism through education. Articles, pamphlets, and newspapers attempted to dispel negative stereotypes and replace them with factual evidence of positive Jewish characteristics. In large measure, the JE belongs to this genre of defense literature as both exemplar and summary."[249]

Both encyclopedias received entries from scholars across Europe and the Americas. While the JE marked the shift of Jewish scholarship from Europe to the Americas, the EJ marked the shift of Jewish scholarship to also include Israel.

Both represent a particular political, ideological, and cultural bias of the scholars' own historical context, religious affiliation, and scholarly methodologies.

Both encyclopedias further represent the incorporation of new archeological discoveries. The JE incorporated the findings of Schechter's Cairo Geniza while the EJ incorporated findings of the Dead Sea Scrolls. Both encyclopedias mark the application of social sciences and emphasis on Jewish history, as well as anthropology, and statistics.

The Jewish Encyclopedia

Singer first conceived of the scope of the JE to demonstrate the role that Jews and Judaism have played in diverse areas of general culture, such as science, art, literature, industry, and commerce. Singer wanted the JE to be scientific in method and without any religious bias. It would serve as a compendium for scholars and as a guide for the Jewish and general public. The JE was to contain a complete survey of Jewish history, literature, and theology, plus material on Jewish communities, sociology, and archeology as well as biographies of prominent Jewish scholars, theologians, poets, businessmen, and physicians. Subject areas of history, biography, sociology, and anthropology comprised the greatest number of articles in the JE. As stated in the *Preface* the objectives of the JE included, "keeping abreast of the times in Biblical matters... to acquaint the student with the results of modern research in many fields that are altogether new and bristling with interesting discoveries... Assyriology, Egyptology, and archeological investigation in Palestine."[250] Singer also wanted the JE to be ecumenical by improving the mutual understanding of Christian and Jew.

The JE marks the culmination of a century of European Jewish scholarly activity. It also is an important source of information about the attitudes, ideals, and concerns of Jewish scholars at the turn of the century. Cyrus Adler, Richard Gottheil, Kaufman Kohler, Marcus Jastrow, Joseph Jacobs, Louis Ginzberg, Morris Jastrow, Gotthard Deutsch, Emil G. Hirsch, Solomon Schechter, and Crawford H. Toy served as members of the editorial board of the JE. Tension arose among the editors at times with coalitions being forged between conservative traditionalists, Cyrus Adler and Solomon Schechter and more liberal reform scholars such as Kaufman Kohler, Isidore Singer and Hirsch. Schechter likened the relationship between Conservative and Reform to that of the English government with two parties in constant opposition, yet dedicated to serving the same cause. Schechter branded reform "Paulinism," while Singer called conservatism, "Roman Catholic Israel." Interestingly Orthodox traditionalists like Judah David Eisenstein used the JE to condemn the JTS and brand it non-orthodox. Eisenstein argued that Ginzberg's article, "Law, Codification" which was approved by Schechter was proof that the leaders of the JTS expounded higher biblical criticism when in fact Schechter expressed disdain for Higher Biblical criticism as "the Higher anti-Semitism." As well as Schechter's dislike for the detrimental effects of hurrying to rush entries, the controversy between Schechter and Eisenstein contributed to Schechter's resignation and he was replaced by Wilhelm Bacher.[251]

The JE sought to incorporate in a comprehensive manner the method, mood, and content of *Wissenschaft des Judentums* scholarship thus fulfilling the desire of many European Jewish *Wissenschaft* scholars for providing a summary of a century of research mostly in Europe. Publication of the JE in the English language marked the passing of the mantle of scholarly hegemony to the United States thereby coming to symbolize the emerging cultural and intellectual independence of American Jewry. The JE more than any other English language encyclopedia incorporates the findings of *Wissenschaft des Judentums* scholarship.

Wissenschaft des Judentums

Wissenschaft des Judentums originated in Germany in the 1800s out of the desire on the part of some university trained Jews to modernize the study of Judaism in accordance with the model of objective critical scholarship. Its founders included Abraham Geiger, Zacharias Frankel, Leopold Zunz, and Heinrich Graetz. Zunz was convinced that the Jew could not attain full emancipation until Judaism was accorded respect and raised to its rightful place among academic disciplines. Frankel and Graetz emphasized the crucial role *Wissenschaft des Judentums* would play in the increase in Jewish self-knowledge thereby creating a recovery of Jews' self awareness and preservation. Significant *Wissenschaft* breakthroughs included Zunz' studies in liturgy and *Midrash*, Michael Sachs' research on Spanish Jewry, Solomon Munk's work on Medieval Jewish philosophy, Graetz 11 volume history of the Jews, Benno Jacob's biblical studies, and Frankel's study of the *Mishnah*. *Wissenschaft des Judentums* sought to expand the depth and breadth of Jewish knowledge and hone new methods for analysis of Jewish texts. The centers for *Wissenschaft des Judentums* research included Frankel's *Judische Theologisches Seminar* in Breslau, Abraham Geiger's *Hochschule fuer die Wissenschaft des Judentums*, Azriel Hildesheimer's *Rabbinerseminar fuer das Orthodox Judentums* in Berlin, and Jews' College in London. Graetz' *Monatsschrift fuer Geschichte und Wissenschaft des Judentums* was a voice of the movement in Europe while the Jewish Quarterly Review was *Wissenschaft's* voice in America. The spread of *Wissenschaft* led to a receptivity to the idea of a Jewish encyclopedia on Jews and Judaism in the world, but evoked criticism by some traditionalists, who are skeptical, if not hostile to the free inquiry of *Wissenschaft* which is not bashful to question tradition in a spirit unencumbered by religious authority. Although Ginzberg was critical of *Wissenschaft* scholars for their late dating of the origins of *Kabbalah* and for their rationalist anti mystical bias, *Wissenschaft des Judentums* exerted a great influence on the scope and overall approach of the JE. The JE is pro-*Wissenschaft*.[252] The only perceptible significant departure from *Wissenschaft* methodology is the inclusion in the JE of Judeo-German (Yiddish literature) thereby overcoming the unfavorable prevalent *Wissenschaft* tendency to pay scant attention to modern Yiddish literature of Mendele Mokher Seforim, I.L. Peretz, Sholom Alekhem, and countless others.

Bias and Unstated Ulterior Assumptions in the JE

The JE reflects a particular political, ideological, and cultural bias illuminating the contributors' own historical context, religious affiliations, and scholarly methodologies. Schwartz argues that the anthropological entries by Fishberg promote the desired integration of Jews into the non-Jewish culture by suggesting that unfavorable traits are not intrinsic to Jews' natures but the result of external conditions. It is assumed that once the external conditions improve for Jews the negatives attributed to their characters will disappear enabling Jews to integrate fully into Western society.

Likewise the entries on American Jewish history also represent unstated ulterior objectives and biases. Schwartz suggests that the motive to show conclusively that Jews were instrumental to the initial settlement of the Americas as well as contributed to Columbus's journey monetarily and through invention of astronomical instruments Jews developed, is fueled by the desire to prove the right of Jews to belong in America so that the Jewish roots in the United States are emphasized. Schwartz further argues that the illustrations and photographs of American synagogues, cemeteries, hospitals, and other institutions is motivated by the desire to give a belief of permanence to the Jewish American community and to promote the view that Jews have successfully adapted in America. Schwartz suggests that the American Jewish history entries are written with a motive to counter anti-Semitic charges of the worthlessness and parasitism of Jews and to promote positive stereotypes. Schwartz contends further that the emphasis on Jewish servicemen in the JE represents the unstated need to refute the accusation that Jews do not do their share to serve their country. It is thus an attempt to demonstrate the patriotism of American Jews. Schwartz writes, "In sum the JE unabashedly sings the praises of Jews and Judaism in America. There is abundant evidence of Jewish roots, belonging, religious development, success, and contribution, more than enough to demonstrate that the Jewish experience in America was indeed different. Here Jews did not labor under the curse of any kind. Here one would find no litany of persecutions. Here an emancipated Jewry could successfully integrate into society while maintaining a creative cultural and religious life. Ample reassurance is given that any deviations from this sanguine picture- either from Jews who do not fit the pattern of successful adaptation or from non-Jews who practice discrimination- are atypical, the exceptions that prove the rule."[253] Schwartz suggests that the tone of the articles are apologetic. The entries dismiss anti-Semitism as the irrationality of medieval prejudices, attributing attacks to ignorance and delirium on the part of the perpetrators.

Schwartz further argues that the articles on Eastern European Jewry emphasize the extent to which Jews originally lived in harmony with other non-Jewish neighbors and display an anti-*Shtetl* mentality which assumes the necessity of enlightenment for Eastern European Jews. Schwartz argues that the articles are written with a typical Russian *Haskalah* perspective which equates the traditional Jewish way of life with ignorance, narrowness, and superstition. The view that "Hasidism is blamed for contributing to mental stagnation and intellectual obscurantism" and the critique of the stifling atmosphere of the *heder* education and *yeshivish pilpul* is an unstated bias of the Enlightenment perspective of the writer. The unstated message is that the Eastern European Jew must be brought out of primitivism and superstition by ameliorating his living conditions.

Conclusion on JE

The JE summarized and preserved Jewish *Wissenschaft* scholarship in English and America. The JE signified the transference of both the center and language of Jewish scholarship. Joshua Trachtenberg saw publication of the JE as the "first great fruit of Jewish learning in America."[254] In 1955 he believed that it still was "unsurpassed as the greatest single achievement of American Jewish scholarship." Salo W. Baron described it as "an extraordinary achievement and turning point in the history of Jewish learning in the U.S., a signal of the entrance of America into the field of Jewish *Wissenschaft* studies with distinction."[255] Shimeon Brisman describes the publication of the JE as a unique event that "signaled the beginning of the American era in Jewish cultural and intellectual history" directly influencing the course of Jewish learning in the United States.[256]

The contributors of the JE felt the need to articulate a modernized Judaism intellectually compatible with current scholarship including Biblical criticism and Darwinianism. The JE broadened the discipline of Jewish Studies by including the nascent fields of the history of Zionism, Yiddish Literature, and Jewish Statistics. It also served as a catalyst for American Jewish History later to be championed by Jacob Marcus. The JE put America on the map as a place for serious Jewish scholarship. The JE provided a forum for scholars like Kohler, Gottheil, Kayserling, Bacher, and Jacob to summarize their research for a broad audience. It also provided the opportunity for young scholars like Ginzberg and Lauterbach to hone their skills. During his time with the project Ginzberg prepared 406 articles and several monograph length entries such as "Allegorical Interpretation of Scripture" and "Law, Codification" which remain classics. The impact of the JE on Christian scholarship was seen concretely in George Foote Moore's book *Judaism in the First Centuries of the Christian Era: The Age of the Tannaim*. The JE thus altered the tone of subsequent Christian scholarship on Judaism.

The JE, although outdated in some respects, continues to be an important reference tool. Joshua Bloch, head of the Jewish Division of the N.Y. Public Library in 1926, noted that "there is not a day when we do not have occasion to make use of the volumes of the JE and to send numerous readers to its pages."[257]

The JE proved to be influential with regard to subsequent encyclopedias of Judaism. It became the standard, providing concrete guidelines for topic headings, entry size, and style. As well as the culmination of previous encyclopedias,[258] the JE became the paradigm with which later Jewish encyclopedias looked. While Judah David Eisenstein's *Otsar Yisra'el* (1907-1913) was written in reaction to the limits of the JE, the later *Russian Jewish Encyclopedia*,[259] the more popular *Universal Jewish Encyclopedia* (193943), the never completed *German Encyclopedia Judaica* (1928-34), and *Encyclopaedia Judaica* (1972) were all influenced by the precedent of the JE.[260] We now turn to the *Encyclopaedia Judaica*.

Encyclopaedia Judaica

The initiative for the EJ came from Nahum Goldman, the last survivor of the board of editors of the Berlin *Encyclopedia Judaica*. Determined that the Nazis should not have the last word, he proposed a Jewish Encyclopedia.[261] Silver notes, "Many in Israel were eager that the never completed German Encyclopedia Judaica receive an appropriate completion. As if to perpetuate that unfinished but invaluable work, a number of articles from it have been translated and placed in the EJ."[262] A small amount of the initial funding, obtained by Dr. Goldmann came from German reparations due for the cessation of work on the Berlin Judaica.[263] Later the Rasco Company in Israel and later the Israel Institute for Scientific Translation in Jerusalem helped with an offer to publish the books in Israel, because of lower printing costs.

Work on the EJ was begun in the United States under the editorship of Benzion Netanyahu (zl) of Philadelphia, then editor of the *Encyclopedia Hebraica*. AA. Neuman (zl) then president of Dropsie College became chairman of the American board of editors, later succeeded by Alexander Altmann (zl) of Brandeis University. Benzion Dinur (zl) of Hebrew University became chairman of the Israeli board.

Work began in 1966 and responsibility was accepted by Keter Publishing House which produced the 16 volumes two days ahead of the scheduled 5 year production date. Many Jewish scholars throughout the world were asked to contribute, but some scholars declined, refusing to hurry and rush through the work.[264] In charge of the board as general editor was Cecil Roth (zl) who died in 1970. In 1970 Geoffrey Wigoder (zl) took his place. The New York office was headed by Dr. Frederick Lachman, who coordinated the departments and divisions whose editors were in North America.

In 1966 the 25,000 entries were determined. The subject matter was divided into 20 major divisions and these were broken down into departments, each with its own editor so that altogether over 300 editors worked on the encyclopedia. According to Wigoder, "every one of the 25,000 entries went through 18 editorial stages and 32 technical stages."[265] The categories treated by the scholars included those such as: Bible, Hebrew, Semitic languages, Second Temple Period, Rabbinic literature, Talmud and Talmudic period, Jewish law, Jewish Philosophy, Mysticism, Medieval Hebrew Literature, Judaism, Jewish History, Zionism, Contemporary Jewry, Holocaust,

Chapter Three 45

Modern Hebrew Literature, Participation of Jews in World Culture, Modern Yiddish Literature, Americana, *Eretz Yisrael*.

The contributors were truly international. For example all four top editors (Drs. Cecil Roth, Louis Rabinowitz, Rabbi Posner) were British while the managing director of Keter Publishing House, Yitzak Rischin was from Australia, while other senior members of the editorial staff included Dr. Alexander Carlebach (formerly of Belfast) and Mrs. Joan Comay (from South Africa).

The work of illustrations and graphics department was headed by Mr. Moshe Shalve. It is reported that some of the photographs for the work were obtained by an American girl who met a Russian student and asked him to get her some slides of illuminated Hebrew manuscripts guarded in Leningrad. The EJ has made them available to the Western World for the first time.[266]

Special features include a 100 year Jewish calendar, a 26 page chart of Jewish history, a 50 page guide to ancient Israelite pottery, a table listing Hebrew newspapers, a full table of places in Israel, a Hebrew grammar, entries on the figure of the Jew in literature, descriptions of the treatment of Biblical figures in art, inserts on aspects of Jewish artistic expression, a selection of autographs of famous Jews, maps, diagrams, charts, and genealogical dynasties of Talmudic masters and Hasidic leaders.

Chapter Three 46

Recent Developments Effecting the EJ

In Ariel we read, "Every field of Jewish scholarship has undergone basic revision in the light of discoveries such as the Cairo Geniza and the Dead Sea Scrolls; the application of the social sciences- sociology, economics, demography- to Jewish history; the perspective of the biblical period afforded by archaeology and the new illumination of the entire Near East of antiquity."[267] The EJ is a result of these new disciplines and approaches. The introduction to the EJ notes, "Social and economic history was barely recognized as a subject for serious research three quarters of a century ago; now it takes a foremost position in historical scholarship."[268]

The following chart can be used to compare the JE with the EJ: [269]

Jewish Encyclopedia	Encyclopedia Judaica
European and American scholars	55% Israeli scholars / 30% U.S. scholars
No index	Computerized index
26 columns on Jewish ethics	10 columns on Jewish ethics
Jewish law classified in Rabbinics	Jewish law as an independent discipline
Legendary material	Legendary material more downplayed
No entry for Kabbalah	Scholem's 120,000 word essay on Kabbalah
Downplay Hasidism	Long essay on Hasidism and genealogical tables
No Jewish life in Muslim Lands	Jews in Muslim lands

Rabbi Akiba essay by Louis Ginzberg	Rabbi Akiba essay 1/3 JE length
26 columns on Jesus	8 columns on Jesus
Sparse on Biblical Archeology	Many findings on Biblical Archeology
Black and White	Color photographs
Pre-Holocaust (post-Dreyfus)	Post-Holocaust

The EJ is the product of developments in the growing understanding of the full significance of East European Jewry in Jewish history, the impact of Jews in Muslim lands, the study of Jewish mysticism by Gershom Scholem, the subject of Jewish law as an independent discipline from Talmud and Rabbinics, the importance of Jewish art, the increased interest in Yiddish language and literature, Biblical Archeology, the field of modern Zionism in all its political, national, religious, and cultural forms, and the Holocaust which has all developed as a result of a still evolving understanding of Jewish studies. Chaim Raphael refers to this expansion of scope in modern Jewish studies as a "changing point in consciousness."[270] *Catholic Library World* notes, "New developments in scholarly research is consolidated into this work: The Dead Sea Scrolls, recent excavations, Masada, the Dura-Europas synagogue in Syria- all relatively recent discoveries are evident."[271]

The contributors of the EJ do not fail in being seriously interested in the past because they view the past as dated and the present superior to the past. Rather the perspective is taken that views all periods equally immediate to God. Many of the contributors survived the Shoah and had no false illusions in the superiority of the present. However we can note the Enlightenment assumption that values "scientific method" above "medieval superstition and backwardness" is probably a bias the EJ does not escape. The perspective of scientific historicism holds itself superior to religious beliefs that can not be proven and which it views as naïve and uninformed.

Traditionalist Unease with the Modern Biblical Approach in the EJ

Chaim Raphael claims that the modern critical treatment of the Bible in the publication of the 1901-1906 JE, was more of a shock in 1906, than in the EJ of 1972. During the 19th and 20th centuries German Biblical scholarship, basing itself on Ibn Ezra and Spinoza had opened the Bible up to a radically different approach that called into question the unitary nature of the Torah as a divinely revealed work written by Moses on Har Sinai. In 19011906 the JE contained three sections in approaching the Bible: Traditional, Legends, and critical.

Raphael asserts that to read the critical section for a traditionally-educated Jew was almost like eating non-Kosher food. He comments, "Even to read it was daring. To believe it, even tentatively, was almost blasphemy."[272] German scholarship had called for (1) comparisons of the Bible to parallels in ancient Mesopotamian Literature,[273] (2) the understanding of religious ceremonies through anthropology and folklore, (3) application of the findings of archeology to parallels with other ancient cultures of the Near East,[274] (4) etymological studies of Hebrew with Aramaic, Sumerian, Akkadian, etc.[275] and (5) the

Chapter Three 49

Wellhausen Documentary hypothesis that the Pentateuch is an amalgam of four sources (JEPD) and the process of editing and redaction.[276]

According to Raphael the passing of seventy years has made the appearance of these views in the 1972 EJ less shocking. Even traditionalists, have become more acclimated to and tolerant of the radical findings of Higher Bible criticism. The EJ still recognizes the difficulty that some of its material on the Bible may have for some traditionalists. It notes, "Special problems were posed in the Bible division in view of the great varied and even radically opposing attitudes to the Bible and Bible Scholarship... It was felt that an encyclopedia designed to reflect all aspects of knowledge relevant to Jewish culture must in the sphere of Bible bring to the reader all views from the most traditional to the most critical."[277]

Nonetheless the 1972 EJ is modern in its capacity to usher the reader into a kind of skepticism and away from the traditional faith placed in the Pentateuch as the word of G-d. For example by showing internal apparent inconsistencies in place names as evidence for a complex multiple editing process or the repetition of certain teachings, themes, phrasing, and terminology by a particular editing school... some readers' faith may be called into doubt. The section on the *Masorites* and *Masorah* also suggests that the Biblical text was subject to subsequent editing and revision. The 1972 EJ does however, contain a postscript by Rabbi Louis Rabinowitz emphasizing that the true traditionalist still believes that the entire Torah is a "unitary document, divinely revealed, and entirely written by Moses (except for possibly the last eight verses recording his death written according to the *gemara* either in a moment of prophecy or by Yeshua ben Nun).

The Differences in Introductions of the JE, The German *Judische Lexicon*, and the EJ

As we have seen one of the purposes of Singer's 1901-1906 JE, as stated in the introduction, was to rebut anti-Semitism, which, it believed, could be corrected by eradicating ignorance.[278] The Enlightenment assumption that reason, knowledge, and argument were the cure to persecution caused by ignorance influenced the motivation for the making of the JE. Singer's naïve view that ignorance is the root of all evil is made problematic by the fact that one of the most educated groups of people in the world, the Germans, were instrumental in trying to exterminate the Jewish people.

The reader of the introduction of the German *Judische Lexicon* which began in the 1920s and the 1972 EJ in English will be struck by the differences concerning the phrasing of the stated purposes of these two works. In the *Geleitwort*[279] of the German Encyclopedia there is emphasis on the urgency (*dringende*) of the need for such a work whose purpose is to gather (*zu sammelnden*) knowledge (*Wissenstoffes*) in immense ascent to a thorough knowledge (*ins Unabsehbare gestiegen, anderseits eine auf inniger Verrautheit*), for a reliable understanding of Jewish Science in all its ramifications (*zuveilissige Kenntnis der Judischen Wissenschaft in allen ihren Verzweigungen*) to promote community awareness (*gemeinverstandlichen*). We read in the *Geleitwort* of the danger (*die Gefahr*) of forgetfulness

(*Vegessenwerdens*) of the Jewish community as a result of small familiarity with the Hebrew language (*Infolge der geringen Kenntnis der Hebraischen Sprache*). It would appear that before impending crisis and catastrophe in Jewish history a pattern emerges whereby a need to provide access to the well springs of Jewish learning is made available in an effort to avert disaster.

The goal of the German *Judische Lexicon* is to widen (*weiten*) the Jewish *circle (Judischen Kreisen)* of access (*der Zugang*) to the sources of Jewish *science (zu den Quellen judische Wissenschaft*) so that Jewish spiritual history (*judischer Geistesgeschichte*) will not be locked (*verschlossen*) and lost to the community.[280] The purpose (*Zweck der Enzyklopadie*) is summed up in the sentence, "*Darum bedeutet die Schaffung* (There is the meaning of the production) *einer modernen Enzyklopadie des Judentums gewissermassen* (of a modern Jewish Encyclopedia to a certain degree*) eine Erlosungswerk fuer* (as a redeeming work for) *viele zerstreute* (disseminating*) und meist unzugangliche* (making accessible the inaccessible) *historische Werke des Judentums* (the historical work of the Jews).

The passionate determination for a "redeeming work" (*Erlosungswerk*) in the German *Judische Lexicon* is substituted by a cool appeal to objectivity in the English EJ. In Ariel the purpose of the work is put this way, "An up-to-date balanced summary of knowledge and scholarship on every subject of Jewish interest- this is the objective of the English language *Encyclopaedia Judaica*."[281] *Booklist* notes a threefold purpose of the English EJ by writing, "The value of this work is in the role it can play in Jewish education and culture; in the spread of Jewish

Chapter Three 52

knowledge... and in the closer linking of Israel with Jews as well as non-Jews the world over."[282] Silver notes the importance of Israel as the center of the EJ's production by remarking, "EJ asserts the claims of Israeli scholarship to primacy in the world of Jewish learning. Germany had its day in the late nineteenth century, which was marked by the *Real-Encyclopaedie des Judentums*; the English speaking world had its day, which was signaled by the JE; and now, Jewish learning centers in Jerusalem, which to the EJ's editors is its natural home."[283]

Positive Reviews of the Encyclopaedia Judaica
Charles Berlin for Library Journal

Charles Berlin calls the publication of the *Encyclopaedia Judaica* "a very welcome event."[284] Berlin writes, "The publication of this work, providing a synthesis of this vast corpus of information, with special attention to the past 75 years (especially the development of the Jewish community in the United States, the destruction of European Jewry in the Holocaust of World War II, and the establishment of the state of Israel), is a very welcome event." Berlin further writes, "A welcome feature that greatly enhances this handsomely bound set is the approximately 8000 illustrations, although frequently the choice of a title page for an illustration is ill-advised, and in many instances it is difficult to justify the space allocated to a particular illustration."[285] Berlin notes that generally consultation with the 560 page index is "well worth the effort." Berlin concludes his review with a positive assessment by writing, "But as the latest, most comprehensive, and in many cases, most authoritative summary of research in all areas of Jewish scholarship, this new encyclopedia should be readily available in, and is recommended for, all academic libraries and medium and large public libraries."[286]

Daniel Jeremy Silver for CCAR Journal

Daniel Silver is generally positive about the EJ.[287] Daniel Silver opens his book review of the EJ with the following positive remark, "Probably the most important event in our scholarly world last year was the publication of the *Encyclopaedia Judaica* (EJ) under the general editorship of Cecil Roth. The volumes are beautifully printed and the pages are full of colored reproductions, charts, maps, and photographs which give the books a live and vigorous air. For those of us who were weaned on the Jewish Encyclopedia (JE), the new EJ emits a sense of life and of the present which the softer print and more modestly styled older set simply did not exude."[288] Silver confesses that the haste of the publication has not made for slovenliness. He asserts that in the hundred pages of the encyclopedia he has read he has yet to find a major typographical error. Silver considers it a good thing that the EJ's emphasis "is on the todays and tomorrows of Jewish life" for "its Judaism belongs to a live people." Silver notes the great advancement to learning in mysticism and *Kabbalah* as the result of Scholem's contribution. Towards the end of Silvers review he concludes on a positive note by writing, "With it all, EJ provides us with a good and valid encyclopedia. Those interested in historic theology and philosophy may find that some articles are not the equal of the JE predecessors. But some are better. The article on Jerusalem is a masterpiece. Any judgement should recognize that the EJ's great virtue is that it is concerned not merely with antiquarian scholarship. JE presented us completed faith.

EJ presents us the Jewish people. It is much more vigorous, alert, and vibrant."[289]

Time Magazine- a popular magazine with a large readership

Time magazine is generally positive[290] and calls the EJ "monumental." It cites the input of Israeli Botanist Yehuda Feliks to illustrate how the exciting field of modern genetics has much insight to offer on the ancient story of Jacob's breeding of monochrome sheep to produce spotted offspring. *Time* magazine implies that the new field of genetics is creatively applied to the interpretation of Jacob's secret as a keen perception of the laws of heredity to mate hybrids so that their recessive genes emerge to produce a maximum of spotted offspring. The reviewer in *Time* magazine positively comments, "Feliks' hypothesis, complete with genetic charts showing the results of the crossbreeding, is one of thousands of examples of the learned, the witty, and the arcane that fill the *Encyclopaedia Judaica*..."[291] *Time* magazine further positively notes, "The result shows few signs of haste. Some entries are so exhaustive as to be exhausting..." Time further is positive when it writes, "Such flaws pale beside the quantity and quality of the material that is included. Historian Arthur Hertzberg's meticulous article on Jewish identity examines every mode of definition, historical, sociological, and religious, carefully setting the Orthodox view against others."[292] *Time* further positively concludes, "David Flusser of the Hebrew University of Jerusalem has written a treatise on Jesus that Christians would do well to read." *Time* considers Gershom Scholem's 83 page article on *Kabbalah* "the most lucid treatment of the complex subject available."[293] *Time* is not alone in noting that the pages of the EJ are interleaved "with magnificent illuminations from medieval Jewish manuscripts and pictures of mosaics and frescoes from ancient synagogues."

Criticisms of the EJ: Zeitlin, Agus, and the Jewish Spectator

Zeitlin

Zeitlin asserted that the Jewish community does not have the reservoir of expert Jewish scholars capable of ascending to the task of the EJ. He writes towards the end of his critique, "The publication of the EJ is not a major accomplishment of world Jewish scholarship. On the contrary it reveals the paucity and decadence of Jewish learning. Many articles are below the standards of a good encyclopedia, they are sophomoric. The items dealing with the early history of the Jews are replete with distortions of historical facts. They may misguide the reader. In the articles on Halakhah and Rabbinics we note the lack of understanding of the text. The contributors are not to be reproved. A person cannot give more then he possesses. Many of the contributors are scholarly benighted. The blame is with the publishers and editors." [Note: Zeitlin critiques the following 12 aspects of the EJ:

(1) The article on Shavuot is inadequate and full of misstatements whereby carelessness and lack of comprehension is demonstrated." (2) The article on the Am Ha-Aretz uses Danby's faulty translation of Hagigah 2:7. Zeitlin points out that the term Perushim in the meaning of Pharisees never occurs either in the Mishnah or in the tannaitic literature but only in the dialogs between Sadducees and Pharisees. He points out the following falsities, (a) the synagogue as a house of worship came into Jewish life after the destruction of the Second Temple, (b)

the name Perushim was adopted under the meaning of exponents or expounders of the law, (c) Pharisees exclusively believed in the coming of the messiah, (d) Pharisees exclusively used the term Bore Olam and HaMakom when referring to G-d, (e) the Talmud quotes halakhah in the name of the Pharisees; (3) The statement made by the author of the article on the messiah is faulty and has Christological connotations. According to Rashi, Zechariah did not make mention of the messiah although the Church fathers interpreted this idea of messiah in verse 12, ch.6 as Jesus; (4) In the article on proselytes the author was careless in quoting the opinion of R. Eliezer or misunderstood the Talmud. The laws of conversion should have been listed; (5) The author of the article on Zealots presents a pseudo-historical essay whereby the author is confused and distorts the writings of Josephus who differentiated between Zealots and Sicari; (6) Zeitlin finds the article on economic history faulty for its using of the Roman term Palestine rather than the Hebrew and Greek term Judaea and the Roman term Dead Sea rather than Sea of Salt or Lacus Asphaltes. Zeitlin writes, "Does the author not know the simple fact that the land where the people lived was called Judaea and the people were called Judaeans." Zeitlin asserts that the article about the economics does not reflect at all the economic situation of the Jews of Judea; (7) The writer of the article on Jewish identity does not cite sources and attempts a much to ambitious subject for such a short space; (8) The writer of the article on Chronology is historically wrong about the Seleucid era; (9) The article on Halakhah is "full of mistakes and misunderstandings about the rabbinic texts, works from faulty translations, and lumped together all the takkanot during existing Jewish history so that there is no presentation of historical development whereby the distinction between Takkanot ha-kahal and Takkanot of Tannaim is blurred; (10) The article on the Dead Sea Scrolls and Qumran community is written from a partisan point of view (note Zeitlin misdated the Dead Sea Scrolls as medieval and not dating from the late Second Temple period); (11) Zeitlin is critical that the EJ should devote attention to items about Jewish gangsters and not important Jewish scholars. He writes, "There is a touch of vulgarism in this undertaking of the EJ. There is an item about Louis Lepke Buchalter, who was an American gangster executed for murder. There is also an item about another gangster Siegel Bugsy whose motto was "don't worry, we only kill each other." However there is not item about the well known Jewish scholars like Dr. J. Teicher and Professor S. Hoenig, and others. I daresay that the inclusion of gangsters and exclusion of Jewish scholars is an affront to learning and Jewish scholarship. It is a sad reflection on the editorial policy."] Zeitlin suggests that publishing of the EJ was an effort in public relations. Zeitlin finds twelve aspects of the EJ which he faults.

Agus

Agus is critical of the EJ for its inadequate treatment of reform and conservative Judaism. Further Agus feels that the Jewish attitudes toward Christianity are too brief and not well developed.[294] Agus writes, "The main failing of the EJ in relation to Christianity is that it does not contain a positive evaluation of the ideals that Christianity conveyed to Western culture, nor does it take up the task of explaining why Christianity succeeded in winning the Roman world, whereas Judaism failed to do so, a question that is certainly in the mind of the modern Jew."[295]

The Jewish Spectator

Like Zeitlin, Trude Weiss-Rosmarin in the *Jewish Spectator* points out inaccurate information and claims the existence of a generally low level of scholarly expertise. The *Jewish Spectator* asserts that the work is laden with errors concerning more traditional Jewish areas of study where faith and *Halakhah* still remain strong. We read, "As for teachers of the *Mishnah* and *Talmudim*, only the more important ones are listed- the *Tannaim* on one folio page and the *Amora'im* on two folio pages."[296] The Spectator implies that the EJ is harnessing authoritative Western modes of scholarship to short change the representation of Judaism's more traditional heritage.

The *Jewish Spectator* is highly critical of the editors of the EJ's penchant for Jews prominent in the world of entertainment while giving less attention to current Jewish scholars.[297]

As for keeping up with recent developments, the *Jewish Spectator* claims that the EJ has failed in that area when treating the work being done on the Cairo *Genizah*, U.S. Jewish communities, the Who is a Jew Controversy, and the Shoah. The *Jewish Spectator* suggests that the editors of the EJ might have achieved their goals more successfully if they had attempted through greater care and thoroughness to compile a shorter reference book of precise factual information rather than a reference book in the French Encyclopedist tradition of numerous book length expositions.

Conclusion:

Both the 1906 JE and the 1972 EJ constitute important compilations of Judaica. Both have sought to catalogue, preserve, and promote knowledge about Judaism and the Jewish people in order to enhance our legacy and to overcome ignorance and antiSemitism. As with all such ambitious and living documents, they have attracted both praise and criticism. The lively debate generated by these works is a testament to the dynamism and vigor of modern Jewish scholarship. It is the constant striving to improve, reformulate, add to, and go beyond these reference works that epitomizes the richness of Jewish Studies today.

Chapter Four
Reverence, love, cherishing of Jewish texts

Introduction:
To better understand the culture of Jewish learning and the reverence this cultural traditionally has in cherishing of the sefer, that the Nazis sought to exterminate along with the textual body of real live Jews, we must pause to consider in a brief historical overview the love for which the Jewish people throughout the millennia in the diaspora have for the transmission (masorah) or what Rav Saadia Gaon calls "reliable tradition", via the written and oral law.

Once we gain a better appreciation how this love is the life blood and essence for Jewish continuity, survival, and a uniqueness that associates itself with preservation of Jewish learning and teachings, we better gain insight into the Nazi keen radically evil perception that in order to murder the "Jewish race" (although Jews are not a race but united via a religion) one must attempt to first annihilate the Jewish raison d'etre which is "learning" (lomdos) that is associated with this love of the Jewish "text"- in its oral and written form. True the Nazis wanted a museum to the Jewish "murdered race" sans Jews. No other genocide encapsulates this Nazi satanic grasp of the importance of burning Jewish books, for the purposes of Judeocide. While the genocide against Native American Indians, however terrible, still continues to allow Native Americans to exist on reservations, the Nazis sought a Judenrein Welt, populated only with cultural museums to the exterminated Jewish race.

Thus the attempt to censor Jewish books, that we will overview in its historical context in the 2nd part of this paper, locating the Nazi censorship of the Jewish text in its wider historical perspective, cannot be understood outside of intuiting how the Jewish book and love of text in general, is a key to Jewish survival across history. Not merely as a form of "identity" but as the life blood of a living people. One academic put it this way: "the Jews love the torah more than G-d". Indeed since the torah is perfect and G-d is perfect then Torah and G-d are coterminous.

A clear connection between the Nazi book burnings, and the gas chambers, exists only if we see in broader perspective, the larger historical scope of Jewish censorship that allows us to better gain insight on specifically how one (censorship of the sefer and manuscript in Jewish history) led to the other (persecution of Jews in general, and Nazi Judeocide in particular). The bonfires of the Hitler boyscouts (HitlerJugende) were a necessary prelude for what was to follow. The burning of Jewish books and censorship of Jewish books for two millenia in Jewish history is inextricably linked and precisely consequential as a providential role in Nazi censorship of a whole Religious and ethnic groups raison d'etra and Haltung, encapsulated in and matrix of Judeocide.

Reverence, Cherishing, and Love of the Sefer
The reverence, respect, and love for Jewish books as the vessels of potential transmission (masorah) of sacred

teaching and knowledge, expanding consciousness (mogen gedolut) via a living teacher is found in Jewish law and custom. Abraham ibn Ezra referred to tomes as "sheaths of wisdom." The Vilna Gaon known as the GRA expresses the attribute of malchut (royalty) in in comparing the 62 tractates of the Babylonian Talmud to the 62 Queens, and the other many 100s of thousands of Rabbinic works to the "maidens who serve the Queens." The GRA also noted that his sacred tomes where his most precious possessions for just as "his feet allowed him to walk in this world, his books allow him to walk in higher worlds, even outside of history and time." The higher worlds to which the GRA refers are the Hechalot, the 7 heavens, or palace of Hashem, where according to Rabbinic texts, angelic doorkeepers guard gates, allowing certain priviledged souls who have attainted the highest levels of intellectuality and cognitive knowledge to enter into rooms where the soul is delighted and refressed by angelic discourses of fountains of wisdom. This motif is found in texts such as Rambam's Moreh Nevukhim chapter 52 Part II linked on our Rambam library guide at: , http://libguides.tourolib.org/rambam and Orhot Tzadikim. Since Kings in antiquity often served as Judges, as did Solomon, the notion of one's fate and judgment being written in a books is encapsulated in the High Holiday liturgy that on Rosh Hashanah it is written, on Yom Kippur sealed, and on Hoshanah Rabbah G-d's heavenly court of angels, deliver the verdict of one's yearly destiny to "G-d's archive." Besides from this book metaphor of providence, Maseket Rosh Hashanah notes there are actually 4 new years- for Kings, for trees, for Grain and of course the new Year. Ibn Ezra understands the importance of the calendar divided into these 4 new years within the context also of the Hebrew birthday corresponding to the Zodiac. [Note: Astral commentary, of 'Sefer ha-Moladot', which addresses the doctrine of nativities and the system of continuous horoscopy in nativities, and of 'Sefer ha-Tequfah', which is devoted exclusively to continuous horoscopy in nativities. The doctrine of nativities makes predictions about the whole of an individual's subsequent life on the basis of the natal chart, and the system of continuous horoscopy in nativities is concerned with the interval between life and [death] and makes predictions based mainly on anniversary horoscopes, which are juxtaposed with the natal horoscope. To Abraham Ibn Ezra's mind, not only are these two doctrines the core of astrology; they also epitomize the praxis of the astrological métier. If the Zodiac is a secret key or Rossetta stone for deciphering G-d as providential shepherd sheperding his flock of angelic hosts whose eyes are the stars which watch and guard meritorious individuals in proportion to the individual's attainment of intellectual virtue who sailing the sea of heavenly space by the constellations of thought, then this work by ibn Ezra enlightens the "eyes of its pupils" with expanded consciousness, light years and parasangs away of the purpose, function, and secrets of the heavenly bodies. Ibn Ezra rains upon us meteor showers of understanding which Jewish tradition has preserved in understanding works such as the Kail Adon which the GRA notes is an encryption for the planets which in Pirke de Rabbi Eliezer are said to move in the heavens like the hakafot on Simchat Torah and which in Menorat HaMaor are represented in the branches of the menorah thus the makloket between Pharisees and Sadducees in Tosefta Hagigah 3,8) (see: Yalqut Pequdei 40, #419; cf. Midrash Tadshe 11, Bet ha-Midrash 3, p. 175: חמה כנגד חמה ולבנה שבעת נרותיה כנגד ז" כוכבים המשמשין את העולם- The Menorah represents the

Chapter Four 64

sun and moon. Its seven lights represent the seven planets which serve the world; See Philo Quis rerum divinarum heres 225 & De vita Mosis 2, 102 & Josephus Antiq. 3, 146)/ Zechariah 4:10- 7 branches~ the eyes of Hashem ranging over the earth... pure diadem on Joshua צניף טהור ergo like מצנפת ציץ]. Indeed esoteric mysteries are hinted at in this work which in material terms can be found in the mosaics of the Zodiac correlating to the Hebrew months in the synagogues of Tzippori, Bet Alpha, and even the Bialastocker shul of New York! To this highly recommended work, a shooting star across our radar, we wish a welcome, Mazel tov! Ibn Ezra was zokeh to a vision of Providence and Hashgahah Pratit, with his naked eye astronomical observations, that today has been obscured, despite our sophisticated technologies for measuring and scientifically mapping phenomena such as meteor showers, Eagle Nebulae, comets, etc. because ibn Ezra's gaze was not obscured by the polluted skies of modernity and despite his genius as a polymath preserved the simple childlike faith of the Psalmist. (see Sela, Shlomo (eds. and trans.), Abraham Ibn Ezra on Nativities and Continuous Horoscopy:A Parallel Hebrew-English Critical Edition of the Book of Nativities and the Book of Revolution. Abraham Ibn Ezra's Astrological Writings, Volume 4, Series, Études sur le judaïsme médiéval, NY: Brill, 2014, xiv, 588 pp)]

In a comic vein, on Purim, little children dress up as a Sefer Torah, suggesting that all human beings are texts yearning to be interpreted and indeed cherished like our holy books. It is the love for the ideas in holy books that bring one closer to G-d that partakes of the books potential to foster Amor Intellectus and Amor Deus.

The Provencal scholar Rabbi Yehudah ibn Tibbon in the 13th century time of the Rishonim, wrote, *"Make books your companions; let your bookshelves be your gardens: bask in their beauty, gather their fruit, pluck their roses, take their spices and myrrh. And when your soul be weary, change from garden to garden, and from prospect to prospect."*

The Spanish poet and physician, Rabbi Yehudah HaLevy wrote, *""My pen is my harp and my lyre; my library is my garden and my orchard.[298]"1* The original line is:

נבלי וכנורי בפי עטי / גני ופרדס ספריה

"My harp and my viol are in my pen / its books are my garden and orchard of delight"

This is from the poem beginning "יונה תקנן" -- that's poem #110 in volume 1 of Brody's edition (Diyan : ye-hu sefer kolel kol shire Yehudah ha-Levi ...'im hagahot u-ve'urim ve-'im mavo me-et Ḥayim Brodi. Berlin : bi-defus Tsevi Hirsh b.R. Yitshak Ittskovski, 1896-1930). See p. 166, line 37-8.[299]

Rabbo Yishaq ben Yosef of Corbeil (d 1280 France) in his Sefer Misvot Qatan composed in 1276-77 in France around 1276 outlines a detailed strategy and plan for the dissemination of his texts by asserting that every community should finance a copy of his halakhic code and keep it so that those who wish to copy or study it will be able to have access on a daily basis.[300] He urges that if a Sofer of a community has to stay in another town in order to copy the book, he should be reimbursed for his expenses from the "public fund" and prescribes the rates. Not only should every community finance a copy of the Rabbi of Corbeil's work and make it available for copying and borrowing on a daily basis, but he further states that if a representative of a community has to stay in another town in order to copy the book, he should be reimbursed for his expenses from the public fund, and even prescribes the rates of expense. This would ensure the distribution of this halakhic code and ensure its standardization. This however was an exception according to Beit Arie in that most books were owned privately by individuals who could afford to maintain collections.

The Spanish statesman, Rabbi Shmuel ha-Nagid wrote, *"The wise of heart will abandon ease and pleasures for in his library he will find his treasures[301]."*2 Rabbi Abraham ibn Daud writes in Sefer ha-Qabbala about Rabbi Shemuel ha-Nagid that he had sofrim who copied Mishnah and Talmudim, and he used to donate these commissioned core texts to students who could not afford to purchase them in the academies in Spain.[302]

In an earlier period Hai Gaon, Head of Bet Din in 998 in Pumberditah commented, *"Three possessions should you prize: a field, a friend, and a book.[303]"* 3 However the Hai Gaon mentions that a book is more reliable than even friends for sacred books span across time, indeed can express eternal ideas, that transcend time itself as later expressed by Rabbi Shimon ben Zemach Duran (Tashbaz) who in his Introduction to Zohar HaRakiah writes, "However when the wise man lies down in death with his fathers, he leaves behind him a treasured and organized blessing: books that enlighten like the brilliance of the firmament (Daniel 12:3) and that extend peace like an eternal river (Isa. 66:12)."

Rabbi Judah Companton, a Spanish rabbi of the 14th century,[304] interprets the verse from Pirke Avot, *"Acquire thyself a companion"* to *"Acquire thyself a book, for a book is* better than companions for the truth and wisdom of man goes farther if one is diligent He who increases books increases wisdom."

The Chofetz Chaim wrote a prayer of intercession for Israel, asking for G-d's mercy on His people solely because they are guardians of the Jewish book:

> Behold, O Thou Master of the Universe, the honor which Thy people Israel bestows on Thee. Just look down from Heaven and see the crowns with which they crowned thy Holy Torah. Thou hast given to They people a Torah small in size, yet see how many mighty towers they have built upon it by writing holy commentaries. Thy studied every word, every letter, and every dot. All of these they have adonred and illumined with ornaments as white as pearls and bright as saphires. Just consider the two Talmudim; and then further chaplets of grace without number: The Midrash, The Zohar, the Sifra, the Sifri, the Mekhilta, the Tosefta, Alfasi, Rambam, Rishonim, Ahronim! Consider also the circumstances under which these expansions of the palace of torah were created: In the long and bitter Exile, between the fire and the sword, under conditions beyond human endurance and yet, they studied, learned, wrote, and relearned. So dear Master of the Universe, why art Thou wrathful with Thy people Israel? Do you have any other nation to compare that cherishes the Hebrew books so much? Therefore how long , how long dear Father in Heaven wilt Thou allow Thy faithful people Israel to endure its sorrows and sufferings[305].

The love and reverence for Jewish books is seen in Jewish law. It is not permissible for a sacred Jewish book to lie on the ground and if by accident a book is dropped to the floor is is picked up and given a kiss.[306] A Jewish books is not to be left open unless it is being read, nor is it to be held upside down[307]. 6 It is not permitted to place a book of lesser sanctity on top of a book of higher holiness, so for example one must never put any book whatsoever on top of a Tanakh. If one says to someone, "Please hand me this book," the book should be given with the right hand and not with the left hand."[308] If two men are walking the one who is carrying a sacred book should be given the courtesy of entering and leaving a room first, as the second is enjoined to pursue knowledge." [309] ." Rabbi David ibn Zimra of the 16th Century who wrote more than three thousand Responsa and volumes on Halkhah and Kabbalah comments, "that if one buys a new book, he should recite over it the benediction of the She-Heheyanu.[310]

Halakists debated the merits and demerits of lending or not lending private books. R. Asher ben Yehiel of Germany (1250 Toledo 1328) even endorsed a legal discussion to fine an owner who refused to lend a book ten gold coins a day testifying not only to the shortage of books, their precious worth, private nature of book ownership, and Rav Asher's personal view that knowledge is a common good and treasury of the Jewish people etc.[311]In a Responsa from Spain one rabbi Asher b Yehiel advocates the donation of books to synagogues, " so that "community books should be available to the poor of the town for studying since it would be a fault if they were to hang around idly for lack of books".[312]Community books therefore stored in synagogues were for the benefit of the poor who could not afford private collections. Yet even bucherim were expected to bring their own texts to school based on private collections as evidenced from a responsum of the head of the Mainz[313] halakhic school in the second quarter of the 11th century and from a responsum in 12th century Provence.[314] A rare example of an early example of a book produced for public liturgical synagogue use is found in the Bodleian Library from the 14th century by a scribe named Yakov.[315] The phenomena of privately commissioned but publicly used liturgical texts in the Middle Ages for the Cantor can be identified for instance in the well known Worms 1272 Mahzor.[316] Even this illuminated Mahzor was commissioned by private patrons. It was kept by its owner and taken to synagogue services. The earliest dedication of a book in a non-Karaite synagogue is a colophon dated 1469 of a siddur privately commissioned in order to place it in a Ferrara Italian synagogue under the condition that the community be able to consult it in the synagogue, but no one, neither "man nor woman" be allowed to take it out of the synagogue unless permitted by those in charge (Parnasim).[317] In the 15th Century two Yemenite ms were written for a synagogue in Sana'a- a biblical codex by sofer Yosef son of Benaya, the most renowed scribe in Yemen, in 1484 for the synagogue.[318] A well known sofer like Joel ben Simeon if he copied and illustrated a Pesah Haggadah without inscribing a colophon according to Beit Arie that is a clue that it was nto commissioned by a specific patron, but by a book dealer.[319] Two dozen colophons exist that were copied for chance buyers by the indication of unnamed patrons, whereby an empty space would be left for inserting the patrons names later, or by addition of a deed of sale by a scribe of an uncommissioned manuscript. Also noteworthy is that some scholars and authors were also highly qualified hired scribes for example Rabbi Jehiel ben Jekuthiel ha-Rofe, the sofer of the manuscript of the Jerusalem Talmud from 1289 (Leiden, University Library,

MS 4720) who was commissioned to copy three other manuscripts and who is identified as the author of Ma'a lot ha-middot, Tanya, and Hilkhot shehitah.[320] The phenomena also exists where persons who had been hired in their youth to copy books to later hire scribes to copy for them.[321] Besides these execeptions, however the majority of Hebrew books were privately commissioned. Beit Arie argues that beginning n the 10th century about half of medieval Jews books were self produced, a proportion unmatched in other civilizations of the codex. This high rate of self-production may be the most important information yielded by the codicological study of colophoned manuscripts shedding light on the transmission and textual criticism of Hebrew texts.[322]

Malachi Beit-Arie writes, ""altogether privatized consumption of handwritten Hebrew books (in Middle Ages) is associated with the entirely personal production and dissemination of manuscripts. This private character fits the individual nature of intellectual life prevailing among the dispersed medieval Jewish communities characterized by the lack of political frameworks or centralized authorities.... Unilke the preservation and concentration of the non-Hebrew books mainly in institutional collections (monastical, ecclesiastical, state, royal, etc), the Hebrew medieval book was initiated, produced, consumed and kept individually."[323] Beit Arie notes that "the European halakhic literature, the Tosafot, response, and various early halkhic works and the Sefer Hasidim of the German Pietist Movement in German, provide the richest information on Medieval books in general and on scribal practices n particular."[324] Beit Arie points out, "The documentary sources on Jewish books comprise mainly lists of books. In Europe – particularly in

Italy- these lists can be found on blank pages in manuscripts, where one of the successive owners registered his private library."[325] Book lists have been identified and classified by scholars.[326]The largest recorded Jewish library in the Middle Ages (226 books) was the library which was owned by the two sons of the banker, physician, Rabbi Abraham Finzi, Yishaq and Mordechai Finzi ofMantua.[327]Other private library ists include 156 books by Rabbi Judah Leon Mosconi in Jajorca around 1375.[328] Inventories of 26 private Medieval Libraries in Jaca (Huesca province of Aragon) were compiled in 1415.[329] Beit Arie emphasizes his thesis again on the private nature of medieval book collections by amplifying, "Almost all the literary and documentary sources relate to books in private possession produced as a private initiative, and to scribes hired by individuals, in order to prepare copies of specific texts for their personal use. All the European and some of the Oriental lists are in fact catalogues of private collections or lists of inherited books. From dedications on books we do learn however that books were kept in synagogues amassed over the years through donations by individuals who commissioned books specially or donated books from their private libraries.[330] The private personal nature of book production, ownership, use, and preservation is further documented by the SFARDATAbase[331] which analyzed over 4000 extant or copied colophons in medieval Hebrew manuscripts assembled by the Hebrew Palaeography project in the context of codicological documentation of dated and undated ms which include indications of scribes names. According to the colophons only a very miniscule # of the ms were commissioned by communities, mostly synagogues. The vast majority were commissioned by private individuals for private use. Scholars, intellectuals, and ordinary literate laymen who wished to obtain a copy of a text had three options: (a) They could aquire the desired book by locating an existing copy in their area and trying to purchase it from an owner as a number of medieval books include deeds of sale in their back matter. A rare case exists documented I the back of a 15th century Prrovencal manuscript where the scribe explicitly states that he wrote the book "for anyone who would like to purchase it".[332] The two other options open to those who wished to acquire a book, from the time of the earliest dated codices (beginning 10th century) involved commissioning tailor made production. One could hire either a professional scribe or casual scribe. The third option was copying the required text themselves. Both ways of producing new medieval handmade manuscripts depended of course on obtaining a model or exemplar for copying. According to Beit Arie, "almost all the literary and documentary sources refer to books in private possession, produced by private initiative, and to scribes hired by individuals to prepare copies of certain texts for their personal use. All the European and part of the Oriental book lists are in fact catalogues of private collections or listings of inherited books. The other kind of book lists found in the Cairo Geniza is deemed to have been book dealers' catalogues and inventories."[333]

With the advent of the printing press many scribes (sofrim) were distrustful of the new technology feeling that smugness would result from evolving from hand copied manuscripts to the printing press. Not to mention also their concern of the prohibition of writing down oral torah, now made more easy by the new printing press technology.[334] Rabbi Joseph Solomon del Medigo worried that the invention of printing would be responsible in a bad way for the increase in and spread of inferior books and confident that the survival of good and noble works would decrease citing Koheleth:

אֵין זִכָרוֹן, לָרִאשֹׁנִים; וְגַם לָאַחֲרֹנִים שֶׁיִּהְיוּ, לֹא-יִהְיֶה לָהֶם זִכָּרוֹן-- עִם שֶׁיִּהְיוּ, לָאַחֲרֹנָה

The great Rabbi Isaac Halevy Herzog, the first chief Rabbi of Israel in 1948, always carried a volume of the Tanakh when walking through the streets of Jerusalem. The rabbi explained that if people would rise in his presence as is befitting before a Talmud Hakham, the implication would be that they were paying honor not to him, but to the ideas represented in the text that he carried and surely knew by heart.

This reverence for the Jewish book translated into great Jewish book collectors like Rabbi Menahem ben Yehudah who in the introduction to his book, Bereita de Rabbi Eliezer and Midrash Agur (Safed, 1587) writes, " From the day I reached manhood I deprived myself of food and drink in order to pursue and purchase books that brought me closer to Hashem"[335] Another avid collector who sacrificed in pursuit of knowledge was the 16th century Rabbi Yosef Shelomo Delmodigo who lived on the Greek Island of Candia who confesses, "I have often traveled hundreds of miles by land and sea in order to search out, and buy, even a small precious volume."[336] In the modern period we do find some Ultra Orthodox concern that the expansion of the palace of torah[337] found in modern libraries widening collection development policies, that include the works of unbelievers (minim), and apkorsin (knowledgeable unbelievers), Karaites, missionaries, and Jews who reject the divine revelation of the torah as interpreted by Hazal constitutes if not in understatement "a challenge" (language of Haskalah) then downright a threat to traditional belief that could lead to the weakening of emunah pashut and bitachon, and even corruption of the youth so that issurim were issued forbidding the devout to visit by entering libraries of the masklim.[338]

For lovers of good books, one's library is something living and dynamic, the pride and joy of their lives, and more importantly provides the sepulchers of wisdom that can open gates in the higher heavenly worlds. Rabbi David Oppenheim (1664-1736) of Prague had a large collection that was acquired by the Bodleian library of Oxford University which views these volumes, some of which were specially printed for Oppenheim on vellum and blue paper, as a glory of its larger collections.

According to Schmelzer at the time of Oppenheimer major Judaica collections were in private hands. Schmelzer writes:

"There were Jewish communal libraries and collections at seminaries in Vienna, Berlin, Budapest, Paris, Cracow, Vilna, Warsaw, and elsewhere, and the library of the Breslau seminary was quite well known for its good collection of Hebrew manuscripts and printed books, obtaining in 1904 18,000 printed books and 400 manuscripts. Still neither of these libraries matched the major Hebraica collections or could have aspired to rival those of the Bodleian or the British Museum. Libraries of Jewish organizations and institutions could not and did not reach the level of Hebraica collection in royal, ecclesiastical, state, or university libraries in Europe. Historically no public Jewish libraries existed before the 18th century; Hebrew books were owned by individuals

> *and frequently significant private collections of Jewish owners were acquired by non-Jewish libraries. Thus two of the finest private Jewish collections, David Oppenheime's and Heimann Michael's were purchased in the 19th century by the Bodleian and by the British Museum; the important private collectionsof Abraham Merzbacher was acquired by the City Library of Frankfurt and that of David Kaufmann by the Hungarian Academy of Sciences- both at the beginning of the 20th century."*[339]

Before the 20th century however as early as the 19th century Jewish public libraries acquired new importance, in their importance being recognized for the dissemination and preservation of a common Jewish heritage, continuity, a loci of memory, and as repositories of the work of Wissenschaft scholarship. Abraham Geiger noted that:

> *The most eloquent witness for the respect of the spiritual work is the foundation and maintenance of a library. A library priveds not only nutrition for the spirit, but is also a monument to the spirit where our ancestors are gathered… A library pictorially represents for us the ties of times, where gray antiquity is intertwined with the bright present.*[340]

During the 1890s Jewish community leaders and members of the Association for Jewish History and Literature mandated estabalishment of Jewish libraries to preserve knowledge of the Jewish past.[341] With the establishment of Jewish public reading halls (**Lesehallen**), the number of Jewish libraries increased further.[342] Lesehallen were founded for example in Berlin[343] in 1894, Franfurt a. Main in 1905, Hamburg in 1909, and Posen in 1900.[344] The Deutsche-Israelitische Gemeindebund, Masonic Lodges,

Juedischen Vereingeschaften, and Jewish societies sometimes subsidized these Lesehallen located in primary urban centers. In the case of Frankfurt am Main a Masonic lodge sought to bring Jewish books to rural areas in the form of a mobile travel lending library.[345] The Montefiore Society, the Verein zur Abwehr des Antisemitismus (Association for the defense against anti-Semitism), and other Jewish educational institutions also sought to establish Jewish libraries.[346] Often modest membership fees included borrowing privileges but often the Jewish public could read books on premises if they did not check items out of the reading room. In the cases of scholarly merit borrowing fees could be waived as noted by Gerschom Scholem who only need to provide a note from his mother (zl) before he could use the collection of the Jewish community Council in Berlin.[347] According to borrowing statistics and patron volume statistics these libraries for example in Berlin example were used very heavily often with standing room only which Scholem attributes to the incredible thirst of German Jews in search for their roots, as a counter reaction to the process of assimilation and acculturation that had begun en masse centuries earlier, as a result of political emancipation and the modern Enlightenment. Discussion of essential core collection occurred regarding the phenomena of the Vereinsbibliothek.[348] The phenomena of the home library made possible by the relative greater ease of publishing, and Jewish thirst for cultural roots as a backlash reacton amongst some assimilated Jews after having attained status in the host society as a result of emancipation, assimilation, and acculturation gave rise to the greater number of Hausbibliothek.[349] Even in the Ghettos this thirst for Jewish roots could be identified in some readers who frequented Ghetto libraries.[350] Some Jewish libraries such as the one in the Nazi Ghetto of Vilna were allowed to function because German authorities felt they would be a useful distraction for ghetto residents.[351] Herman Kruk in considering the psychological attributes of the ghetto reader, classifies how books might still have any kind of relevance to their harassed, persecuted, and worked to death readers.[352]

Rabbi Mathias Strashun (1817-85) collected a magnificent library in Vilna as did the Hebrew bibliographer Heimann Joseph Michael (1792-1846) in Hamburg. Michael's collection is now in the British Museum in London. The great collection of Austrian scholar Solomon Halberstam (1832-1900) was incorporated into the library of the JTSA. German Abraham Merzbacher (1812-85) library later became part of the library of Frankfurt am Main,[353] many of whose books the Nazis collected for a museum to the "murdered Jewish race" and which ended up in the Offenbach depot, before being sent to libraries throughout the Jewish world, as described by Gershom Scholem, who was sent by the Israeli government to the Offenbach depot to bring back Hebrew books to the JNUL in Jerusalem.[354] The burning of Jewish books was all the rage by the boy scout Hitler Jugend who when the Fuhrer became chancellor of Germany on May 10, 1933 ordered the conflagration of more than 20 thousand Jewish books in the Square at Unter den Linden in from of the University of Berlin. The German bibliographer Eliezer Rosenthal (1794-1868 of Hannover was accessioned by the University of Amersterdam. Moses Friedland (1826-99) built the Bibliotheca Friedlandiana which was bequeathed by the Asiatic Museum of the Imperial University of St. Petersburg. The Russiah Jewish Orientalist scholar Baron David Gunzburg (1857-1910) library is know as the

Gunzburg collection in Moscow. In the English speaking world great Jewish private collections were built by Elkan Adler of London, Mayer Sulzberger, Dr. A.S. W. Rosnebach of Philadelphia, David Cassel, Moritz Steinschneider, and Jacob Schiff.

Jewish books are more precious than rubies, the bastion of Jewish survival, a survival kit enabling the perpetuation of Jewish existence and religion. In Sefer Iyov, amongst Job's afflictions he affirms, "But as for me I know that my redeemer liveth," who giveth solace in the written word, "Oh that my words were now written!/ Oh that they were inscribed in a book!/ That with an iron pen and lead/ They were graven in the rock forever! (Iyov 19:23-25). Heinrich Heine referred to the Jewish book as the "Jews portable homeland" for the Jew found surcease from his sorrows and persecutions and resilience and strength to survive from Jewish books. This is attested in Rabbi Joseph Teumin, in his introduction to his book Peri Megadim, which quotes from a letter sent to him by a Jew named "Levi the Poor Hebrew teacher": When I wake up during the long cold winter nights and my wife weeps because there is no bread for the children, and my mind is filled with agonizing thoughts, it is then that I sit down to open a book and to learn. The book then becames my city of refuge and my bastion of courage."[355] Shmuel Yosef Agnon who was also a great book collector, reminissed in recalling his grandfather's library in Eastern Europe and writes repeatedly of the sanctity and saving power of the Jewish book.[356]

Gershom Scholem in referring to his own library which he donated post humously to the JNUL, in a letter to Agnon cites a remark of the Besht, founder of modern Hasidim. He writes, *"all a persons' household items, his dwelling and his surroundings are filled with the sparks of his soul and are waiting to be lifted up."*[357] It is the librarian's job to raise these sparks of light,[358] to elevate them. And in the process a burning fire of the light of past generations continues to illuminate the present and into the future, the sefer becoming a sepulcher that not only can as Rambam notes, "draw one closer to Hashem" but also the bridge (gesher) between generations and the historical phenomena of the historical spirit of past "cultural harvests" (see Emerson, Ralph Waldo). The sparks of the souls of the wise of old who attempted to transmit their findings and knowledge to the future generations by writing their ideas down in books, presents the challenge of "raising up these sparks." However once a good reference librarian who has helped prepare access to patrons to access the sparks, the conflageration of cognitive illumination, shines and grows, nurtured by the librarian as a Platonic guardian. This glow indeed shines to recuperate the hidden secrets and intellectual treasures of the past, spanning generations, so that we might witness a "hadlikah" as intense as that on Lag B'omer at Meron, on the Rashbi's yahrzeit. To preserve the glow of these embers of wisdom, is the librarians job, not only to guide patrons to access the light of this wisdom. Such is often a thankless job, but great librarians like Alexander Marx and others, who supervised countless dissertations and donated countless hours to helping researchers navigate the coal bed of the glowing embers, deserve credit, for the light they have enabled to continue to shine into the future.

Even the secular Jew who shared a love for books with Gershom Scholem, his friend Walter Bejamin describes unpacking his library in quasi mystical terms of entering into a zuaberkreis (magic circle) as he creates a space of a house of books. Benjamin's 1932 essay, "Ich packe meine Bibliothek aus: Eine Rede ueber das Sammeln." Alberto Manguel writes in "the art of unpacking a library," February 1, 2018 of the Paris Review:

> *In 1931, Walter Benjamin wrote a short and now famous essay about readers' relationship to their books. He called it "Unpacking My Library: A Speech on Collecting," and he used the occasion of pulling his almost two thousand books out of their boxes to muse on the privileges and responsibilities of a reader. Benjamin was moving from the house he had shared with his wife until their acrimonious divorce the previous year to a small furnished apartment in which he would live alone, he said, for the first time in his life, "like an adult." Benjamin was then "at the threshold of forty and without property, position, home or assets." It might not be entirely mistaken to see his meditation on books as a counterpoise to the breakup of his marriage.*

The sages comment that in a divorce the altar weeps. Likewise in the destruction of the Beit HaMikdash the aggadata brings down: When in 587 B.C. Nebuchadnezzar set fire to the First Temple in Jerusalem, the priests gathered with the keys to the sanctuary, climbed to the burning roof, and cried out, *"Master of the world, since we have not merited to be trustworthy custodians, let the keys be given back to you!"* They then threw the keys toward heaven. It is told that a hand came out and caught them, after which the priests threw themselves into the all-consuming flames." A book and a whole library's books can serve as a "key" (mafteach) to opening the secrets in shamayim.

Alberto Manguel highlights how Benjamin experience flashbacks as the act of unpacking his books brought memories of recollections in sadness of where and when he acquired these relics in the past, a kind of noetic sketch of his life of book collecting and gathering, what in Yiddish is call the process of Kinus. Manguel points out *"Because a library is a place of memory"*, as Benjamin notes, *"the unpacking of one's books quickly becomes a mnemonic ritual. "Not thoughts,"* Benjamin writes, *"but images, memories"* are conjured in the process. *Memories of the cities in which he found his treasures, memories of the auction rooms in which he bought several of them, memories of the past rooms in which his books were kept. The book I take out of the box to which it was consigned, in the brief moment before I give it its rightful place, turns suddenly in my hands into a token, a keepsake, a relic, a piece of DNA from which an entire body can be rebuilt."* Ernest Hilbert in the Wallstreet Journal April 13, 2018 writes, "Walter Benjamin wove a spiritual aura around his books as he prepared to shelve them in a new home." He ruminated about *"the spring tide of memories which surges toward any collector as he contemplates his possessions"* and declared that the "acquisition of an old book is its rebirth." Hilbert reviews three books: (1) Alberto Manguel, Packing my Library (Yale), (2) Burkhard Spinnen's The Book: An Homage (Godine), and (3) Unpacking My Library, Edited by Jo Steffens & Matthias Neumann Yale). Hilbert writes, *"As all three volumes attest, a book's very presence, combined with its contents—tales, images, evidence—cast a peculiar spell on the owner."* Books have been written on the status alone of "the signed book," (im Hatimah), "the loaned book," "the right book", "the burned book," (i.e. the Talmudim) and even "the forbidden book" (censored books), and books that can "change, or end, a life" (i.e. the Sorrows of Young Werther *by Goethe caused a wave of suicides in Germany).*

Unpacking Benjamin's library in his short lived nomadic life where he encountered much antisemitism in the German University system, Benjamin says that he cannot march up and down the ranks of his books um im Beisein freundlicher Hoerer ibnenen die Parade abzunebmen, to pass them in review before a friendly audienece. Unpacking his books yet again leaves his mood expectant. Benjamin calls collectors (of books) Physiognomiker der Dingwelt or the physiognomists of the world of important godly objects, who once they step into the magic circle (zauberkreis) of the acquisition, become readers of their newly owned objects' provenance, the whole background for which becomes *"a magic encyclopedia whose quintessence is the object's fate."* Book culture and owning books for Benjamin enters mystical terms and the realm of magic when he refers to the phenomena as the stuff of a childlike Bezauberung or enchantment. Benjamin cites the Latin phrase habent sua fata libelli as the collector in whose hands a book both materializes and rematerializes is a mystical act of rebirth and renewal in potential for the soul that learns from the wisdom in the books. He writes, *"To a book collector you see, die wahre Freiheit aller Buecher irgendwo auf seine Regalen, (the true freedom of all books is somewhere on his shelves."* The most distinguished trait of a collection will be its Vererbarkeit or "transmissibility" for the fate of books is bound up with their provenance. For Benjamin "ownership" of a book is the most intimate relationship one can have with objects which more than coming alive through their collection, er selber ist es der in ihnen wohnt, *"it is he who lives in them."* You see when a book's contents are internalized they transform one's soul and ergo one's way of perceiving in the world leading to action influenced by great ideas in books. For examples the terms Kafkesque, Orwellian, or Kantian gesture to a body of thought that is life changing and ultimately redemptively determining as the soul aligns itself with a way of knowing, a way of seeing, a way of understanding guided by the books contents and arguments and demonstrations. Then one's relationship to the book becomes not owner but custodian and caretaker and guardian. In fact very frum Jews don't write their name in a book signifying ownership but rather write liHashem. The contents are so precious to the owner that the book itself is from Hashem. Benjamin's essay refers to book gathering not collecting ultimately to make a castle or fortress *"into which one might disappear inside as is only fitting."*

Simon Dubnov breaks down the cliché of intellectuals *"sitting at their desks, in scholarly solitude, with only old books to keep them company."* Instead, they worked — and saw themselves as part of — complex networks that sustained them. The scholars books are extensions of the tools of his intellect not just material objects. YIVO recently held an exhibit featuring Dubnov's musings on packing his library in 1921 in Petrograd and what the library meant to him[359]:

Notably Jewish scholars besides Scholem like Simon Dubnow, Salo Baron, Harry Austen Wolfson, and Saul Lieberman have also described their book and sefarim collections in quasi mystical language also. Thus a creative writer like Borges describes imagining heaven as a great celestial library in shamayim. Being without a library by deduction is like being in its opposite place.

A scholar librarian without a love for great books is like a surgeon without his equipment. The feverish enthusiasm and labor of love to gather and assemble and collect for instance every printed edition bearing even an indirect relationship on one's scholarly interests is a lifelong mission. William Osler for instance kept every edition of the work Religio Medici, for medicine and science were a calling for him, not just a 9 to 5 job, but as the title suggests yes a religious on science and medicine. So too Jewish scholars like Scholem who collected in niche areas such as Jewish mysticism are a great boon to future researchers. Scholem made Herculean efforts for instance to bring together all printed and manuscripts on Kabbala, Sabbateanism and Hasidism. This task required great bibliographic knowledge and detailed in depth knowledge of the history of the printing press and incunabula, as well as typography, lexigraphy, and paleography. Bibliographical research for any scholar librarian is a handmaiden to their research. It is not a separate area, what Nietzsche calls a pleasant sideline of diitantism. Rather it provides for, grounds, and is the foundation for any serious scholarly achievement. Bibliographical/librarian knowledge is not just the materials of a scientists laboratory to be coldly dissected by the scholar of the history of ideas with a philological scapel. Rather it is a growing, organic, and alive field of force that constitutes a base of knowledge requiring an emotional draw of electromagnetic pull and reach. The bibliophile of Jewish texts is not just someone who owns or possesses books. S/he has a "relationship" with texts, as alive and vibrant as any human relationship. Yet while friends may betray one, a book always is not static and provides further levels of understanding every time the scholar engages with it, so that eventually its contents become a matter of existence outside the physical, constituting a realm of the discmbodied intellect. Thus Rambam refers to the Moreh Nevukhim not only as "a key that may open gates of understanding in the 7 palaces of shamayim, into the chambers of which, the soul will be delighted and refreshed by angelic celestial discources that expand consciousness, and like Eliyahu naNavi clear up contradictions in textual sacred understanding, but for the Rambam he tells his star pupil Yosef, for whom the guide was written, that this work (as well as a key) should become so familiar to his soul, that eventually just recalling the chapter headings, will unwind upon his mind thoughts that "go up" into the worlds (olomot) of emet. It will come up on the mind the cognitive topos of the noetic world redeemed by truth and its pursuit. Thus the disctinction between function and essence, between the vesel and its contents, become blurred and cognitively coterminous, a triple point analogously were water exists as both: liquid, gas, and soldid. For a real lover of Jewish books, the pursuit of them, is almost irrational likening as a kind of sensual enjoyment. Before payday funds are allocated for the acquiring a special certain sefer.[360] The mission is a desire "without an end to desire." But this is no Faustian quest and Goethe describes. Rather the stakes are so high that they are ultimate. The quest could pivet on a world redeemed by the attainment of hokmah-binah-vedaas or not. That is why Rambam in Hilchot Teshuva notes that Biolam ha-bah the tzadikim sit with crowns on their heads, enjoying the ziv Shekhinah, The crowns on the heads representing one's eternal reward however are directly proportional to the hokmah bina vedaas achieved in olam hazeh. Thus this is not a game with words, not rhetoric, and neither mere game theory reducing all intellectual matters to "play." What is at stake is eternal redemption- or not.

Vulnerability to Censorship of the Jewish Sefer across History: Preservation of the Sefer as a form of Resistance to Censorship

Censorship of Jewish Books

Censorship is an important topic in library science. In this blog entry I hope to amplify and expand upon that Newsletter essay by noting further examples of *"enemies of the Jewish book."* Whenever persecutors of the Jews arose they also vented their destructive hate on the Jewish book.[361]

In the time of the Macabees, Antiochus Ephiphanes burned Jewish books.[362] The Mishnah notes *"among the five calamities that befell our people on the 17th of Tammuz was the burning of the Sefer Torah".*[363]

In the days of the Hadrianic persecutions Torah study was forbidden and the Talmud records the fate of Rabbi Hanina ben Teradyon who was one of the 10 Holy martyrs murdered by the Romans as memorialized on Yom Kippur in the Eleh Ezkera:

> *The Roman soldiers found him sitting and learning Torah, publicly gathering assemblies and keeping a Scroll of the Law in his bosom. Straightaway they took hold of him, wrapped him the Scroll of law, placed bundles of branches around him and set them on fire. They then took tufts of wool which they had soaked in water and placed them over his heart, so that he should not expire quickly but have a more prolonged and protracted execution. His daughter exclaimed: "Father that I should see you in this state!" He replied: If it were I alone being burnt it would have been a thing hard to bear, but now that I am burning together with the Scroll*

of the Law, He who will have regard for the plight of the Torah will also have regard for my plight." His disciples then called out: "Rabbi what seest thou?" He answered them, "the parchments are being burnt, but the letters are soaring high to heaven".[364]

In the medieval ages in June 1244, 24 cartloads of Hebrew books were committed to the flames. This holocaust was eulogized by Rabbi Meir of Rothenburg, on the 9th of Av. The kinnus lament prayer opens, *"O, ye who are seared in the flames, pray for the peace of thy mourners!"* [365]

The Spanish Inquisition under Tomas Torquemado further burnt many Jewish books as recounted by eyewitness Rabbi Abraham Sebag who notes that possession of a Jewish book warranted execution.[3666] Many Jews did not escape and were found owning Hebrew books and burned at the stake.

In Rome, Italy on Rosh Hashanah 1553 all found tomes of the Talmud were set to flames at Campo dei Fiori, and the eyewitness of Rabbi Judah Lerma in his book Lehem Yehudah (Sabionetta, 1554) writes:

> *On Rosh Hashanah the Curia of Rome issued an edict in all countries and they burned the Talmud and all works allied thereof. Also on the month of Marheshvan my authored books which were recently printed, 1500 volumes in all, were set to flames. So I was forced to begin all over again and to write it from memory.*[367]

Jonathan Rose writes, "*the mass slaughter of Jews was accompanied by the most devastating literary Holocaust of all time.*"[368] In Nazi Germany, less than 5 months after the Fuhrer became chancellor of Germany, on the eve of May 10th, 1933 he ordered his boyscouts (Hitler Jugend) to make a great conflagration of more than 25 thousand Jewish books, in the Square at Unter den Linden in front of the University of Berlin. Similar book burnings were staged throughout Germany which were a prelude to the burning of synagogues on Kistallnacht which took place on Nov. 9th, 1938 and was named a *"birthday present (geburtstag schenken) to Martin Luther's call to burn down synagogues and murder the Jews"* based on Luther's hateful works, Die Juden und Ihren Lugen, and *"Shem HaMephorash."*[369] A sign invitation in Munich[370] titled, *"einladung zum verbrennugssakt am Konigsplatz"* shows an announcement for one of many Nazi book burning rallies [371] 9

Unfortunately thousands of incidents like the one described in Chaim Kaplan's, Scroll of Agony, a diary account of the Warsaw Ghetto, go undocumented regarding the destruction of Jewish libraries under the Nazis radical acts of censorship. Rabbi Poznanski was the rabbi of the Tlomackie Synagogue in Warsaw, the largest population of Jews in Eastern Europe rivaling Vilna and Minsk. R. Poznanski served as the head of the library and was an important scholar of tekufah of the Geonim. Poznanski served as librarian of the Tlomackie synagogue which under Poznanski grew to a collection of 40,000 books including manuscripts. At first the library was in a number of rooms but then it expanded to a separate building. Despite Solomon Schechter invitation to Poznanski to join the JTSA faculty and to become its librarian in 1902, Pozanski refused to abandon his congregation in Warsaw. The destruction of the library is depicted In the Warsaw Ghetto diary o Chaim Kaplan, retitled The Scroll of Agony, we read:

> "The day before yesterday (Oct. 23), like true Vandals, the conquerors entered the Tlomackie Library, where rare spiritual treasures were stored. They removed all the valuable books and manuscripts, put them on trucks, and took them to some unknown place. This is a burning of the soul of Polish Jewry, for this library was our spiritual sanctuary".[372]

Systematically the Nazis sought to burn and confisgate Hebraica and Judaica. Kohut recounts the news heard about the Nazi destruction of the Kohut library in Vienna by writing:

> I can remember clearly the day a letter arrived from Vienna telling me that the Nazis had burned the books of the Kohut foundation there (in Vienna). In my distress I turned to Professor Marx, who rushed to my home as soon as he received my call. Words cannot describe Professor Marx's grief as he read the letter. Each one of the books of the Kohut library was like a treasured friend; the loss was irreparable.[373]

As Nazi hordes took over occupied lands in a campaign of pillage, robbery, confisgation, and Einsatzgruppen mass murder of Jews, the Nazis set aside some Jewish books, for a future Museum to the murdered Jewish race. After WWII this collection of Hebrew books at the Offenbach Depot was confisgated by the allies, and the scholar Gershom Scholem was sent to salvage and bring back to the Jewish National Library in Israel precious tomes.[374]

Prior to the Holocaust Marx of the JTSA anticipated destruction so in the 1930s the rescue of European Jewish treasures was sought. The transfer of ritual objects and Sifrei Torah of the Danzig Jewish community to the Seminary in 1939 is documented by the Jewish Museum.[375]

Schmelzer cites a letter of Doctor Israel Schapiro to Marx as follows:

> *I take this opportunity of bringing to your attention a proposal of Leo Winz, former editor of Ost und West in Berlin, and now a resident of Tel Aviv, Palestine. Mr Winz in a ltter recently received states that the Jewish library in Vienna was burned by the Nazis, and that other great Jewish libraries and cultural collections in the Reich stood in similar danger.*
>
> *Mr. Winz suggests that such valuable collection as those in the Rabbinical seminary at Breslau,[376] the Hochschule fuer die Wissenschaft des Judentums and the Hildeschiemer Seminary in Berlin, as well as the library of the Juedische Geminde in Berlin could be ransomed for a moderate sum and brought to this country or to Palestine. He cites the German need for foreign exchange as a probably inducement for the Nazis parting with these collections at a reasonable figure and thinks a committee should be formed in this country to collect the monies. I do not know whether you have already been approached on this matter or you thought it practicable.[377]*

In the Former Soviet Union for many decades there was a ban on printing, distributing, or owning Jewish books. As Rabbi Yitzchak Zilber notes learning Hebrew and Rabbinic texts had to take place in secret. [378] During the Stalin regime the purge of Jewish intellectuals, poets, writers, and philosophers who were often murdered or sent to Siberia, also involved the confissgation of Jewish literary treasures.

These salvage efforts were not undertaken and it is not known according to Schmelzer what steps in any were taken by the JSTA or other organizations.[379] In the post

WWII aftermath the Jewish Cultural Reconstruction Organization headed by Salo Baron and administered by Hannah Arendt was responsible for the distribution of many thousands of Judaica and Hebraica works looted by the Nazis and recovered after the War from the Offenbach warehouse, intended to serve as a stockpile to a Museum of the murdered Jewish race.[380] Schmelzer quotes te 1955 librarian Gerson D. Cohen who reports that 28 thousand volumes arrived in the library in one year.[381] Schmelzer thus deduces that it is no wonder that in 1958 the librarian Nahum Sarna referred to 55 thousand uncatalogued books and an equal number of tomes in need of binding.[382]

The Koran calls the Jews, *"the people of the book"* but indeed the Jews are "the people of the books" and Jewish survival is inextricably linked to the preservation, learning, and internalization of the contents of those written and (oral) sacred texts.

As shown in the Houston AJL presentation, it is during times of crisis that oral traditions are written down as illustrated by the Mishnah in 210 by Rav Yehudah haNasi, Rashi and Tosofot during the Crusades, and the Rambam's transmission of ma'aseh merkavah and ma'aseh bereshit during his own times of crisis as encapsulated in the Moreh Nevukhim. As Heinriche Heine noted, when books are burned then people can be burned[383] as illustrated in the Hadrianic, Rav Terydion one of the 10 martyrs during the Roman persecution who was wrapped in a sefer torah with wet wool and lit on fire, and Nazi Jewish text burnings. Censorship in general is not new to the Jewish people but will continue to be waged against Jewish texts as long as there is hatred of Jews and their traditions. It will be resisted as long as there are those scholars who revere, cherish, and love the sefarim... as the gateways to coming closer to Hashem.

Conclusion

Heine was correct that burning of Jewish books would inevitably lead to burning Jews. But if we stop there with this platitude we fail to better understand the secret dynamic of how the Jewish spirit is inextricably tied to the Jewish learning represented in Jewish texts, oral and written, and how censorship of those texts, is the first step for any enemy in the ultimate censorship which is to censor Jewish lives. That is one of the lessons we learn from the account of the eleh ezkareh martyrs recalled in the liturgy for the day of Yom Kippur. We who do have utmost high regard for the plight of the Torah because we revere, cherish and love Jewish living text, are prudent to recall the last words of Rabby Terydiyon who was wrapped in a sefer torah with wet wool for a protracted cruel painful death:

> *If it were I alone being burnt it would have been a thing hard to bear, but now that I am burning together with the Scroll of the Law, He who will have regard for the plight of the Torah will also have regard for my plight." His disciples then called out: "Rabbi what seest thou?" He answered them, "the parchments are being burnt, but the letters are soaring high to heaven"*

What the gemara calls *"Black fire on white fire,"* is perhaps the paradoxical estoric mystery of this "fire of censorship" that is the encrypted riddle that perhaps explains a tincture of the inextricable link and essential bond for the infinite love-reverence-and cherishing of text by Jewish scholars, and Why censorship of any form of those texts, is so tragic, and indeed the first step in any planned

Judeocide. From the spiritual annihilation planned by the Greek Antiochus, to physical planned annihilation by the roman Censors, to the Crusader thugs storming across Europe, to the Inquisition fixated to ferit out heresy, to Nazi boyscout book burnings, and more recent censorship of Jewish books in the former Soviet Union, censorship of text leads to censorshop of Jewish persons as texts yearning to be interpreted as what Derrida calls a field of force. By placing the Nazi censorship of Jewish books that led to utlimate censorship of Jewish lives, in its historical context we better understand the dynamic of European Jewry rabbinic culture and its love-reverence for text either in the written or oral form. Thus the relationship of the text in general and the Jews as a universal eternal unique people, and the book and the victims of the holocaust in particular, come center stage as the secret esoteric dynamic that makes Nazi Judeocide or any attempted Judeocide in history, not only unique because of the Jewish people's unique rabbinic heritage and cultural treasury, but because the "text", however we understand the term text in its deepest most sublime depths, is the merkavah (chariot) that conveys the unique and singular unique destiny and spirt of the Jewish people on the stage of history. Just as Eliyahu ha-navi ascended on a chariot of fire to the heavens, transmogrified alive to the heavenly court, as witnesses of Nazi book burnings we too if we understand the importance of remembrance-perservation- and internatalization of "jewish texts", proclaim with Eliyahu's disciple Elisha, "My father, my father, the chariots of Israel and the horsemen thereof!"[384] The rabbinic riders of the heavenly chariot who descend to the merkava (yored li-merkava) to ascend to the 7 heavenly palaces, are indeed the expert 'horsemen' of a spiritual chariot unique to the Jewish people. Just as there is an earthly chariot below there is a heavenly chariot above, and just as there is a court below there is a court above, and just as there are voices below there are heavenly voices above (kolot elyonim). When the traces of Hazal's wisdom are committed to flames in the attempt to wipe out these righteous sages memory, and more importantly the transcending substance of their eternal teachings, by attempts to reduce the sepulchers of their torah preserved in the shells (klipot) of books to mere ashes, for certain the angels of Hashem will revive those ashes with the dews of resurrection, transported on the wings of angels, to the throne of glory, before the King of kings, who remembers the past-present-future simultaneously and even beyond time itself, the particular destiny and spirit of salvation that makes for redemption, the unque mission of each precious soul of his holy people Israel, also likened to each letter of the Torah, which itself is an encryption of Hashem's holy name(s), proclaiming the symphony of Divine Creation from the beginning of beginnings, thru revelation of Shir HaShirim, to find eschatological redemption biyamei Aharonim, to even beyond the doctrine of shemitot ha-olamot, or the 50,000 year of the Universe's Creation, after the 7 worlds lasting 7000 years are enacted on the stage of temporal unfolding, indeed the year of the disembodied intellects, the heavenly unfolding of ultimate Binah emanating from the sefirah of Malchut, malchut hinted at on the Yahrzeit of Dovid HaMelech on Shavuos, the 50th day of the Omer corresponding to the ultimate Yovel when Hashem will be One and His Name will be One, and the Text of the generations of the heavens finally written as told on Rosh Hashanah, Sealed on Yom Kippur, and delivered to Hashem's eternal "archive" by the heavenly archons/malakchim, on Hoshanah Rabbah. Hoshanah Rabbah was purposely along with Tish B'av chosen as the day for mass murder of millions of Jews. The Nazi logic was ingenious, demonically clever, and completely consistent with divine providence- The Jew and text are one?

Chapter Five

The Ethics, Hermeneutics, Politics, and Theology of Hebraica Translations -

The Cases of Shir HaShirim, Akedat Yitzhak, Isaiah's almah vs. parthenos, Michaelangelo's mistranslation of keren, and kelei zemer in Tehillim

Across History in the Targumim, Septuagint, Peshita, Vulgate, Tafsir (Arabic), Yiddish, Ladino, Biur of Mendelssohn, and Rosenzweig's Die Heilige Schrift und ihre Verdeutschung

Description:
We will consider translations from the perspectives of library science, philosophy (epistemology), philology, theology, linguistics, and politics. We will look at some of the differences between the Tanakh (Hebrew), Targumim (Aramaic), Septuagint (Greek),Vulgate (Latin), Tafsir (Arabic), Peshita (Syriac), Judeo-Spanish (Ladino), Judeo-German (Yiddish), Beur (German of Mendelsohn), and Die Schrift und ihre Verdeutschung (Rosenzweig and Buber). We will consider theological choices in translation and we will explore the politics

of collecting translations and the difference between literal and poetic translations.

Are all Translations[385] Interpretations[386]- Is the Library a Tower of Babel?:

The Politics, Hermeneutics, Theology, an Ethics of Translations Across History in the Targumim, Septuagint, Vulgate, Tafsir, and Beur Walter Benjamin remarks regarding the "Art of the Translator"[387] set the question of "translation" as it relates to book culture and libraries out as a major topic for modern philosophy. So too in Israeli culture thoughts regarding translation and book culture abound. Agnon comments, that "anyone who translates is a liar, but anyone who doesn't translate is a thief"

גזלן הוא מתרגם שאינו מי כל אבל שקרן הוא שמתרגם מי כל

As well as Bialik's humorously remarks, that "reading a translation is like kissing the bride through a veil, etc."

את לנשק כמו זה תרגום ללמד צעיף דרך הכלה

In this article I hope to show that translations are often interpretations and the important ramifications this has for the library as the home of memory for the translations of different cultures. The library is not a tower of Babel that will collapse in its quest to serve as a gateway linking patrons closer with divinity, but rather the libraries offering of sanctuary to the translations of different and diverse cultures makes the library stronger, more fortified, and enriched as a castle of memory shedding light on the diversity of different ages, cultures, and histories of the reception history of texts.

The following six examples demonstrate that translations are often interpretations:

(1) In Rav Sadia Gaon's Arabic translation of the Hebrew Bible on Genesis 22 (the Akedah), the rabbi changes the tense of a verb with theological consequences. The Akedah raises the question of predestination and G-d's foreknowledge (*yedidah*/ידידה) and *hashgahah pratit*/ (פרטית השגחה) and free will (*bihira*/ חפשית בחירה) which is encapsulated in the mishnaic dictum, "Everything is foreseen but freedom of will is given (*HaKol Tzophuyey veReshut Nitanah*). The Hebrew texts include the verse after Avraham passes the test (*nisiyon*/נסיון) something to the effect, "Now I know that you fear HaShem"

Rav Saadia is uncomfortable with the suggestion of this Hebrew construction that there was any lacunae or absence in Hashem's knowledge/omniscience and therefore uses the verb in Arabic _ARAFTU_ which suggests that G-d already knew Avraham would pass the test before the angel said "do not sacrifice Isaac" (*al tishlach yadchah el hanaar*). The *Degel Yehudah* is comfortable with the original Hebrew and suggests that the test was meant to educate Avraham himself and the world that Avraham is a "knight of faith" (Kierkegaard) despite Louis Jacob's objections to Kierkegaard's Christological underpinnings.

However Rav Saadia changes the tense in the translation from Hebrew to Arabic so as to suggest that indeed "Everything is foreseen (*Hakol Tzephuyey*/ נתונה והרשות צפוי הכל) since G-d knows the past, present, and future simultaneously although paradoxically we must act as if we have free will so that there is human accountability and responsibility for moral actions. The translation is clearly an interpretation.

Chapter Five 99

(2) In the Septuagint or Greek translation of the Hebrew Bible the text draws on an opinion in *Midrash Rabbah* that clearly changes the meaning of the original Hebrew text. In the Hebrew text Batya, or Pharoah's daughter is said to extend her own hand (amahtah) to retrieve

Moses in the basket on the Nile

However in the Rabbinic Midrash on which the Septuagint draws, Batya is said to send out her maidens who retrieve Moshe. Clearly the translation is again another interpretation.

(3) In the third example the discoveries of archeology shed light on the translation of the word for "harp/stringed instrument" in the Hebrew Bible, Greek *Septuagint*, and Latin *Vulgate*. In the Hebrew text King David is said to play the *kinur* to cure Saul of his meloncholy and in the Talmudic Tractate *Maseket Berachot* 3b-4a[388] we are told the *Aggadic* tale that King David hung his harp above his bed and at midnight a magical breeze blew upon the harp making magical music which woke King David, who would play music until the sun rise (literally sparkling of the dawn.) Biblical archeologists have found Mosaics, vase paintings, oil lamp illustrations that show the word for harp in Hebrew "*kinur*" to be 2-3 cubits long. So too in the Greek period (310-160 B.C.E.) the word for harp is transliterated "*lyre*" and again the archeological record testifies to an instrument roughly 2-3 cubits long.[5] However when we move into the Roman and Byzantine period up until the 18th century where Latin was the academic language of learning in the western world, the word for harp is "*psallere*" and the archeological evidence in mosaics, paintings, etc. represents such an instrument to be over [Note: See Braun, Joachim,

Music in Ancient Israel: Archaeological, Written, and Comparative Sources, Erdmans Pub. Co., 2002; in David B Levy's library guide for TC Jewish art David writes why music is the most spiritual of the all the arts:

While the fine arts are in essence corporeal, music as an art is purely of the spirit and the most spiritual of all the arts. The work, "Ta'amei HaTa'amim" (The reason for the trope), authored by the Masorite Asher ben Asher who lived in Tiberia sometime in the 7th century likens the art of cantillation to giving "soul" to the letters of the text. In this work when the baal korei chants the text correctly according to musical trope this act of music "opens the gates in Shamayim." While the letters of the text are the body of the torah, the music is the soul according to the Masorite Asher ben Asher. Music in antiquity was employed by many prophets in order to prophecize and go into ecstatic trances as noted by Dr. Moshe Idel and King David is said to have cured the meloncholy Saul by playing the harp. Dr. Joachin Braun has noted the differences in size of musical period instruments in antiquity such as the harp during the 1st temple (kinur), 2nd temple (lyre), and Roman and Byzantine periods (psaltrium) whereby the size, pitch, and harmony of the instrument was changed by differences in the representations of the instrument in these different time periods. For instance the magrepha is a strictly 2nd Temple instrument which is mentioned in the mishnah said to be shaped like a shovel and some sort of percussion instrument.

Music is magical and represents the spirit of a people. According to the rabbis of the Talmud "one had never seen a beautiful sacred building if they had not gazed upon the Beit HaMikdash, and one never heard "sublime music" if they never heard the Levites singing on the steps, the sweet singers of the Temple litrugies. Indeed Josephus tells us that the Beit Hamikdash was made of marble that was painted Mediteranean sea blue, and when the sun rebounded off of the gold dome, the blue painted marble had the appearance of shimmering Mediterrean pure sea waters. Thus Rabbi Akiva in Maseket Hagigah says, "al tamru mayim mayim" because the shimmering appearance of the illusory play of light on the blue marble is not indeed water, but marble painted blue in the sunight. So too the music of the Beit HaMikdash was even more holy and we learn many insights about this music from the Talmudim. One remark notes that when the Levites were taken in slavery to Babylon one Levitical family that excelled in instrumental music cut off their thumbs so that they not be able to teach music to their captors. "On the rivers of Babylon there we sat and wept, when we remembered Zion" for the Levites refused to sing a new song of an old land in a land of captivity in deference to the music of the Beit HaMikdash, and indeed in the rishonim period Rabbinic halakhah proscribed the use of music instruments even at weddings in order to remember the true and final place for sacred music to be sung by the Levites in the Temple as expressions of kedushah and spiritual elevation. Thus the book of Lamentations (Eikah) is chanted in a minor key representative of dirges in musicology to express the deep emotion of and feeling of ultimate loss caused by the Hurban. Psalms during the 1st and 2nd Temple periods were set to music. We know this by many musical instructions innate to the language of Psalms such as "selah" which indicates an ascending scale on a stringed instrument. Sol Finesinger has written an excellent article titled, "Musical Instruments in the Tanakh" in which the scholar notes the differences in language for musical instruments mentioned in the Tanakh as theiy appear in their latter translations in the Targumim (Aramaic), Septuagint (Greek), Vulgate (Latin), Tafsir (arabic), Ladina (Judeo-Spanish), Le texte sacre (French),

Die Heilige Schriften und Ihren Verdeutschung (German) etc.

All periods of Jewish history gave rise to expressions of different cultures of Jewish music from Ladino songs, Sephardic pisgomim, to Yiddish folk songs. These music traditions are rich in beauty and deep in expressing the whole gamut of the emotions from sadness to ultimate joy and happiness. Music is the food of love indeed because it is the opposite of anything corporeal but wholly and holly an expression of the eternal spirit of human beings striving to reach the stars and G-dliness. Maimonides wrote a teshuvah on "listening to music" that was recently republished in this century by Dr. ISrael Efros, past president of the Baltimore Hebrew University, and from this teshuvah we learn that the Rambam distinguished between good and bad music. Bad music is lude, vulgar, and a thing of common people who live at the level of animals deriving no pleasure except from eating and things of the body while on the other hand good music serves a number of functions including, lifting one's spirits from meloncholy i.e. a thereapeutic function, and ultimately giving expresion to the ultimate longing and desire of the human being "for dwelling closer to Hashem."

A Hasidic rebbe is said to have been so influenced by music's power that the Rebbe at seudah shelishit, when various Hebrew songs are sung, actually practiced a mystical technique of allowing his soul in musical ecstasy to "go out and not return" (yotzei ve bili teshuv) and the Rebbe song a niggun on particular shabbos seudah shelishit with all devotion to hashem in ahavas Hashem, ahavas Torah, and ahavas olam, that the Rebbe's soul did indeed go out and depart to the higher realms. We learn from esoteric Jewish texts that the Jewish souls (neshamah, ruah, chayah, and nefesh) are defined by musical ratios represented on stringed instruments, and indeed the transmigration of the soul (gilgulim) is sent on its journey to a song. Rabbi Yehudah HaLevy poetically and philosophically wrote in a poem that one turn one's life into a song, and it is through music that all transcendance is possible. While as Kohelet notes there is a time to sing and time not to sing, the piyutim (liturgical poems) that adorn and pepper the Rosh Hashanah and Yom Kippur Mahzor, representent the varous angels of varous hierachical ranks, in fact intoing celestial sublime song, which is not just fitting praise of Hashem who is leilah leilah (beyond all praise) but because of Hashem, who created the spirit of the soul, which can only find its ultimate expression in song.] five feet tall, the size of a Celtic Harp, etc. Thus the translation is an interpretation again.

(4) In the fourth example we find controversy with regards to the translation of the word *"almah"* in Isaiah 7:14. In Hebrew _almah_ can refer to either a virgin (*betullah*/בתולה) or maiden. On can translate Isaiah 7:14 as, *"Lakhain yitain Adonai hu lakhem ot. Hinei haalmah harah viyiledet bein vikarat shemo Emmanuel"*
אות לכם הוא אדני יתן לכן עמנואל שמו וקראת בן וילדת הרה העלמה הנה

The Septuagint translation uses the Greek word _parthenos_ which means *betullah*, and Christological exegesis saw this as a foreshadowing of the birth of *Yeshka* by the Virgin Mary, while Rabbinic commentary *insinuates* that she was not a virgin or was impregnated in a bath in which someone named Jeremiah had ejaculated. Both Ibn Ezra and Redak refute the Christological inferences from this verse. Since the sign was given to Ahaz to allay his fears of Israel and Aram, it does not make sense that he should be given a sign of something to occur over four hundred years later. Moreover, verse 16, which foretells the defeat of Aram and Israel before the child knows to reject evil and choose good, proves conclusively that the child was to be born in the immediate future. Likewise the translation "virgin," for *almah* is completely erroneous. The word is used for a young woman, regardless of whether she is a virgin or not. As proof, the masculine, *elem*, which, obviously is not related to virginity.

(5) Among the most famous translations that resulted in the change of meaning of the exoteric Biblical text, is the translation of the Hebrew word "*Keren*/ קרן," which has several meanings, as "Horn/ שופר ." "*Keren*" in the Hebrew text meant to imply "beam of light." As a result of the Vulgate of Jerome the mistranslation and different meaning came into being so that as a result, artists over the ages have depicted Moshe Rebbenu, the giver of the *nomos*, with horns growing out of his forehead. Michelangelo's sculpture of Moses is one of many depictions. In Europe, Christian anti-Semites need not rely on such recent Renaissance depictions to spread hatred of *Jews*, claiming the Jews were devils with horns, for Joshua Trachtenberg has demonstrated in the _Devil and the Jews_ that there is a long folk tradition associating the Jew with the demonic. Even before these folk tradition we find in the gospel of John the phrase in Greek, "*Ioudais diabolica*," which is often translated that the Jews are "the spawn of the devil" as well as hypocrites, vipers, evil, guilty of deocide, original sin, and transgenerational

guilt. Holocaust testimony bears witness that the Nazis made the murder camps into hell by making Jews burn bodies and turn them with pitchforks. Thus The Nazis willed onto the Jewish experience, what for centuries had been represented in medieval iconography and paintings by Bosch and Bruegel of Jews in hell, with tales and horns turning bodies with pitchforks. The Nazis essentially willed onto the Jews the Christological view that Jews are devils. Once a group is dehumanized and demonized then strict logic leads as a slippery slope to their extermination because they are not human.

(6) The sixth example regarding the argument that translations are often interpretations is apparent from the following chart which represents the uses of different words in Hebrew, Greek, Aramaic, and Latin for *kelei zemer* in the Septuagint (G), Peshita (S), Vulgate (V), Targum (T):

כנור (42)

G	S	V	T
κιθάρα (20)	קָרָא (37)	cithara (37)	כִּנָּר (21)
κινύρα (17)	omitted (5)	lyra (2)	כּוֹנֵר (6)
ψαλτήριον (4)		psalterium (2)	קִינָה (1)
ὄργανον (1)		organum (1)	

חצוצרה (29)

G	S	V	T
σάλπιγξ (27)	קָרָא (15)	tuba (27)	חֲצוֹצְרָא (11)
omits (1)	omits (5)	omits (1)	
mistranslates (1)	mistranslates (4)	tuba ductilis (1)	
	conflate readings (5)		

נבל (27)

G	S	V	T
νάβλα (14)	נִבְלָא (13)	psalterium (17)	נִבְלָא (10)
ψαλτήριον (8)	קָרָא (4)	lyra (4)	נִבֶל (2)
ὄργανον (2)	נֵבֶל (2)	nablium (3)	קָרָא (2)
κιθάρα (1)	omits (6)	cithara (1)	
mistranslates (1)	mistr. (2)	mistr. (1)	mistr. (1)
σκεῦος ψαλμοῦ (1) =כלי נבל		vasum psalmi (1) =כלי נבל	

Many of these different words for selected three musical instruments are different instruments in shape, sound, and effect of music played, etc. and therefore the meaning of the text undergoes a metamorphosis. The pitch, tone, and harmony, etc. of an earlier period instrument is not necessarily that of its later representative progeny. Not represented in this chart are for instance the *magrepha* which the *mishnah* says looks like a shovel and also figures in the NT. Next to each instrument is the frequency of the number of times the word appears.

While many more examples can be supplied to show that all translations are interpretations, we will wrap up this article with the notation in the introduction to the *Zohar* composed by Rabbi Shimon bar Yohai and

Chapter Five 107

written down by Rabbi Moses DeLeon, with permission of de Lattes, that anyone who attempts to learn this work composed in Palestinian Aramaic outside of a language of Palestinian Aramaic is an uncivilized person, the likes of someone who might be eating raw "horse feed" i.e. barley or oats.

חיות מאכל לאכול כמו זה בתרגום הזהר את ללמד

To learn the Zohar in the original Palestianian Aramaic is like enjoying the cooked *Hallah* of a very fine gourmet grain called a Gluskin (see *Maseket Pesahim*). Thus the Zohar sets up the hermeneutics of esotericism, secrecy, whereby only a few initiates who can learn, understand, and comprehend this mystical text in *Kabbalah* in the original language will be best able to appreciate its secrets, wonders, and delights. Reading the Zohar in a language outside of Palestinian Aramaic the introduction suggests is not only another interpretation, but almost like reading a wholly different text than the original.

As the topic of translation relates to libraries, we must thereby conclude that a library that is open to persons who speak many different languages and come from different language backgrounds should include various works in translation. For example the great translations of a seminal text of the Bible include: the

Tanakh (Hebrew), *Targimim* (Aramaic),[389] *Septuagint*[390] (Greek), *Vulgate*[391] (Latin), *Tafsir* (Arabic), *Peshita* [Note: Peshita (Eastern Aramaic)- the term Peshitta means "simple, straightforward, direct." The term was first used by Moses b. Kefa (d. 913) and then by Gregory Bar Hebraeus. Christian tradition ascribes the origin of the Peshitta to Abgar, king of Edessa, who is said to have sent scholars to Palestine. Wichelshaus argues that Abgar is identical with King Izates II of Adiabene who with his family converted to Judaism.

The Peshitta (Classical Syriac: ܦܫܝܛܬܐ pšîṭtâ) is the standard version of the Bible for churches in the Syriac tradition . The consensus within biblical scholarship, though not universal, is that the Old Testament of the Peshitta was translated into Syriac from Hebrew, probably in the 2nd century

Wikipedia notes regarding the etymology of peshita: The name 'Peshitta' is derived from the Syriac *mappaqtâ pšîṭtâ* (ܦܫܝܛܬܐ ܡܦܩܬܐ), literally meaning 'simple version'. However, it is also possible to translate *pšîṭtâ* as 'common' (that is, for all people), or 'straight', as well as the usual translation as 'simple'. Syriac is a dialect, or group of dialects, of Eastern Aramaic, originating around Edessa. It is written in the Syriac alphabet, and is transliterated into the Latin script in a number of ways, generating different spellings of the name: Peshitta, Peshittâ, Pshitta, Pšittâ, Pshitto, Fshitto. All of these are acceptable, but 'Peshitta' is the most conventional spelling in English.

Regarding the Syriac old testament Wikopedia continues: What Theodore says of the Old Testament is true of both: "These Scriptures were translated into the tongue of the Syriacs by someone indeed at some time, but who on earth this was has not been made known down to our day".   Crawford Brukitt concluded that the translation of the Old Testament was probably the work of Jews, of whom there was a colony in Edessa about the commencement of the Christian era. The older view was that the translators

Chapter Five 109

were Christians, and that the work was done late in the 1st century or early in the 2nd. The Old Testament known to the early Syrian church was substantially that of the Palestinian Jews It contained the same number of books, but it arranged them in a different order. First, there was the Humash, then Iyov , Joshua, Shoftim, 1 and 2 Shmuel, 1 and 2Melachim, 1 and Chronicles, Psalms, Proverbs, Ecclesiastes, Ruth the Shir ha shirim, Esther Ezra Nehemiah Isaiah followed by the Twelve Minor Prophets, Jeremiah and Ekah, Yehezkel and Daniel. See 253 hits in RAMBI as of 7/7/19 traditions assign the work to the time of Solomon, and ascribe the translation to an order of Hiram, king of Tyre, or to the priest Assa sent by an Assyrian King to Samria (II Kgs. 17:27-28)] (Syriac), Beur392 (German translation of Mendelsohn), Die Heilige Schrift und Ihren VerDeutschung (German translation of Buber and Rosenzweig), L'Ecrit Sacre (French).

The question of offering literal versus poetic translation is another matter, and a comprehensive library should make an effort to collect many types of translations. For example Marvin Fox's English translation of the Bible prides itself on literality. For example Fox translates the word, "*Rakiah*" not as firmament as the JPS and King James editions do, but rather as "copper beaten dome" directly from the cognate Semitic language of *Akadian*, where the term *Rakiah* suggests that this ancient people believed that G-d put a "copper beaten dome" as a *capula* on the earth that constitutes the outlines of the sky as if the earth is a astrological planetarium.

Translations also reveal ideologies and politics. For

example the Reform Movement's translation of the Hebrew Bible of Plaut, will differ from the Conservative Movements *Etz Chaim* edition, which will differ from the Orthodox movements editions such as the Stone edition, Judaica Press edition, and Aryeh Kaplan's _The Living Torah_ edition. One Orthodox reviewer of the *Etz Chaim* Edition of the Conservative movement in Commentary magazine raised the question of whether an Orthodox Jew's reading from this edition would be the equivalent of eating a "ham sandwich!". So too the JPS Torah Commentary largely done by scholars with an Ancient Near Eastern Studies background such as Tigay, Millgrom, and Sarna also represents a certain method, approach, and has its own biases. The JPS 5 volume commentary prides itself on forging traditional commentary with modern Biblical scholarship, including higher Biblical criticism which Solomon Schechter called the "higher anti-semitism"[393].

The use of the word "wall" in *Shir HaShirim* 9-10:10 also reveals the politics of translation. The Stone edition renders the Hebrew according to Rashi as, "If her faith and belief are as a wall withstanding incursions from within, we shall become her fortress and beauty, building her city and Holy Temple, but if she waivers like a door, succumbing to every alien knock, with fragile cedar panels, shall we then enclose her. My faith is firm as a wall, and my nourishing synagogues and *Beit midrashim* are strong as towers! Then, having said so, I become in His eyes like a bride found perfect." The Hebrew text reads:

אם-חומה היא נבנה עליה טירת כסף ואם-דלת היא
נצור עליה לוח ארז .
אני חומה ושדי כמגדלות אז הייתי בעיניו כמוצאת שלום

Gersonides understands the metaphor of the walls and doors to that relating to the proper scientific method that the soul must employ in moving in logic and rhetoric from accepted premises to true premises only i.e. a mushal of intellectual cognition which is most ultimately attained by metaphysics which the Rambam equates with *ma'aseh merkavah* and requires many prerequisites[394]. Rabbi Moshe Alshekh interprets the *pesukim* according to an allusion to the walls of *Yerushalayim* and the *Beit Hamikdash*. Thus the rich olfactory metaphors (נרד,קנמון, כרכום , קנה) and allusion to spice aromas in *Shir HaShirim* are allusions to the *keturet samim* shehikteru avotanu in the *beit HaMikdash*/

הסמים קטורת המקדש בבית אבותינו שהקטירו.

The Malbim notes that a person should make their own body like a holy temple so that the *Shekhinah* can dwell within. The JPS translation is more literal and does not plumb the depths of these veiled hints at esotericism. It renders the verses as,

> "We have a little sister whose breasts are not yet formed. What shall we do for our sister when she is spoken for? If she be a WALL, We will build upon it a silver battlement; if she be a door, We will panel it in cedar. I am a wall, My breasts are like towers. So I become in his eyes as one who finds favor..."

The JPS was commissioned by HUC and JTSA at a time when they eliminated from their *siddurim pesukim* wishing for a restoration of the *Beit Hamikdash* which is the ultimate longing of every Orthodox Jew expressed in phrases such as *"VeHasheiv et haAvodah LeDevir Betechah (Amidah)"* and *"Kail Boneh Kail Boneh*

Boneh Betchah Bikarov (*Pesah Haggadah*), etc. The *pusek* "*Shuvi Shuvi HaShulamit*" further refers not to the woman Shulamit who should return to her lover Shlomo, but the Jewish people who should do collective teshuvah so that the *mashiach* can come if they observe two *shabbatot*.

Shir HaShirim over the last 2000 years has been interpreted as a mushal. Rashi sees the beloved Shulamit as representing the Jewish people. Philosophers like Alamono in Italy have interpreted the Song as a mushal for longing for union of the active intellect with HaShem. This Maimonidean and Gersonidean mode of rationalist interpretation has a long tradition. Joseph ben Judah ben Jacob ibn Aknin wrote a commentary in Arabic in North Africa with this theme,[395] and Samuel ibn Tibbon (d.c. 1232) in the introduction to his unpublished commentary on Koheleth, maintains that all of Solomon's books "expound the problem of the human soul and the sekel hapoal."[396] Samuel was followed in this approach by his relative Jacob Anatoli, and by his son Moses ibn Tibbon of Montpellier whose writings date from the period between 1244 and 1274 who further describes Shir haShirim as the love of the human intellect for the Active intellect.[397] A similar approach is taken by Immanuel ben Solomon of Rome (c. 1261-1328), and older contemporary of Gersonides.[398] Joseph ibn Kaspi (b. 1279/80), who wrote a very short introduction to Shir Hashirim based on Maimonides' comments in the Morch Nevukhim 3:51, reads the text as an allegorical account of the conjunction (devekut) between the material intellect and the Sekel haPoal.[399] Menachem

Kellner notes, "In Gersonides (Provence, 1288-1344) pirush the text is not a dialogue between two physical lovers, nor as the Talmudic rabbis had read it, as a dialogue between HaShem and the House of Israel, but as two dialogues. In Gersonides' view the first dialogue is between the human material intellect and the Active Intellect, a kind of conjunction with which is a human being's highest perfection and greatest felicity. The second is between the faculties of the soul and the material intellect. These discussions relate to the desire of the material intellect to approach the Sekel HaPoal and its attempts to enlist the willing aid of the other faculties of the soul in this quest."400 Gersonides writes that the purpose of Shir HaShirim in part is to lead one away from physical lusts, for these perfected individuals will employ stratagems to lead people away from being attracted by their lusts so far as possible, in a way which will cause them to perfect their endeavors and reach human felicity."401

Mikubalim see the Song as a *Mushal* for union with the *Sefirot* which are determined in emanation (*azilut*/עצילות) correlating to the astral constellations/ מזלות . Within the cosmos of the *Mikubalim* verses such as

"a garden shut up is my sister, my bride/ a spring shut up, a fountain sealed (4:12) refers an emanation of the sefiroth, as it says, "and a river went out of Eden to water the garden/

יוצא והנהר הגן את להשקות מעדן
(Gen. 2:10)."402

As reported by Rabbi Solomon Rybek, Rav Soloveitchik in oral lectures taught that *Shir Hashirim* as the holy of holies, has no *peshat* but only *Remez*,

Derosh, and *Sod* that make up the *Pardes*.[403] The Rav said, "there is no peshat/ פשט, only remez/ רמז, derash/ דרש, vesod/ סוד". In fact Rav Soloveitchik's monumental work, *Kol Dodi Dofek, brings this pusek from* Shir HaShirim to refer to the new state of Eretz Yisrael as the "beloved who knocks" i.e. requires support from the American Jewish community. [Note: This essay originated as an address delivered in Yiddish by the author to the Religious Zionists of America on the occasion of the Eighth Anniversary (May 1956) of Israel's independence. It was subsequently elaborated upon, rewritten in Hebrew and appeared in an anthology entitled *"Torah U-Meluchah"* published in Jerusalem in 1961. As my review of this work indicates, the Rav's metaphor of *Eretz Yisrael* as the beloved who knocks for American Jewish financial support marked the Rav's turn at that time from the *Aggudat Yisrael* Part which at that juncture in Jewish history was not (as) Zionistic. The Rav discusses the religious significance of the creation of the State of Israel and obligation that its existence imposes upon Jews. The Rav refers to six knocks of the beloved- the first knock is political whereby the United Nations approved Israel's right to exist. The second knock was on the battlefield when the small Israeli military miraculously defeated a larger Arab invading attack. The third knock is on the theological dimension and the need of Christians to support the Israeli state. The fourth knock is for the perplexed youth who are confused and suffering from *hester panim*. The fifth knock is the most important and it is one to balance *Hashgehah pratit* with the right of Jews to defend themselves after the Shoah. This is beautifully encapsulated in Modern Hebrew literature in the literary repartee between Bialik in his poem *"the City of Slaughter"* and Agnon's Midrash on it in the story *"Ma'aseh ha-ez"* *(story of the goat). Bialik in his poem, which was commissioned to memorialize the Kishneff pogrom, takes a Maccabean stance that Jews should fight back with weapons, and not "hide like mice" in the face of hate and violence. Agnon qualifies this stance and argues that we also need to outsmart our enemies. The plot of Agnon's story involves a very poor family that relies on a goat for cheese and clothing. The father is out in sleet and snow trying to earn a *parnassa* for his family. For the Bar Mitzvah of the son the mother must knit her own talit for the bar mitzvah out of goat's hair. When the wave of pogrom thugs hit their town the family sacrifices the goat and dips the *talit* into the blood of the goat to use it as a decoy by hanging it on the porch of the house, so the thugs think the house has already suffered violence. Images of the *ketunat passim* in the Yosef story are employed. The family survives through the decoy. In this way Agnon drawing on images from *Had gadya*, corrects Bialik's macho stance that muscle alone will be enough to defeat the enemies of the Jews. The Rav acknowledges the place of muscle however when Moshe saw the Egyptian smite a Jew... he struck down the Egyptian (Ex. 2:11-12) and *lex talionis* is meeted out when the order of Pharoah "every Hebrew male child born shall be cast into the Nile" is reciprocated with drowning of the Mitzrim in the Sea of Reeds. While we do not celebrate the downfall of our enemies, i.e. the halakhah is to pour out a drop of wine when reciting the plagues in the Pesah Haggadah, ."]

Catholics have seen the beloved not as the "forsaken Jewish people" but as Christians, the virgin Mary, or *Yeshka* Himself. With the rise of the Reformation, the beloved was seen as the Protestant break off church. Christian scholars like Max Engammar, Ana Matter, Ann Astel, Ulrich Zwingly are juxtaposed to modern Jewish scholarly interpretation of Michael Fishbane, Sholom Rosenberg, Ephraim Urbach, C. David Ginzberg, Sigmund Salfeld, Robert Alter, Ephraim Shmueli, and others who are cognizant of the classic traditional Rabbinic commentaries which have been bibliographically compiled in a collection by Barry Walfish. The *Targumim*, Rashi, ibn Caspi (1 page), ibn Ezra, *Saftei Hakhamim, Seforno, Metzudath Dovid, Metzudath Zion*, Likutei Anshei Shem, Ramban (see Chavel) *Ashkenazi, Alamano, Alshek, see Shir HaShirm* as *mushal* / allegory (Παράβολη) / metaphor which is a vehicle hinting at something else beyond the erotic love poetry between a man and woman of the surface. Indeed Rabbi Akiva's proclamation of *Shir Hashirim* as the *holy of holies* invites the interpretator to equate its significance and meaning with immense importance of all of messianic eschatological redemption in the restoration of the *Beit HaMikdash*. If the poem were just an erotic love song then the "bedroom would be the holy of holies" as enacted by Titus when he had a *ma'aseh biah* with a *zonah* there, and clearly this is not the intention of traditional interpreters for one is to make their own home with a wife like a *beit hamikdash me'at* where Hashem's presence can dwell, as it dwelled in the *Beit Hamikdash* on *har habayit* by creating a relationship of *ahavah*/ אהבה (*gematria*=13) and *akhdut*/אחדות (ehad=gematria=13)[13=13=26= *gematria* of *shem hamiphorash*/ המפרש שם] which brings the *shefah* of the *Shekhinah* down to dwell, as it dwelled in the *kodosh kodoshim*. One should approach life in one's own home with the sanctity, kedushah, and purity as that in the Beit HaMikdash. Thus the pesuk from Shir HaShirim (7:3), *"Thy body is a heap of wheat, hedged with roses"* (בשושנים סוגה חטים ערמת בטנך) is seen as a *remez* by the rabbis as an injunction to follow the laws of family purity as *Midrash Tehillim* 2:15 indicates by carrying over the metaphor of the *red rose*: "A man marries a woman. She says to him: I have seen what looks like a *red rose*; and he separates from her. What kind of wall is there between them? What sort of serpent has stung him? What is it that restrains him?- the words of the Torah!". The *Shekhinah* dwells in the marriage *Shir HaShirim* is indicating as it dwelled in the Beit HaMikdash if there is attention to purities. The *pusuk* from *Shir HaShirim* 4:13, *"Your progeny shall be like a pomegranate orchard- Pardes Rimonim*

(חכמה מלאי יהיו בניכם כמו הרמון מלא בתרי"ג

(גרעינים) "

is interpreted by the *Metzudas Dovid* as, "Your children shall be full of wisdom as a pomegranate is full of (613) seeds." *Pardes Rimonim* is not only the title of a work by the Remak (Rabbi Moses Cordoveros) but a more recent work by HaRav Moshe David Tendler, shlita, on family purity. Thus *Shir HaShirim* is again seen as the makor for attaining holiness, sanctity, and purity in marriage on the anology of the Beit HaMikdash where these three principles were the essence of the priestly life.

As you can see there is not only politics in translating WALL in *shir hashirim* in many modalities, but the deeper understanding of Rabbinic tradition (i.e Rabbi Moshe Alshekh) opens up the redemptive history which fulfills the longing and purpose of Jewish existence i.e. our restored *Beit HaMikdash* on *Har Habayit*[404]. Obviously the Orthodox believe the rabbinic interpretations of seeing *Shir HaShir* as a *nevuah* for the building of the *beit Hamikdash biyamei Hamashiach* is not just "an interpretation" but the true esoteric hidden ultimate meaning of what looks to Reform and Conservative Jews merely as an erotic love poem between Shlomo and Shulamit. The *Tefilah ahar Shir Hashirim* speaks of the Song as the holy of holies in the merit of its verses, letters, punctuation, meanings, names, forms, hints, secrets, purities, awesome wonders, etc. The prayer enjoins that the reader read the Song for a blessing by interpreting it traditionally in the manner of the *Tzadikim* and Hasidim revealing its wondrous secrets[405]. *Shuvi Shuvi haShulamit* is therefore in Orthodox interpretation not the enjoinder of a call to Shulamit to return to her lover after wandering through the streets of Jerusalem and exchanging dialogue with the gatekeepers, but an injunction upon the Jewish people as *Klal Yisrael*, a 13 petalled rose, to return to *HaShem* in repentance (*teshuvah*). Indeed the Zohar in citing *Shir HaShirim* opens with the metaphor of a rose in the context of the *pesak*, "My beloved is like a rose amongst the thorns."[406] (כמו אהובתי החוחים בין השושנה) Theologically this *pesak* is given practical *halackic* meaning and extra valence by being interpreted as a reason for the *minhag* of holding a *kiddush* cup in the palm of the hand. The rose symbolizes *Keneset Yisrael*, as the rose among thorns is tinged with red and white, so the Community of Israel is visited now with justice and now with mercy, as the rose possesses thirteen leaves, so *Keneset* Israel is vouchsafed with 13 categories of mercy which surround it on every side.

The five fingers in which the Kiddush cup as rose bud is surrounded not only represent 5 petals but 5 *sefirot of atzilut* (emanation) or 5 ways of salvation which are 5 gates. This is alluded to the in the verse "I will raise up my cup of salvation" [אקרא ה' ובשם אשא "ישועות-כוס] (Ps. Cxvi, 13). This example is what Jacob Katz notes is the interplay between esotericism and practical *halakhah*.

Sometimes translations represent the glory of the reception history of a work and its refraction within the warp of time over historical periods. German philosophy calls this the "destinyladdenness of language (*Schicksalladenkeit des Languesprache*). For example Rambam's *Moreh Nevukhim* was written originally in Arabic as the *dalat al-harin* which Rabbi Yehudah ibn Tibbon translated into Hebrew as the Moreh Nevukhim. An interesting letter exists where the Rambam told Rabbi ibn Tibbon that the only time they could meet to discuss the questions of translating this great philosophical work would have to be on the Sabbath because the Rambam was so busy during the middle of the week with his duties as a court physician in Cairo Fostat. The Rambam confesses that he leaves his home before the sun rises on a donkey and returns after it has set, only to be faced by patients who are waiting for him in the Jewish quarter. The Rambam notes that he is so tired that he must prescribe medicines while lying on a couch from fatigue at night.[407] Nonetheless the life of this text lives long after the Rambam's dates of 1135-1204 and it has seen other Hebrew translations by Bedersi and Rabbi Yehudah Alharizi. A French translation with notes in Arabic has its own special qualities by

Shlomo Munk who also discovered the lost text of the *Mikor Hayim* in the *Bibliotheque Nationale* in a Geniza which had only been know in Latin Translation (*Fons Vital*) for much of the Middle Ages. A Latin translation of *the Guide* exists titled _Doctor Perplexus_ and was the edition that St. Thomas Aquinas read from when encountering Maimonides. So too the English translations of Rambam's Guide for the perplexed also reveal interpretations and ideologies and methodologies. Shlomo Pines translation for University of Chicago Press is a very excellent academic translation with an excellent article by Leo Strauss as well. The Friedlander edition was done by an orthodox Jew in England and is unique also. Different editions of the text in Hebrew will also reveal many things about the readers and their audiences. For example the Rav Kook edition includes parallel manuscripts, as does Louis Finkelstein's edition of *Sifre*, or Solomon Schechter's text of *Avot de Rabbi Natan*. However a classic Rabbinic edition of *the Guide* will include the commentaries of the Abarbanel, Efodi, and Crescas, because of the importance of the Rabbinic tradition's emphasis on "an authoritative chain of transmission"[408] and refracted through rabbinic commentaries and super-commentaries. Thus the type of edition or translation of the Guide reveals much about the interpretation of the reader community that might select that particular edition over something else. The many languages into which Rabbi Shneur Zalman of Liadi's *Tanya* has been translated testify to the importance of the work within the messianic trajectory of dispersing the well springs of Torah to the four corners of the world, for according to the Besht, the messiah cannot come until the *Quellen der Torah* are disseminated/permeated everywhere.

In conclusion libraries should include translations of works from diverse time periods and cultures because those translations reveal much light upon the mind sets, methods, cultures, interpretations, and aspects, and modalities of being of their host cultures. Libraries are not a *Tower of Babel* that will collapse by representing texts in the "70 languages of the world." Rather libraries as Rabbi Yehudah HaLevy (ztsl) notes are gardens and orchards with fountains of wisdom, palaces of understanding, and trees of knowledge to delight the mind, illuminate the soul, and bring us closer to divinity. Libraries are the homes of historical memory and as such serve as gateways where we can pursue wisdom, understanding, and knowledge, and this activity which is more than just education, but a striving for achieving the proper balance between intellectual, moral, and spiritual virtue, is so high, so noble, and so worthy a quest for it makes possible the redemptive active of the understanding of understanding, what Aristotle calls *noesis noesis*. May all our patrons enjoy this quest, and may the library serve as a conduit where patrons can "translate" their own longings, hopes, thoughts, feelings, and desire for wisdom, understanding, and knowledge into the reality of cognitive growth and development. Searching for wisdom, understanding, and knowledge may itself be a translation process. Translating oneself to another person is a dynamic process of human relationships. Thus translations are not only texts, but the self is a text itself yearning to be deciphered by others. One sage was regarded as a basket of books, but in reality all of us may be texts in our own right. *Text* is not just a print document, but a field of force, a modality of being, as Jacques Derrida has revealed in his Deconstruction philosophy. At Purim it is certainly humorous that children often dress up as walking Torah scrolls, which indeed suggests that we are all texts waiting to be deciphered, read, and discovered by others. Shakespeare's Prospero in the Tempest, remarks, "My library is not dukedom large enough" and escapes from his library where he created magic and alchemy, and returns to civilization in Italy, because he comes to the realization that human relationships are just as important as learning book texts, and reading the text of others, is ultimately more important than reading book texts only, for we cannot love G-d via intellectual pursuit from books, until one learns to love others.

Chapter Six

Reel Librarians:

Images and Stereotypes of Librarians and Libraries in film, television, and literature

Images and stereotypes[409] of librarians in film has evolved over the decades as has the image of libraries. Stereotypes change as has that of fiction writers as "either old fogy bookworms" or unreasonably efficient[410]. Stereotypes of librarians have "ranged from the bespectacled mousey male of the 1800s to the 1900s shushing spinster complete with bun."[411] The image of the Spinster is common.[412] Sable writes of the stereotype, "the librarian is unfailingly and eternally middle aged, unmarried, and most uncommunicative. She exists to put a damper on all spontaneity, silencing the exuberance of the young with a harsh look or hiss. Her only task seems to be checking out books or collecting fines. Books to her are best left upon the library shelves[413] where they do not become dirtied or worn.... There at the desk she will stay, stamping out her books until her retirement."[414]

Libraries have many images associate with them. Some have likened them to crypts[415] as found in films like Stephen King's The Policeman and Asimov's Forward the Foundation, and cemeteries where ghosts hang out (**ghost busters**), to palaces in heaven as per Louis Borges, "The Library of Babel". The image of the library as cemetery and crypt contrasts Louis Borges who commented that he imagines heaven and the afterlife as a large library in the palaces of G-d beyond. The head of the Library of Congress also has a positive image of libraries as "temples of learning."[416] The architecture of the LC and other great libraries has been noted to convey the awe and sanctity of great cathedral like houses of worship.[417] In the Book, *the Alexandrian library: Glory of the Hellenic world*, it is noted that one head librarian Callamachus was accidentally locked in the library overnight and testifies that he heard ghosts and demons so that whenever he frequented the library again he wore garlic around his neck. The Alexandrian Library figures in ***Cleopatra*** (1963) where Elizabeth Taylor as Cleopatra fights her way into Caesar's chambers to announce the Alexandrian Library is on fire, an event which resulted in the loss of Aristotle's work on Comedy tandem to his *Poetics* on Tragedy

As we move from high culture to low brow culture, In ***Ghost Busters***, the first place in all of the city to be visited by ghosts is the NYPL which is guarded by lions.[418] Two librarians appear in the film. The first (a ghost) is shown as the stereotypical old spinster with her hair in a bun, conservatively dressed, a mean look on the face, and constantly Shushing. In fact a constant pattern of the stereotype of the librarian in film is that of shelving, stamping, and shushing. The fact that often women are portrayed in this manner is due to many factors.[419] The second librarian in *Ghost Busters* is the victim of a visitation when the card catalog is attacked. She is portrayed as a mousy neurotic who when asked if there was any family history of mental illness, comically replies, she had an uncle who thought he was St. Jerome. In this popular Hollywood film Ghostbusters much comic play is made of a card catalog where cards are flung out by some demonic ghost power, which causes the stereotypically dressed librarian in a conservative suit, glasses, hair bun, to flee in terror.

Filmclip Ghost busters (popular culture)

Stereotype of Library as Respectable Job

In Imitation of Life (1934) Fredi Washington's mother asks her why she is working as a dancer in a club when she told Mom that she had a "Respectable Job in a library." In Imitation of Life (1959) Susan Kohner tells her mother that has a job cataloging books at night in a public library. Her daughter on the opposite pole actually has a job in a strip joint singing and dancing.

In Party Girl, the main character is show as first arrested but her relative gets her a respectable job in the NYPL which causes the main character to become more subdued, docile, and a proponent of order. When she catalogs her roommate, a DJ's record collection, he criticizes how the library job has made her an order freak. When in Party Girl, Mary grapples to understand the classification system of the Dewey decimal system she reads about its stated objective, "classification systems provide a system for organizing a universe of items be they objects, concepts, or records" suggesting the power of the classification system is total, massive, and comprehensive. Its goal is to organize thereby control the "whole universe of items." As new discoveries such as the Dead Sea Scrolls in the 1950s or new findings in genetics, stem cell research, and cloning become available today the system merely expands and includes these new findings in its expansive or enumerative capability to describe what Wittgenstein might call in the TLP, "all that is the case." The message is that arbitrary and uncontrolled discourse will either be excluded or pinned down as so many butterflies or lego pieces glued or nailed to a board. The institutions of the library has the authoritative control to determine what shall fall within the universe of discourse defined by the boundaries of its classification system. The order of the stacks and catalog express this control. The system may assume that without mechanisms of control or order, the discourse becomes dangerous and uncontrollable. Thus the discourse of control can be seen to limit the freedom of unique creativity. This contradicts Jennifer Summits characterization of libraries as verily places of creativity.[420] Even A dissertation with an ambiguous and equivocal title for instance on "nothingness and nothing in literature and Philosophy"[421] will be pinned down historically to the topic of meontology stemming from ancient Greek thought.[422] For the stereotype of the librarian as order-freak lurks the unspoken fear of discourse becoming undefinable that cannot be traced to an identifiable origin, and the ambiguity of multivocal and equivocal discourses that emit multiple meanings that may even contradict each other. Like Koheleth's contradictions this gives the text a secret vitality and as Walt Whitman remarks, "Do I contradict myself, so I contradict myself, I contain multitudes."[423]

As well as becoming a fetishizer of order the main character in Part Girl also ends up humiliating a patron attempting to reshelve a book he has pulled from the shelves. She is seen at the reference desk surrounded by piles of books, mechanically stamping books. She looks up and seeing a young male library patron says, "Excuse me what are you doing?". The patron raises his hand to his chest in a gesture that says, "Who? Me? Mary continues, "Yeh, you...." Singling him out so that he is noticed by other patrons sitting at desks. She asks sternly, "Were you just putting that book away?". The young man stands frozen while other patrons approach the desk for help. Mary comments strongly, "IT looked like as though you were putting that book away". The patron looks around with a shocked expression. The people at nearby tables raise their heads. Sarcastically Mary says, "I guess you didn't know we had a system for putting books away here?". Mary continues, "Now, I'm curious.... Your just randomly putting that book on the shelf, is that it?". The patron looks lost, helpless, and trapped, unable to speak. Mary raises her voice and says loudly, "You've just given us a great idea. I mean why are we wasting our time with the Dewey Decimal System when your system is so much easier, much easier. We'll just put the books (again raises voice) anywhere!". Mary turns to the people at the reading desks, "Hear that everybody? Our friend here has given us a great idea. We'll just put the books any damn place we choose!". Mary is shouting very loudly now and loosing it. She bangs her fist on the desk. She pushes it further by saying, "We don't care, right? Isn't that right!". Mary has evolved from a carefree party girl to a order freak librarian not afraid to assert her authority. This scene follows a scene where Mary has an epiphany when grasping the Dewey Decimal system for the first time. Mary takes the patrons' misshelving of a book as a personal affront. She takes her job shelving books very seriously. Mary should have quietly come from out behind the reference desk and tactfully whispered to that young man that she could assist him in reshelving the book. Instead she chooses to stand behind the desk and shout sarcastically and embarrass the patron. She embarrasses the patron in public. She the librarian seems to enjoy her authority and the public humiliation she has caused. [424]

Humiliating someone in public in Jewish law is called *Halbanat panim*. Rav Nachman equates such an act of embarrassing someone to public as the equivalent of murder or spilling blood.[425] When one is embarrassed "*Azilsumakav' atihivara,*" the features lose their red color and turn white; thus, the Talmudic term for humiliation, "*halbanat panim,*" whitening of the face. David HaMelech's retort to his tormentors included the admonishment that one who shames others in public forfeits his eternal reward.[426] This notion is in fact stated authoritatively a number of times in the Talmud. [427] The Talmud displays an exquisite sensitivity to the potential of even an accidental misplaced word to cause great anguish: This attitude is also evidenced by countless enactments of the Rabbis designed *"sh'lol'vayesh,"* not to embarrass. Shakespearean sonnet 94 speaks of a great souled individual who chooses not to harm someone in public by embarrassment via stoicism.[428] This is clearly low humor where librarians engage in intimidation, bullying, and embarrassment, but it is a pattern in a number of images represented in film.[429]

Stereotype of Librarian as Nerd
In A Tree Grows in Brooklyn (1945) Peggy Ann Garner goes to the library where she is involved in a project to read all the books in order of the card catalog.

Library as retreat for refuge
The silence of the library provides refuge from the busy loud work a day world outside its walls. Joan Nixon writes: "That cocoon of whispery hush (with) an atmosphere of reverent silence."[430] The silent tone of the hypnotic hush can be peaceful and solemn for some, but it can evoke fear in others.[431]

Even in the recent film *Foul Play* (1978) Goldie Hawn is a librarian divorcee with post traumatic divorce stress syndrome, pursued by detective Chevy Chase and finds refuge from his harassment by immersing herself in her library work. The library is also a refuge in Whisperers (1967) where eDith Evans plays a confused old lady who spends her time warming herself in the local library as a refuge. Feminists critique how the notion of library of refuge plays to patriarchal oppression of women. To make the library like a home or refuge attributes to the library an air of domesticity. Women in the West, [unlike the east where in china for instance women work in the fields, and men stayed at home in medieval times], are associated with "domesticity, emotionality, nurturance, and the like" while men are associated with "publicity, the mind, rationality, and higher mathematics, etc."[432] Librarianship has been stereotyped as a "feminized profession" characterized by semi-professional field which is female dominated in numbers but male dominated in organizational control."[433] This is the way patriarchal society according to some feminists maintains hegemony through constructing hierarchical systems of difference, but not difference as Derrida means and understands. The social construction of masculinity and femininity is the subject of much feminist critique.[434] See for instance Mary Hunter's work, The Face of Medicine.[435] Feminists seek to resist and change this hierarchy of hegemony in the name of social equality of men and women. Librarianship has been considered a feminist profession in which feminist has been used as a negative valance rather than a positive epithet.[436]

Detective Genre: Sleuthing murder

The classic *Young Sherlock Holmes* (1985) represents Holmes and Watson meeting as teenage students with several scenes in the library. In my test case, In Umberto Eco's novel *The Name of the Rose* the medieval library is likened to a labyrinth which one upon entering risks never escaping.[437] The semiotic novel by Eco was made into a film. Mysterious deaths occur at the monastery in Northern Italy in the 14th century.[438] The detective search for clues to the ambiguous murder mystery leads the main character played by Sean Connery to the monk who supervises the scriptorium named Malaki and the closed stacks of the library. The monastery library is very old as Machi says, "the library dates back to the earliest times.... And the books are registered in order of their acquisition, donation, or entrance wthin our walls." William remarks, "they are difficult to find then?". Malachi replies, "It is enough for the librarian to know them by heart and know when each book came here. As for the other monks they can rely only on his (the librarians) memory."[439] In this way there is a masorah of knowledge transmitted from head librarian to head librarian across centuries.

Eco's novel is a murder mystery set within the confines of a male 14th century abbey in Italy. The abbey library is at the heart of the novel and the community. It is a fortress containing a labyrinth with secret passageways, booby trapped rooms, hidden doors, and a system of organization that is known to only a single librarian. The abbot describes the library as following:

> The library was laid out on a plan which has remained obscure to all over the centuries, and which none of the monks is called upon to know. Only the librarian has received the secret, from the librarian who proceeded him, and he communicates it, while still alive, to the assistant librarian, so that death will not take him by surprise and rob the community of that knowledge. And the secret seals the lips of both men. Only the librarian has, in

> addition to that knowledge, the right to move through the labyrinth of books, he alone knows where to find them, and where to replace them, he alone is responsible for their safekeeping[440]

Eco's fortress library is a place that orders and protects texts and limits access to texts. The librarians role as keeper of the texts extends further for it is the library who knows the secret of all secrets of all texts. The abbot comments on the nature of the library in the monastery which houses holy texts[441] and is the loci of love of learning ideally[442]:

> And so no one except for two people enters the top floor of the Aedificium...?
>
> The abbot smiled, "No one should. No one can. No one even if he wished would succeed. The library defends itself immeasurable as the truth it houses, deceitful as the false hood it preserves. A spiritual labyrinth, it is also a terrestrial labyrinth. You might enter and you might not emerge " (p.38)

Thus the library is set up as a place you might not emerge and thus a place of mystery, danger, and death. It is a place of fear, and a place to be feared.[443] The image of the labyrinth is found also in Sifrei Kabbalah where a letter mem (possibly representing mayim or just speaking to the middle as it is the middle letter of the alphabet and when surrounded by Aleph and Taf (first and last) spells Emet) is at the center of a maze like trajectory towards which the pilgrim ventures. The idea of the journey of life as if in a maze like labyrinth with the goal of reaching the

Chapter Six 133

center of ayn sof if common in Jewish mystical (Kabbalistic) art.

The abbot describes the system of control which is more than just protecting the physical texts. The library and librarian is not only a repository of physical texts but the loci of arbitrating between truth and falsity. We read:

> The other monks work in the scriptorium and may know the list of the volumes that the library houses, But a list of titles often tells very little; only the librarian knows from the contents of the collection of the volumes from its degrees of inaccessibility, what secrets, what truths or falsehoods, the volume contains. Only he decides how, when, and whether to give it to the monk who requests it; sometimes he first consults me (the abbot). Because not all truths are for all ears, not all falsehoods can be recognized as such by a pious soul[444]

The abbot is suggesting that the librarian is a gatekeeper. He knows the truth of an individual text through his knowledge of its place in the organized system of the library, where the text is located in the labyrinth of knowledge echoed in the labyrinth of the library. But more importantly the chief monk librarian understands the contents of the texts in his labyrinth library and knows their secrets and the chief librarian is said to have an overbearing countenance and eyes that see into one's soul

> The librarian came to us. We already knew he was Malachi of Hildesheim. His face was

> trying to assume an expression of welcome, but I could not help shuddering at the sigh of such a singular countenance He was tall and extremely thin, with large and awkward limbs. As he took his great strides, cloaked in the black habit of the order, there was something upsetting about his appearance. The hood, which was still raised since he had come in from outside, cast a shadow on the pallor of his face and gave a certain suffering quality to his large melancholy eyes. In his physiognomy there were what seemed traces of many passions which his will had disciplined but which seemed to have frozen those features they had now ceased to animate. Sadness and severity predominated in the lines of his face, and his eyes were so intense that with one glance they could penetrate the heart of the person speaking to him, and read the secret thoughts, so it was difficult to tolerate their inquiry and one was not tempted to meet them a second time.[445]

The Chief librarian Malachi not only knows how to access the texts but more importantly what they mean hermeneutically and what secrets they contain. Consider further the exchange between William and another monk in the Name of the Rose:

> This cordial conversation with my mater must hav put Nicholas in a confiding mood. For he winked at William (as if to say: You and I understand each other because we speak of the same things) and he ninted, "But over there"- he nodded toward the Aedificium- the

section of learning are well defended by works of magic....

"Really?" William said with a show of indifference. "Barred doors, stern prohibition, threats I suppose…"

"Oh no. More than that…"

"what for example?"

"Well I don't know exactly; I am concerned with glass not books. But in the Abbey there are rumors… strange rumors…"

"of What sort?"

"Strange Let us say rumors about a monk who decided to venture into the library, during the night, to look for something, Malachi (The librarian) had refused to gie him, and he saw serpents, headless men, and men with two heads. He was nearly crazy when he emerged from the labyrinth."[446]

In the detective program *Miss Marple* (1962-1965) Mr. Stringer is the village librarian who serves as Miss Marples faithful helper in solving many detective crimes just as in the Night Strangler (1972) a timid researcher in the newspaper library helps Darren McGavin solves a strange series of murders. Likewise in Shadow of a Doubt (1943) Terese Wright researches a murder in Santa Rosa California public library as portrayed also in *Anatomy of a Murder* (1959) that shows lawyers using a library. In *Bridge Across Time* (1985) Librarian Adrienne Barbeau helps solve murders. In Hidden City (1988) Cassie Stuart is a film librarian uncovering evil doing in London with the aid of Charles Dance. In Maxie (1985) a flapper from the 1920s inhabits the body of a 1980s woman. Two librarians resolve the plot. In *Web of Evidence* (1959) a librarian assists a young man trying to prove his passed on father innocent of murder.

To return to the detective novel and film the Name of the Rose, A suspenseful scene in the *Name of the Rose* has Connery trying to learn the classification system and solve the murder mystery which ends in a clue whereby the secret of the library depends on the decipherment of a text in Greek.

Filmclip Name of the Rose (high culture)

The library as the locus of knowledge for detective sleuthing is also found in the film *Homicide*.

David Mamet's film *Homicide* which portrays the existential crisis and journey of the main character, a policeman named Bobby Gold, in search of his own Jewish identity that evolves in the process of his solving a murder case which he wrongly assumes is fueld by anti-semitism rather than economic class hatreds. Fischer suggests that Mamet warns of the perils of assimilation with the example of the main character Bobby Gold, a police detective, who goes on a journey with regards to discovering his own Jewish identity in the process of solving a detective case. Gold engages in what Charles Pearce and Umberto Eco identify as a "hermeneutic of semiotics" to decode 'signs that signify signifiers' to uncover the encryption of clues that lead to solving the motive for the murder. Bobby discovers a piece of paper at the crime scene with the words GROFAZ which turns out to be a red herring although pursuit of trying to understand the meaning of this clue leads to Bobby's heightened Jewish identity and understanding. Bobby's assumption however regarding the antisemitic implications of this clue prove wrong and the film ends with Bobby uncovering that the motive for the murder of a Jewish person was economic class resentment and not per se antisemitism. Thus the film plays upon the act of misreading semiotic signs in the library and over reading their significance.

Filmclip Homicide (Jewish Culture)

In a different modality a kind of detective sleuthing appears in the Israeli film The Matchmaker written and directed by Avi Nesher inspired byt Amir Gutfreund's novel When Heroes Fly set in the Haifa cityscape . The main character Arik a gawky teenager (played by Tuval Shafir) gets drawn into an old I.B. Singer world of a poor diverse world of immigrants, Arabs, ex kibbutniks, black marketers, gamblers, sailors, and Shoah survivors suffering from post-traumatic stress disorder Yanekel Bride has a day job as a matchmaker for hard to match misfits and at night smuggles goods and running illegal card games. During the day Arik plays detective following Yankeles clients to check their veracity. This parallel's the pulp fiction recommended to him by a mousy public librarian named Meir (Dror Keren) who recommends detective thrillers. Sylvia a from a dwarf family that survived Aushwitz and owns a movie theater that shows cheap romances and Hindi love stories, hires Yankele, insisting that he find her a soul mate. Clara Epstein (Maya Dagan) is the shiduch coach of Yankele's clients and hosts a gambling parlor. The librarian, the timid Meir pursues Clara instead of the matchmaker's arrangement it sets off a combination of comic and tragic events.

Genre of Burning books and libraries

While in Name of the Rose, In the end the monastery symbolizing the loss of sanctuary or refuge,[447] burns down there is a pattern of library and book burnings in films that represent attacks on discursive authority posed by the Foucaultian written text and what it represents. Thus in *the Breakfast Club* (1985) students serve detention time in the library as a symbol of rules can't be broken. Thus the title from the medieval poet, after the rose dies only the name is left, evoking a semiotics of essotericism. Interestingly A number of diverse films depicting libraries end in the burning of the library from Fahrenheit 451 (1966) to *the Book Thief*. Fahrenheit 451 is not about libraries but their absence as the totalitarian Big Brother Orwellian society burns books.

Filmclip Fahrenheit 451 and the Book Thief

Positive Representations of libraries and librarians

In Spencer's Mountain (1963) later developed into the wholesome program the Waltons, the eldest son, needs a scholarship to go to college and in his summer vacation sets up a public library run for the benefit of the community.

Library as Locus of Knowledge= Power

The library as a locus of knowledge is portrayed when Diane Keaton in *Baby Boom* (1987) uses the library to research the market for her baby food.I *Indiana Jones and the last Crusade* by Spielberg (1989) Dr. Henry Jones states that half of anthropology is done in the library" and finds Note also the copy of RQ o Michael J. Fox's bedroom book shelves in *Back to the Future* (1985) as Fox's time travel is based on library research. the clue to the location of the lost chalice in the library in Venice. In *Soylent Green* (1973) Charlton Heston represents a 2022 situation where librarians have all the power as they are the only ones who know how to access information. In *China Town* (1974) Jack Nicholson uses the county archives in search for knowledge as does Charles De Gaulle in *Day of the Jackel* (1973) who uses the Reading Room of the British Museum to study old newspapers of WWII which drives the rest of the plot. In Misery (1990) the local sheriff uses the library to solve crime. Likewise in *The Deep* (1977) the library is used to find info about sunken treasure found while skin diving. In *Defence of the Realm* (1985) Gabriel Byrne uses newspapers in a public library to trace evidence of a cover up. In My Side of the Mountain (1969) a boy consults a local librarian on who to run away from home to be closer to nature. In *Paper Chase* (1973) set in an East coast law school the students use the library to succeed. In Rollerball (1975) James Caan uses the public library to seek info about he infamous game of which he is the star. The info is restricted. Later he goes to the central computer which has all info of the world except it has los the 18th Century. This is kept in Switzerland and features Ralph Richardson as the absent minded librarian- a stereotype for a Professor also. In *Somewhere in Time* (1980) Christopher Reeve falls in love with a girl in a photo. The Librarian helps him find info about her. In *Zardoz* (1974) Sean Connery finds in a forgotten library the book that helps him find the secret of Zardoz.

Censorship of Library materials

In the *Music Man* where Marian the librarian makes available then scandalous works by Balzac and Chaucer, that are too riskee for the small town which wants to censor them, but she sings while she stamps books.

The library is positively portrayed as a part of the research process as it is for baseball fans in *Field of Dreams* (1989) where Kevin Costner spends time in the library researching a 1960s radical writer, although parents try to remove books from the school reading list. The motif of censorship of library materials is also represented in **Storm Center** (1956) where a fiery small town librarian fights censorship and suppression of free speech by refusing to withdraw a book on communism. In Return to Peyton Place (1961) Robert Stirling the school principal is fired when he refuses to remove Carol Lynley's novel from the school library. The issue of censorship and privacy is found in the film *All the President's Men* (1976) where a librarian gives circulation records to reporters Redford and Hoffman.

In *Hand that Rocks the Cradle* (1991) a friend of an unfortunate mother uses newspapers on microfilm in a public library to find out the origins of an evil nanny in a background check. In War Games (1983) Matthew Broderick goes to the library to find info about the computer programmer. Libraries and librarians are thus seen as the loci for knowledge as in the Handmaid's Tale (1990) where a general is beaten in scrabble by former librarian, and the general says, "I knew you would be good at this. You used to be a librarian."

Negative images of librarians an libraries

In the film Ragtime (1981) the film concludes with a takeover of the J P Morgan Library in NYC and features the director of the library as a bombastic yet cowardly curator. This disrespect for librarians is also seen the fact that for much of the history of librarianship librarians are underpaid, underutilized, undervalued, underappreciated, and often disregarded as having little or no contribution to make to the wider goals and aspirations of educational institutions.

Library esoteric repository of the occult

In *Big Foot and the Henderson's* (1987) John Lithgow asks for books on Bigfoot. In *Carrie* (1976) Sissy Spacek searches through her high school library looking for books on mental telepathy. In *The Dunwich Horror* (1970) librarians of a College library locate a rare book on the occult which leads to horror filled adventures. In the sci fi film *IT* (1990) the lead character is a town librarian but "IT" comes and makes all the books fly off the shelves. This respect for the library as a place for research is also seen in a number of films that identify the library as the loci of knowledge of the occult.

The kid teen TV series, *Buffy the Vampire Slayer*, where the librarian of a High school allows the slaying of vampires, demons, ware wolves and monsters by his access and knowledge of the occult books in the library on kishuf, wizardry, and black magic. Rupert Giles is the high school librarian referred to as "the watcher." . He is the source of training, counterintelligence, and guidance for high school student Buffy Summers, the one of her generation chosen to be Vampire Slayer Buffy draws on Giles not only for emotional support but for research necessary to do that for which the Vampire slayer has been chosen. Buffys fellow high school friends meet and conduct much of their research in the library where they consult vampire and demon lore, the occult, witchcraft, spellcasting, etc. Giles stereotype of that of tweedy (wears tweed coat), sometimes befuddled, well dressed, intelligent, stable, friendly, supportive, and wise. Giles is also creative in that he engages in translations and recasting what he reads into stories, tag lines, and aphorisms that make sense to the teens he helps. Giles speaks to the faith of the importance of the library where answers can be found in the pages of books. His character and role speaks to the belief that "knowledge is the ultimate weapon." The show portrays books as central and the knowledge therein as key to the struggle against evil forces. It shows that research is hard work as Giles is depicted as pulling all nighters doing research from midnight to six am In order to defeat vampires. With Spinoza who proclaims knowledge a virtue as opposed to Goethe's Faust where its pursuit is ultimately unachievable, the show holds that to know the forces of darkness, to classify them, and defang them is a good to defeat evil. Giles himself dropped out of Oxford to pursue high magick, but then moved to the British Library and then to Sunnydale California. He reads multiple languages. Giles is gentle and genteel, literate, sensitive, and devoted to his patrons. Yet Giles is not a techy. He is bookish and reserved, and a bit technophobic. He lives in the world of books and print culture. HE confesses to Buffy that computers fill him with "Childlike terror." Jenny gently chides him for living in the Middle Ages, and assures him he will enter the new century with a few years to spare.[448]

Likewise the horror genre features a librarian when in *the Horror of Dracula* (1958) an investigator is sent to Dracula's castle on the pretext of cataloging the Count's rare books. In a Jewish key this magical aspect of books in the library containing esoteric secrets is found in The Chosen (1981) which has several scenes in the library "like they used to be" with lots of dark wooden shelves and individual study desks by the windows. In John Le Carre's detective thriller *The Spy who Came in from the Cold* (1965 film) Clair Bloom works in a library and is also devoted to the occult. In the spy thriller The Thief (1952) Ray Milland loosk for microfilm hidden in a card catalog drawer in the library of Congress. In Whicker Man (1967) an investigator goes to the library to investigate pagan rituals and discovers info that leads to the films surprising ending.

On the flip side of the library housing the occult in Buffy the Vampire slayer, an atmosphere of White magic is portrayed by such films as, *Wings of Desire (Der Himmel Uber Berlin)* (1988) where the Socrates like Peter Falk meets angels who like to hang out in the Berlin library facilitating learning in the reading room:

Film Clip Wings of Desire

Library as bureaucratic maze

In *Citizen Kane, Orson Welles' masterpiece,* the library vault guarded by a fierce bureaucratic librarian whose authoritative protocol for access is quite overwhelming and imposing. Thus the dialect is set up in Citizen Kane of the library trained to thwart off the protagonists access to vital information or they may be the facilitators of knowledge.

Filmclip Citizen Kane

Library Reference Interview

This assumed pompous authority of the stereotypically depicted librarian also surfaces into a different modality in Sophie's Choice. Let us turn to a few examples from representations of Jewish librarians. In the film *Sophie's Choice* starring Meryl Streep as a Polish Shoah survivor living in Brooklyn, She has discovered poetry of Emily Dickinson in an English language class and comes to the the library to take out a poetry book. Sophie goes to the library to for a book by her beloved Emily Dickinson. In her Polish accent she innocently asks the mousy librarian with a bowtie and don't bother me attitude for a book by this American poet. Sophie has misunderstood the name of the poet to be Emil Dickens. The librarian an overly confident surly young man with thick glasses lambasts her for her alleged "ignorance" because it is "common knowledge" that Charles Dickens was not an American nor did he write poetry but rather novels. William Styron writes:

But the incredible emotion evaporated swiftly. It was gone by the tie she entered the library and long before she encountered the librarian behind the desk- a Nazi. No of course he was not a Nazi, not only because the black and white nameplate identified him as Mr. Shalom Weiss but because- well, what would a Nazi be doing appropriating volume after volume of the earth's humane wisdom at Brooklyn College Library? But Shalom Weiss, a pallid dour, thirtyish man with aggressive horn-rims and a green eyeshade was such a starling double of every heavy, unbending mirthless bureaucrat and demi-monster she had known in years past that she had the weird sense that she had been thrust back into the Warsaw of the occupation. And it was doubtless this moment of déjà vu, this rush of identification, that caused her to become so quickly and helplessly unstrung. Feeling suffocatingly weak and ill again, she asked Shalom Weiss in a diffident voice where the catalogue file would be in which she might find listed the works of the 19th century American poet Emil Dickens.

"In the catalogue room, first door to the left," muttered Weiss, unsmiling. Then after a long pause he added "but you won't find any such listing."

Won't find any such listing?" Sophie echoed him puzzled. Following a moment's silence she said "Could you tell me why?"

"Charles Dickens is an English writer. There is no American poet by the name of Dickens."

His voice was so sharp and hostile as to be like an incision.

Swept with sudden nausea, light-headed and with a perilous tingling moving across her limbs like the faint prickling of a multitude of needles, Sophie watched with dispassionate curiosity as Shalom Weiss' face sullenly inflexible in its graven unpleasantness seemed to float way ever so slightly from the neck and the confining collar. I feel so terribly sick, she said to herself as if to some invisible solicitous doctor, but managed to choke out to the librarian, I'm sure there is an American poet Dickens." Thinking then that those lines, those reverberant lines with their miniature sorrowing music of mortality and time, would be as familiar to an American librarian as anything as household objects are, or a patriotic anthem, or one's own flesh, Sophie felt her lips part to say, "Because I could not stop for Death..... She was hideously nauseated. And she failed to realize that in the intervening second there had registered somewhere in the precincts of Shalom Weiss' unmagnanimous brain her stupid contradiction of him, and its insolence. Before she could utter the line, she heard his voice rise against every library decree of silence and cause a distant shadowy turning of heads. A hoarse rasping whisper – querulous, poisoned with needless ill will- his retort was freighted with all the churlish indignation of petty power. "Listen, I told you," the voice said, "there is no such a person! You want me to draw you a picture! I am telling you , do you hear me! [449]

The novel brings out in ways the film does not that the encounter with the librarian related to triggering her previous experiences at the hands of bureaucratic Nazis. Sophie feels powerless in the face of the librarians authority and is made to feel ashamed. The librarian does not attempt to ask Sophie to clarify her request, but assumes that she is ignorant. He publicly humiliates Sophie, in a manner somewhat similar to Mary's tirade in Party Girl and the physical violence and killing in Conan the Librarian. These portrayals are exaggerated for the purposes of comic effect, but the deep discourse is one of fear.

This is a classic example that could be shown to every MLS reference librarian as an example of a botcher reference interview. Sophie emerges from this reference interview intimidated and bullied. Sophie probably won't return any time soon to the library after he bad experience. This confirms with Swope and Katzer findings that users who have bad experiences in the library are afraid to approach the seemingly ever- busy librarian because they think that their questions may be a bother or that they may appear stupid.[450]

The imposing male librarian, dressed in a starched white collar, like clerical garb, is perched on a high pulpit like reference desk. He looks down upon all who appear before him. Sophie is not only intimidated by the high ceilinged Cathedral like architecture in which her footsteps echo on an expansive highly polished marble floor, but also by the stand offish reference librarian. Sophie hesitatingly asks the reference librarian for help. In the interaction with the smung and overly confident librarian Sophie's initial intimidation by the architecture of the library is confirmed by this frightening encounter of the botched reference interview.

Filmclip Sophie's choice (Jewish Culture)

Another film where the image of the librarian engenders fear is Stephen King's The Library Policeman. The library policeman sparks fear. We read:

> *I had loved the library as a kid- why not? It was the only place a relatively poor kid like me could get all the books he wanted –but as I continued to write, I became acquainted with a deeper truth. I had also feared it. I feared becoming lost in the dark stacks, I feared being forgotten in a dark corner of the reading room and ending up locked in for the night. I feared the old librarian with the blue hair and the cat' s eye glasses and the almost lipless mouth who would pinch the backs of your hands with her long, pale fingers and hiss "SHHHH!" if you forgot where you were and started to talk too loud. And yes, I feared the library police.*[451]

The library police will break into houses if persons have not returned library books and these "faceless enforcers who would actually come to your house if you didn't bring back your overdue books.[452] The librarian Ardelia Lortz admonishes Sam in an intimidating way to return his books on time, threatening that if he does not he will be visited by the library Policeman:

> *"The books are not renewable to be sure to get them back by April 6th." She raised her head and the light caught in her eyes. Sam almost dismissed what he saw there as a twinkle... but that wasn't what it was. It was a shine. A flat hard shine. For just a moment Ardelia Lortz looked as if she had a nickel in each eye. "Or?" he asked and his smile suddenly didn't feel like a smile- it felt like a mask. "Or else I'll have to send the Library Policeman after you," she said.*[453]

Sam then has anxiety when he is late to return the books. He has nightmares that the librarian Ardelia Lortz is under his bed or in his closet. She is seen grinning happily secretly in the dark wiggling fingers tipped with long sharp nails, her hair sprayed out all around her face in a fright wig. She looks like a monster. Sam thinks his bones will turn to jelly if she whispers at him. The library policeman who later visits sam is also ghoulish. He wears a trenchcoat like an axe murderer and has a bad pale complexion and a white jagged scar lying across his left cheek, below his left eye, and over the bridge of his nose. The following description makes the policeman into a typical horror demon:

> *His mouth was set in lines of ultimate passionless authority and Sam thought for one confused moment of how the closed library door had looked, like the slotted mouth in the face of a granite robot. The Library Policeman's eyes appeared to be silver circles that had been punctured by tiny shotgun*

pellets. They were rimmed with pinkish-red flesh that looked ready to bleed. They were lashless... [454]

The description continues equating the library policeman with "all authority, all power, all force. He was judge, jury, and executioner." The library policeman ends up pricking Sam's neck with the tip of a knife at the flesh of his throat. "It was like being pricked by an icicle." A single bead of scarlet blood oozed out and then froze solid, a tiny seed-pearl of blood. King is writing in the horror genre. The librarian and library policeman fit that characterization. Sam the child is terrified not just by being shamed and humiliated by the authority figures of the librarian and library policeman but in the end bodily harm. King is know to write novels that evoke childhood fears. The portrayal of the library policeman as a specter, contributes to this fear. Like Conan the Librarian wielding a dangerous sword against library uses who he splits in half for the sin of overdue books, King's library policeman also threatens murder.

Stereotypes of librarians from literature, art, and film

Giuseppe Arcimboldo (1527-1593) represents in a painting an image of a librarian that is a man made out of books[455].

As Pirke Avot refers to one sage as a basket of books, the portrait above actually a man who is the sum total of books that have influenced him. He himself is a kind of book yearning to be interpreted perhaps.

In the first issue of American Library Journal (Sept, 30, 1876) Dewey himself wrote of the stereotype of the mousy and nerdy librarian. Dewey writes: "The time was when a library was like a museum and a librarian was a mouser in dusty books." In 1907 Edmund Lester Pearson further enumerated the stereotype by writing:

> *Is there some particular look of weakness or ill health that marks librarians as a class? Some astigmatism, stoop of the shoulders, pallor of the complexion or general dustiness of appearance that labels us like one of our own books?.... What is the badge by which one knows the librarian? Some will immediately answer "a pair of spectacles, a black alpaca coat, silk skull cap, straw cuffs, and rubber heeled shoes".*

Pearson then comments on the fondness for a pince-nez that is fastened to the hair by a small golden chain.[456]

Stevens further elaborates on the stereotype of the woman librarian as follows:

> It was that of an elderly- or at least middle-aged- woman of an obviously unmarried persuasion who wore glasses, put her hair in a bun, often with a pencil stuck firmly in the bun; wore a sour look on her face; and constantly enforced the rule of silence by pursing her lips while saying "Shhh" or "Hush". She was not a friendly person by any stretch of the imagination.[457]

The librarian stereotype of a finger on the lips shushing the patrons to be quiet emphasizes that silence is the key to controlling spoken discourse that has no place in the temple to discursive order.[458] In general the female librarian is portrayed in older films not favorably but according to rigid stereotypes. Manley writes, "The image of the librarian as a "little old lady with the bun, the shawl, the wire specs, and the pencils sticking out of her hair" are a repeated trope in early film.[459] Sometimes the female librarian is stereotyped as "a fussy old woman, myopic, repressed, brandishing or perhaps cowering behind a date stamp."[460]

In a number of movies from the days of silent film the ticket out of spinstedom among the stacks for the librarian is romance leading to marriage. Thus the library is a safe job while waiting to find Mr Right.

In some films male librarians are stereotyped as "failed something elses" or are too dreamy and vague to hold down another kind of job.

In Hollywood movies of the 1930s and 1940s the local town library and its librarians were viewed as essential to the fabric of the community. The library was wise and a source of great knowledge. Thus lawyers are draw to the library for research and many movies featuring lawyers have a scene in the library where an attorney and detectives search to find the elusive precedent that will solve the case.

In comedies scenes in the library frequently stereotype the librarian as a professional "shusher."

In science fiction librarians often fair better than negative stereotypes. Foucaltian equation of information and knowledge equal power enhances the respected role of the librarian. Librarians in sci fi often are trained to thwart the villains access to vital information or to facilitate it for the forces of good. Notice that in Star Trek all captains of all Enterprises carry books, often solid leather bound editions, adding a serious tone to their image.

With revolutions in technology such as the internet, websites, database construction, digitization the stereotype of the image of the librarian as a cyber jockey, computer geek, or other images developed. The stereotypes of obsession with detail, card catalogs, dates stamp authoritarians are being replaced with librarians of know-how who use electronic information retrieval technologies in a post-modern setting. Stevens classifies these stereotypes to include: "The Lipstick Librarian", "The Belly dancing Librarian", "the modified Librarian", and "The Librarian Avenger." Stevens argues what destroyed the early stereotypes of the mousy nerdy male librarian and spinster eye glass bun female librarian with rubber bands around her wrists to bind card catalog cards were economic and technological changes in librarianship. This includes the "decline of women in librarianship and the reemergence of (IT) men as the predominant force in the profession."[461]

While acknowledging that stereotypes do violence to individuals in their Derridean "difference" the question may arise "Do the vast majority of people who become librarians really have traits attributed to them in stereotypes?"[462] and if the library profession happens to attract these people with such aspects of character.[463] Many are offended by the stereotypes and work to change them.[464] Some feminists analyze the stereotype of the female librarian and deconstruct how such representations do violence to women often as repressed and exploited persons. The work of Michel Foucault has been employed to undertake this deconstruction although historian Wayne Wiegand notes much more should be done.[465] Foucault's analysis of power-knowledge regimes and the totalitarianism of patriarchal logocentric discourse has many applications to deconstructing the female librarian stereotypes.[466] Foucautian feminists include Judith Butler and Wendy Brown who argue that his work has "fueled self-critical impulses within feminism that are indispensable."[467] The convergence of Foucault and feminist critique[468] of the female library stereotype is implied by Irene Diamond and Lee Quinby who point out, "Both (feminism and Foucault) bring to the fore the crucial the crucial role of discourse in its capacity to produce and sustain hegemonic power and emphasize the challenges contained within marginalized and or unrecognized discourses. And both criticize the ways in which Western Humanism has privileged the experience of the Western masculine elite as it proclaims universals about truth, freedom, and human nature.[469] Feminists are concerned with pervasive culture stereotyping.[470] The stereotype of the subservient female librarian welcomes Foucaultian analysis in that Foucault explores the relationship of knowledge, power, freedom, domination, control, and truth. The library represents the place of master discourses that has institutionalized control of the great proliferation of discourse "in an attempt to relieve the richness of tis most dangerous elements."[471] Foucault's description of power, order, and knowledge indicates that that the suppressed voice and power of the female librarian stereotype is a function of a male system of power and rationality that is not of her own making. Foucault urges us to ask, "Who is speaking through the stereotype of the female librarian? And to what ends? Whose interests does the female librarian stereotype serve? How can women change the image of the female librarian as powerless and subservient. What system of hegemonic power made the stereotype possible and how to do we change this system? It goes to the roots of not only the disrespect and devaluation of the librarian profession itself but its analog of the disrespect and devaluation of women in society. According to feminist philosophy women are considered subservient, what Simone de Beauvoir calls Le Deuxieme Sexe.[472] Women according to feminists are meant to feel that they should assume low status.[473] Perhaps through Foucaultian analysis the voice[474] of the female librarian can be reclaimed and better heard in a structure not dictated by dominating masculine interests and agendas. Foucault also explored the relationship between order, knowledge, and madness. Since the librarian can be viewed as a "conservator of order"[475] and representative of rationality or discourse of reason[476] and this discursive rationality according to Foucault has led to the suppression of women and other marginalized groups, no better place than to look at the library and stereotype of the librarian to unpack this Foucautian equation. Foucault is in line with Pawel when describing Kafka's work[477] that in its effort to be creative wages war against the bureaucratic "nightmare of reason."[478] In the library each item has a fixed place according to a classification system. It stands in an apriori relationship to every other item. The library is like a butterfly mounter who fixes his object into an irreversible static place. The rage for order is what psychologists call typical of the obsessive authoritarian personality illustrated by the Milgrom in his obedience studies, also studied by critical thinkers like Adorno.[479] The library is either viewed as a refuge of order away from the storm of life, or a totalitarian symbol of man made organized classified humanly constructed knowledge regimes. According to Adi Ophir the library is a space of knowledge. It is related to social space. However "the former did not contain the later, any more than a book contains within its volume the space of its fiction, or an observatory the sky observed in it."[480] For Ophir the collection development policy and how it is applied determine a power of relations of a specialized privileged discourse. The edifice of order and rationality embodied by the library puts in tension those domains that are outside and not represented within the library. According to Castillo the alternative to the ordered knowledge of science and the library is the storm of madness.[481] Madness in part is a departure from the mainstream normative discourse and evokes the dissolution of all boundaries and form. Madness evokes the hegemony of appearances and thus the library makes sense only against the presence of the lurking madness in its shadows. These shadows of potential erupting madness are the domain of the "other" that has not been collected, ordered, and systematized but is outside the reigning discourse or discourses that are authenticated as legitimate. Thus the drive to create and maintain order can be in part a drive to exclude and marginalize the forces of madness. In this Foucaultian equation[482] the library patron becomes the other. The other may not be under the direct control of the order of the library when they choose to leave the library space but they can never really escape this discursive order that speaks with authority of legitimacy and agendas that managed to make their way into the order system. For Foucault the library is viewed as an institution for control of knowledge and truth.[483] The library also for Fourcault represents the management of fear. This management of fear in part according to Radford constitutes a Foucaultian dynamic of the librarian as gatekeeper between order and chaos. Radford writes:

> The library as an institution falls squarely into the lived tensions of this discourse, and these tensions are made apparent in the themes of the threshold: the librarian as formidable gatekeeper between order and chaos, the other-worldliness of the library, the library as cathedral, the humiliation of the user, the power of surveillance and the consequences of disrupting the sacred order of texts. The discourse of fear is a language and a vocabulary. It is a way of speaking about the library and librarian that transcends any specific image or portrayal...[484]

Foucault describes a fundamental relationship and dynamic between control, discourse, and fear. For Eco and Foucault the library is a symbol of authoritative power of discourse.[485] Foucault exposed the politics by which certain discourses became honored and legitimate while others were pushed to the margins of power.[486] He is thus involved in the role institutions play in the process, production, and maintenance of authority, knowledge, and power of discourse. For Foucault all knowledge is controlled Radford points out, "This control is not that of a transcendent Orwellian thought-police, but control produced by the constraints of particular discursive practices, such as the examination in the prison, the confession In the church, the presentation made at an academic conference, the article written for an academic journal, the lecture made at the University, or the reference encounter in the library."[487] Thomas Kuhn[488] likewise has shown that scientific discourse can become structured and limited through the constraints of the paradigm, until paradigm shifts occur by revolutionary scientific discoveries by the likes of physicists such as Copernicus, Galileo, Newton, Einstein, and today string theory and Quantum Mechanics or stem cell research, cloning, and genetic discoveries in the Biological sciences.

Foucault's genealogical projects stemming from Nietzsche's method in *Genealogy of Morals*,[489] as described in Foucault's Discipline and Punishment[490] and *The History of Human Sexuality*[491], describe the institutionalization of discourse, and discursive strategies that respond to the fear of institutional control (Gestell). This fear is the fear of uncontrolled discourse and what it may result in such as mob rule, revolution, and mob violence or what Hobbes calls a state of nature where it is each against each and life is nasty brutish and short. Heidegger too argues there is an anxiety (angst) as to what discourse is, when it is manifested materially as a written or spoken object.[492] Thus before Dasein and das nicht (nothingness) persons talk. For Foucault this fear that leads to anxiety before *Dasein und das nichts* is the realization that discourse is "transitory existence, destined for oblivion ultimately" in what Ramban might refer to what is the 50,000 year of *shemitatot ha-olamot* of disembodied intellects, at the gate of sharei binah.[493] Yet as a short story of James Thurber, notes after people perhaps all that remains are gadgets and the name of Ideas themselves? The discourses housed in the library speak and can be celebrated long after their authors have passed on. The grandeur of library buildings often speaks symbolically as a temple[494] of the discourses of the past generations still effect the present and future generations note a a millennium before Foucault in a different context by the Tashbaz.[495] Institutions produce discourses which they attempt to control, select, organize, and redistribute according to a number of mechanisms to sometimes in totalitarian states configure mass upon at will by spin doctors employed by political regiems to control the masses. Such can be the nature of propaganda from the left of Stalin or right of the Nazis and Hungarian Arrow Cross. This control of discourse harnesses its power and yet neutralizes the chaos of uncontrolled and unformed unconscious opinions that can form into an institutionalized discursive regime of hegemony. Thus the library is more than a repository of texts. It is rather a key mechanism in the preservation and control of fear of discourse. When we say in French, "donner la parole" (to give the right to speak) we mean an institution controls that right an legitimates what discourse is valid and which is delegitimate. Who can speak, when to speak, and what can be spoken for Foucault is indicative of discursive control (gestell). The library plays a decisive role in maintaining this discursive control or privileged discourse. Foucault devoted much analysis as to why some discourses are marginalized and pushed to the side. Foucault described how in modernity the discourses of Darwin, Freud, and Karl Marx became institutionalized and serve as central for certain discursive regimes today.[496] The library of the institution guards against the immediate transitory nature of discourse by providing a temporary where hegemonic discourse can be kept. For Foucault the library preserves some sense of order and continuous tradition to its patrons by preserving "that tiny fragment of discourse- written or spoken- whose fragile uncertain existence can give meaning to patrons lives ideally. For Leo Strauss such Foucaultian analysis is an attack on the great books program Strauss influenced to be taught at St. Johns. Strauss holds that discourse knowledge is not temporary but rather the best classical representation of this discourse is eternal true for all people at all times regardless of cultural-economic-political- and social differences. Thus for Strauss discourse does not divide us as for Foucault but unites all humanity and its mission for the benefit of all mankind. Thus for Strauss the library is the center of any educational institution. The library safeguards against the possible dangers of uncontrolled discourse through complex mechanisms of order such as indexes, catalogs, controlled vocabularies, retrieval systems such as databases, and the digitization of certain discourses allows for a shared and common heritage for all persons by making this content available on the web. However for Foucault the idea that the library is beneficient in serving to provide access to discourse is at odds with the controlling nature of institutions and the process of institutionalization that occurs under Kakfquesque bureaucratic mindlessness all in the name of control and efficiency. For Foucault libraries represent a Umberto Ecoian labyrinth of taboos, barriers, thresholds, and limits that deliberately are disposed to the reigning order, which can become fascist or totalitarian if a demagogue or tyrant comes to power. Thus the library within the institution preserves yet defangs the dangerous elements of uncontrolled discourse. It organizes its disorder. It is a war against the marginalized discourses that are not brought center stage to even be considered fit for inclusion within the master logocentric discourse that make the "cut" into the repositories of order.

If the other, librarian patrons, writes or creates something that is eventually included in the hegemonic discursive order, then they have altered the relationships of the system of order. They have effectively changed if in only a small way the structured values of the reigning order that works via Heideggerian control (gestell) which in turn can be a force of suppression to the marginalized voices, outside the hegemonic order. Thus a library collection can never be truly complete. It never can contain all, for the existence of creation is outside of any humanly constructed order. The librarian is a diplomat of order. Every text has its place. The librarians work place assumes a space where all is accounted for. It can be a refuge to some or prison to others. Its space is an enclosure. In this way it is what Coleridge describes as a Kubla Khan Pleasure dome, a human made system.[497]

Order and knowledge for Foucault work in tandem. Jorge Luis Borges in his short story "The Library of Babel" expresses this dialectic. We read:

> *When it was proclaimed that the Library contained all books, the first impression was one of extravagant happiness. All men felt themselves to be masters of an intact and secret treasure. There was no personal or world problem whose eloquent solution did not exist in some hexagon. The Universe was justified, the universe suddenly usurped the unlimited dimensions of hope"*[498]

For Borges to have knowledge of the secret order was tantamount to having the status of a god which contradicts the negative images and stereotypes of female librarians as a "dull, earnest body... with glasses, her hair in a bun, wearing sensible shoes, support hose, tweed skirt, and droopy sweater."[499] We read further of Borges positive portrait of the librarian:

> *On some shelf in some hexagon (men reasoned) there must exist a book which is the formula and perfect compendium of all the rest: some librarian*

*has gone through it and he is analogous to a god….. Many wandered in search of Him. For a century they exhausted in vain the most varied areas. How could one locate the venerated and secret hexagon which housed Him?*500

The hexagon clearly is a form of the sefiroth structure and architectonic that emanate from heavens distant gardens (die Himmel Ferne Gaften) pleromatically. In Sifrei Kabbalah this structure of emanation of the aspects of the manifestations of G-d, the DNA of G-d in the Universe is represented as such[501].

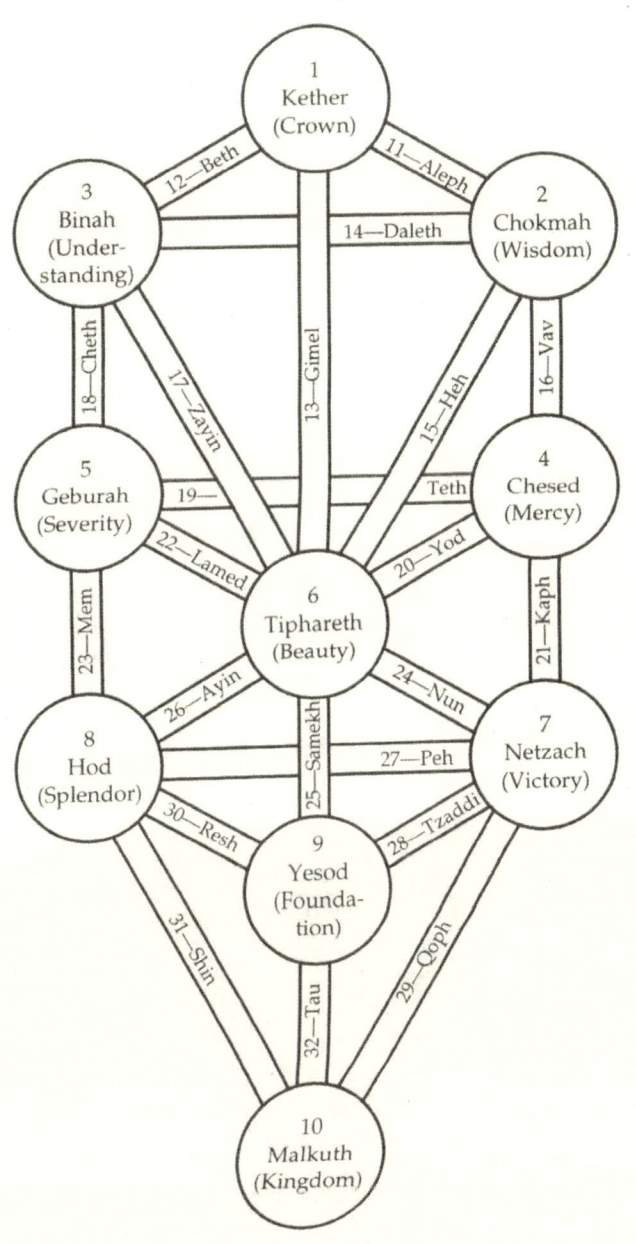

```
                    1
                  Kether
                  (Crown)
         12—Beth        11—Aleph
    3                              2
  Binah        14—Daleth        Chokmah
 (Under-                        (Wisdom)
 standing)
   18—Cheth  17—Zayin  13—Gimel  15—Heh  16—Vav
    5                              4
  Geburah      19—    Teth      Chesed
 (Severity)                     (Mercy)
   23—Mem  22—Lamed        20—Yod  21—Kaph
                    6
                 Tiphareth
                  (Beauty)
         26—Ayin  25—Samekh  24—Nun
    8                              7
   Hod          27—Peh         Netzach
 (Splendor)                    (Victory)
         30—Resh    28—Tzaddi
                    9
                  Yesod
                (Founda-
                  tion)
         31—Shin  32—Tau  29—Qoph
                   10
                 Malkuth
                (Kingdom)
```

So this it is the Ideas behind this image that all the library texts eventually converge and describe? The semiotic of the closed and hidden secret thus becomes an open secret with anyone capable of hermeneutically decoding the encryption above, which for the Ramban is the torah as the encryption of G-d's divine names. Thus the title of the name of the Rose based on a pusek in a medieval poem: After the death of the rose all that remains is the name. This emphasis on the incorporeality of the rose itself but rather its name is found in Rambam's insistence as well on the incorporeality of God and His angels according to Charles Touti.[502] Decoding this enigmatic riddle from this medieval poem would take us too far afield but the importance on the concept of name is well known to all in Judaism, when G-d himself is known as "The Name (Hashem)."[503] The Baal shem tov was said to be the master of the Name. The Besht could Davon and by uttering permutations of the names of the G-d head could effect theurgically persons success in health, parnasa, and shiduchim for instance. For Borges the library is a labyrinth or maze where all leads to the utterance of the Name. Only the initiated have the key, thus a semiotic of esotericism is established with taboos set in place. Mystery surrounds the enigma of the Name. Spells and incantations according to Hechalot texts can open gates to rooms in the palace of G-ds seven heavens, where the soul is refreshed and delighted by the celestial knowledge it hears emanating from the names of angels. It is knowledge of the unity of the Name, and its subsequent various permutation that encrypt for this Name requiring decoding that makes for redemptive knowledge. For Borges the librarians are the gatekeepers of this knowledge, or at least know the path o the journey of life in how to arrive upon its manifestation, according to the Talmud, which is revealed once in 7 years, preferably at a flowing body of water or waterfall, to only those who can learn on their own. Thus the Name is not easily accessed nor attained by the man *ad captum vulgi*. There are Talmudic prohibitions as fences regarding prerequisites required for even questing for this name that hinge around the concepts of *ma'aseh Merkavah*[504] and *ma'aseh bereshit*.[505] Revealing the secrets of these topics is prohibited in Rabbinic thought.[506] One may not discuss the merkavah except in the presence of three and if the persons can learn on their own.[507] Madness awaits those who are incapable intellectually of receiving the shefa of such revelation, and taboos set up to discourage its seeking out.[508] Only a living masorah was fit to transmit these secrets and their writing down prohibited.[509] Rabbinic tradition promises that the ma'aseh merkavah constitute comprehension of the whole[510] and this is not for the hoi polio or n'importe qui, but only an elite. Perhaps the anti-Maimonideans such as Rabbi Judah Alfakar of Montpellier and his disciples keenly perceived the danger to rabbinic authority if the ma'aseh merkavah secrets were to be popularized and thus Dubnov represents a dialogue of Rabbi Alfakar prouncing that the Moreh HaNevukhim and parts of Sefer Mada of the MT. should be censored or burnt.[511]

The User as disrupter of Order

The library user has the potential to disrupt order. She can prevent the ideal of the complete library. She can recreate order. Providing the patron with services to access and circulate the texts can introduce disorder. Institutional authority of determining library policies for borrowing materials, which materials may be borrowed, length of circulation, fines that accrue for later items, etc. are all necessary but as Chelton has shown in her study of communicative production of institutional authority within library services, this establishment of hierarchies of authority and order is not always objective or value neutral.[512]

The library represents order. Some patrons are overwhelmed and awed by the library- not by sheer volume of texts, but by the overpowering sense of order and rules and procedures that the library demands.[513] One enters the library as a space of order rather than a creative space or what recently in the literature is called "a maker space." The stereotype of discoursive order that the library represents is that knowledge and order are not to be tampered with. This is far from the model of a knowledge lab. The library traditionally is not to be disturbed. The knowledge-order architectonic cannot be transgressed against the taboos. For Foucault the librarian is the symbol of the supremacy accorded the reigning order or what Foucault calls logophilia. The librarians role is to serve, to be subservient. Not like a good teacher to foster and enable and facilitate new ideas being born to life in the mind etc. The stereotypical librarian stamps, shelves, and keeps order in the domain of rational knowledge. The librarian is a symbol to show the patron that discourse is within the established order of things or rational knowledge. This place that houses the discourse of order and control honors it by giving selected discourses space, but defangs or disarms the potential of discourse by relegating authority to the librarians to give it its power by selecting it for preservation.

These feminists note that stereotypes risk putting a box, limit, or frame around people and denying their differences, vitality and ability to change like all living organisms that undergo processes of metamorphosis.[514] Hanningan and Crew have called for the application of feminist theory to the critique of the stereotype of the female librarian. Showing that it provides a theoretical framework for a rethinking of the philosophy of librarianship.[515] It is clear that women librarian stereotypes do not take seriously womens' interests, identities, and issues, nor recognize women's ways of being, thinking, and doing as valuable as those of men. The Saturn commercial's stereotype of the female librarian for instance is seen as damaging to librarians and the profession.[516] Case studies have shown that there is no doubt that film and Television create stereotypes of the flat images of librarians. Some argue that behind the triviality of the library stereotype librarians have failed to correct and rewrite it. Thus Ala has referred to waging war against it.[517] The Saturn commercial neutralizes the power of the female librarian by making fun of her stereotype. While the female librarian may be fearsome and the gatekeeper of much knowledge, beneath the stern exterior the commercial suggest there is nothing to fear, only an elderly women with a bun, glasses, and conservative outfit. The fear evoked by the female librarian in the Saturn commercial is a source of humor, ridicule, and face by the male voice-over. There is not respect for the female librarian in the Saturn commercial. Thus in this commercial the rationality of the hegemonic discourse controls and limits the female librarians potential and power. This power control dynamic enforces the female librarian stereotype. The stereotype portrays people who are possessed and obsessive compulsive with the order that rationality demands of them. They are presented as persons who fetishize efficiency.[518] The female librarian is stereotypically portrayed as having an impulse to extreme orderliness, introversion, and naivete.[519] Such a flat character is more to be pitied than revered and respected.

Film clip of Saturn librarian commercial

Afterword in a Comic Key: Seinfeld

The disruption of order can be seen in an episode of the television situation comedy Seinfeld entitled, *The Library* televised in the Autumn of 1994. Seinfeld has not returned the controversial book Henry Miller's Tropic of Cancer, which was a book that was censored when it came out. Seinfeld has it in his possession overdue since 1971. Thus Seinfeld has had it illegally for 23 years. Seinfeld goes with friend Kramer to the NYPL to plead his innocence.

The two friends have no understanding that taking books and not returning them denies the use of these books to fellow borrowers. Instead they mock the small fine associated with lateness:

> *What's amazing to me about the library is – now here's a place where you can go in and take out any*

book; they just give it to you and say bring it back when your done with it. It reminds me of like this pathetic friend everybody had when they were a kidthat would let you borrow any of his stuff if you will just be his friend you know. Tahts what the library is: it's a government funded pathetic friend. That's why everybody kind of bullies the library: I'll bring it back on time. I'll bring it back late- oh, what you gonna do? Charge me a nickel?[520]

Like Stephen King's story The Library Policeman, the Seinfeld episode treats the consequences of not returning a book on time. However this time the genre is comedy not horror. The stereotypically appearing female librarian engrossed in stamping a pile of library books. The librarian looks disapprovingly at Seinfeld's overdue notice and tells him his case has been turned over to a "librarian policeman" named Bookman.

Bookman comes to Seinfeld's house to intimidate, bully, and bully Seinfeld in determining where the book has gone.

Bookman: you took this book out in 1971

Jerry: Yes, and I returned it in 1971

Bookman: Yeh, 71. That was my first year on the job. A bad year for libraries a bad year for America. Hippies burning library cards, Abbie Hoffman telling everybody to steal books. I don't judge a man by the length of his hair and the kind of music he listens to- rock was never my bag. But you put on a pair of shoes when you walk into the NYPL, fella!"

Jerry: Look, Mr. Bookman, I returned that book. I remember it very specifically."

Bookman: You're a comedian. You make people laugh."

Jerry: I try

Bookman: You think this is all a big joke don't ya?

Jerry: No I don't

Bookman: "I saw you on TV once; I remembered your name from my list. I looked it up. Sure enough it checked out. You think because you are a celebrity that somehow the law doesn't apply to you? That your above the law?

Jerry: Certainly not!

Bookman: Well let me tell you something funny boy! You know that little stamp? The one that says NYPL? Well, that may not mean anything to you, but it means a lot to me. One whole hell of a lot. Sure, go ahead laugh if you want to. I've seen your type before. Flashy, making the scene, flaunting convention. Yeh, I know what your thinking; what's this going doing making such a big stink about a library book? Let me give you a hint, junior! Maybe we can live without libraries, people like you and me, maybe. Sure we're too old to change the world. But what about that kid, sitting down, opening a book, right now in a branch of the local library, and finding pictures of pee-pees and wee-wees on the cat in the hat, and the five Chinese brothers? Doesn't he

Chapter Six 172

deserve better? Look, if you think this is about overdue fines and missing books you'd better think again. This is about that kids right to read a book without getting his mind warped. Maybe that turns you on, Seinfeld; maybe that how you get your kicks, you and your good-time buddies. Well, I got a flash for you, joy-boy! You got seven days, Seinfeld. That's one week! (to return he book).[521]

The library policeman in Seinfeld is a hard natured cop with a brusque and lecturing tone and rough manner. He has a condescending attitude to Jerry and his profession and alleged lifestyle. The policeman is an idealist who takes keeping the library collection intact as an ultimate principle. The cop also has been surveilling Seinfeld when he refers to having Seinfeld "on his list." Like the librarian the policeman has the power to humiliate, shame, and bully.

Bookman takes his job personally and seriously. He is adamant in cracking down on overdue books for idealistic reasons that others are denied access and there is a primal violation of the sanctity of the collection. Bookman feels that he himself has been violated by Seinfeld's overdue negligence.

Conclusion

Many negative images of librarians and libraries have been presented. A stereotype found in the *Saturn* commercial and *Ghostbusters* is that of the librarian as an old scowling repressed spinster with her hair in a bun, wearing glasses, and drunk with her authority to stamp, check out books and demand fines for late books. Such a stereotype is one also of an order freak who fetishizes the classification system in the library as ultimate authority. The primary duty she seems to enjoy is Shusshing all the patrons.

We also encounter the librarian as a stereotypical bully, intimidator, and humiliator. For example in *Sophie's Choice,* Sophie is shamed by the librarian Sam Weiss at the Brooklyn College library who botches the reference interview. He assumes Sophie refers to Charles Dickins who was not a poet, when Sophie is really requesting the poems of Emily Dickinson. The library Sam Weiss does not listen carefully and likes to throw his authority around and insinuates that the bullied Sophie is dumb. We also see bullying to a further extreme in Stephen King's *The Library Policeman* where the library policeman in the horror genre is a kind of monster or ghoul who nicks Sam the library patron with knife in his throat threatening worse if he does not return his overdue book. In Conan the library there is not hesitation to kill as Conan splits apart patrons who have late overdue books. Richie in the cartoon the *Pagemaster* is also intimidated by the library and librarian. In the Seinfeld episode of the library policeman, Mr. Bookman is also a bully who tries to intimidate Seinfeld who has not returned a copy of Henry Millers, Tropic of Cancer for 23 years. But this time the encounter is not horror or threats of violence but rather comic relief. We seen also the librarians penchant to humiliating library patrons in the character of Mary in the *Part Girl* who shames a young man who has attempted to reshelve a book himself (in the wrong place). What unites all these negative depictions of librarians is the underlying current of fear behind authority. This discourse of fear lends itself to a Foucaultian analysis of power-knowledge regimes that control and make the library possible by legitimizing hegemonic discourses while marginalizing others.

The purpose of this study into the images of libraries and librarians in film and literature is not to suggest there is validity to these stereotypical representations. Rather we merely point out and note these negative images based on ignorance of what librarians really do and contribute to their institutions. We do not mean to suggest that any individual libraries or librarians have any of the characteristics attributed to them by the Foucaultian discourse of fear. The discourse of fear is a cultural code caused by the misnomer of being anti-authoritarian. Libraries are symbols of authority because of their being associated with metaphors of control, tombs, labyrinths, morgues, dust, ghosts, silence, and humiliation. Rather the goal is to deconstruct these simplistic reductions into stereotypes to point out the complexity of classifying any particular type of profession or individual which is always a limiting of their freedom and acknowledgment of the dynamic of change and development of the complexity of human beings.

So what makes for these negative stereotypes? From what ground soil do they grow. Mostly ignorance and what Foucault calls a discourse of fear, which is not fear of libraries and librarians but what they represent, which is logocentrism and the power of authorized discourse itself.

Films that portray the library and librarians in a more favorable light associated with knowledge, wisdom, light, happiness, comfort, and joy include *Wings of Desire* and even The *Name of the Rose*. In Eco's the *Name of the Rose* the librarian definitely has secret knowledge of the key to solve the secret of sercrets the mystery of mysteries and the library as labyrinth reinforces the librarians esoteric abilities to understand the maze of the labyrinth in the journey to ultimate knowledge of the crime solved by hermentic detective sleuthing employing the science of semiotics of interpretations of signs. Thus in *Name of the Rose* the act of reading and interpretations leads to the solving of the mystery while in the film homicide overreading leads to almost not solving the Detective "who done it" and the reasons and motivations of the murder. In popular sitcoms like *Buffy the Vampire slayer* we do find another popular portrayal of the librarian as the locus of esoteric knowledge also. Here the librarian is young, energetic, feindly, collegiate, and helps Buffy fight ware wolves and vampires by providing knowledge of the occult kept in books in the library. This positive stereotype is also accompanied by more recent images of the librarian as computer jockey, and know it all who posseses practical wisdom which is consulted by characters such as lawyers, detectives, and policemen.

More study and investigation of the grounds from which the stereotypes of libraries and librarians springs is needed. Such research will undoubtedly reveal that these negative images arise because what librarians do and the purpose of libraries is not understood fully by the general public and even administators at libraries. We are seeing today the further trend of the devaluing and disrespect by institutions that are liquidating their libraries in the name of the equation of practical cost efficiency and bottom line thinking, because the role of the library and librarian is not understood but devalued, disrespected, and dishonored. Such findings will undoubtedly uncover that the systems of power, legitimation, and regimes of authority that maintain all the discourses of institutions that house libraries are themselves in need of further library education not only in being proficient in library science skills but better appreciating the value added by librarians and the existence of libraries for the overall mission of any academic or educational institution.

Certain changes have led to the devaluing and dishonoring of what librarians do and the purpose that libraries serves. Certainly one of these is specialization, technology, and other facts. We might recall in conclusion the words of Stephen Reif who notes some of these changes in his acceptance speech in Cleveland of a AJL award:

Professor Stefan Reif's response to the AJL award made in June 2008

Once upon a time, dear colleagues, it was not unusual – it was perhaps even perfectly regular – for those with responsibilities for great libraries or outstanding collections of books to function all at once as librarians, bibliophiles, bibliographers, researchers, and managers. What is more, some of the greatest names in the history of modern Jewish scholarship, including Moritz Steinschneider, Abraham Berliner, Adolf Neubauer, Alexander Marx and Gershom Scholem,[522] played such a variety of roles, not so much because they were imposed upon them but rather in response to what 'book learning' meant to them.

Alas, at some point in more recent decades, libraries and the educational institutions of which they are a part have taken to splitting such functions and assigning each of them to a different post, while at the same time adding additional breeds of librarians whose sole function is technology or fund-raising. When seen in the broader bibliographical context, this may or may not be a favorable development. What is beyond question is that it has led to a most unfavorable suspicion of any member of the profession who attempts to be the kind of factotum that was once the norm.

For reasons which I have attempted to explain elsewhere and with which I shall not detain you further in this context, my career led me to a commitment to a multi-faceted librarianship and a dogged determination to combine scholarship with bibliography, research with cataloguing, lecturing with fund-raising, and paleography with technology. Because this was not always understood or appreciated by the colleagues, institutions and societies with which I came into contact in the world of learning, I sometimes seriously doubted whether I had made the right decision or whether I could have recorded greater achievements had I pursued a more conventional interpretation of the librarian's role.

There is little that could have given me more pleasure than knowing that those responsible for many of the world's greatest collections of Hebraica and Judaica have come to the conclusion that what I and my colleagues (including my wife, Shulie) did in the Taylor-Schechter Genizah Research Unit at Cambridge University Library in a period of a third of a century merits special recognition. To have heard from the Association of Jewish Libraries that it values my work and that of the Unit as the kind of contribution to research in Jewish studies that it wishes to acknowledge publicly and internationally sets the seal for me on a lifelong chronicle of efforts to improve the availability and understanding of a great scholarly resource. As such it is deeply appreciated and warmly received. In addition to expressing my gratitude it is appropriate for me to state that it could not have been achieved without the remarkable industry of generations of researchers in the Unit, the involvement of like-minded individuals at institutions around the world with broad vision and a distaste for parochial considerations, and the close cooperation of generous libraries and librarians such as those that are represented by your Association.

The fact that intellectual like Umberto Eco and Louis Borges would center their creative works around the mystery of the library lends credit to the respect and reverence for which libraries and librarians should be regarded. However the demise of respect for the function and breadth of librarians as scholars is in part due to what I addressed in my presentation and paper at the AJL conference in South Carolina titled, "Learning from Scholar Librarians." There I write:

We have much to learn today from Scholar largely autodidact librarians Drs: Moritz Steinschneider, Abraham Berliner, Abraham Freidus, Solomon Schechter, Umberto Cassutto, Alexander Marx, Jacob Dienstag, Rabbi Efraim Oshry, Chaim Leib Aryeh Vilsker, Gershom Scholem, Haim Maccoby, Stefen Reif, Malachi Beit Arie, and Menachem Schmeltzer- M.S. to MS.

These scholar librarians should serve as inspiring models to Judaica Librarians for the proper integration and fusion of scholarship with practicing Judaica Librarianship. These extraordinary scholarly librarians' research gave mission, guidance, and purpose to their being great Judaica Librarians. These scholar librarians show us that there is no substitute (especially mechanized automation) for authentic subject knowledge, seeing back-stretched interdisciplinary connections, and wide-reading background and autodidacticism, that allows one to cast a wide cognitive net in familiarization with a broad range of Judaica subjects, disciplines, and methods that benefits the field of Judaica librarianship. Until Judaica Librarianship again `values' the importance of Jewish scholarship as an essential key component working in tandem with serving as a Judaica Librarian, the profession will be less for this myopic lack of vision. The understanding of these scholarly librarians shines as a beacon paradigm for weathering the fashions of ephemeral technological changes that morph into the truncated type of professional librarian specialist technocrats. Because these scholar librarians know

> the substantial content of books, manuscripts, and journals in their collections etc rather than `getting by' as task master technocrats, proficient in merely "accessing information" ad captum vulgi, their examples serve as standards by which Judaica Librarianship should set high the bar.

Today scholarship has also suffered from specialization and other factors. The *film the footnote (He'arat Shulayim)* provides a window into some of these trends. The two main characters are a father and son. The father Elliezer Skonnick (Shomo bar Aba) is an old time scholar who spends most his time in the library meticulously researching in a thorough comprehensive, and systematic way variants of Talmudic manuscripts, leading his life in almost obscurity with no one really aware of the importance of his research. His deciphering of minute inconsistencies in various girsa of the Talmudim is hard work. He has not received much recognition except for one time a great legendary scholar cited his findings in a footnote. Eliezer is bitter, anti-social, and envious of his son's popularity and resentful of his own lack of recognition. Eliezer is a secular philologist who treats the Talmudic text like an archaeologist to be dated and identified, spending 30 years of drudgery work carefully alone verifying the source of a particular section of the Talmud. The father spends most of his time in the library. He is bitter that his meticulous evidence in the form of a proof was overshadowed by a competitor (Grossman) chance discovery, so that his research was condemned to a footnote. Grossman is Eliezer's bureaucratic nemesis who blocks his recognition.

In contrast, the son is out and about. Religiously observant the son is concerned with the meaning of the words of the Talmud and makes them accessible to the public. The son is a new type of scholar. He is a populizer of Judaic lore, whose books are best sellers and whose presence is often seen on TV and talk shows. The son is in the limelight and has a popular public pesonna. The son has a *je ne sais quo* and is likable and carries charisma. Both scholars however seem to be covetous of fame and honor. The greatest honor to many academics in Israel is the Pras Israeli. Eliezer receives a call congratulating him on having won this prestigious prize. Vindication at last for a lifetime of pain staking scholarship. When Uriel is told this remarkable development that the father is announced as the winner the son realizes that the caller actually intended to award the prize to the son. The chairman of the committee and old curmudgeon Grossman (played by Micah Lewesohn), meets with six other judges to discuss the mix up. The exchange is hilarious. An apparent solution is arrived at by Grossman, who is a lifelong saboteur of Eliezer's work. During the meeting Uriel says he has been submitting his father's name for the Israel Prize every year, and accuses Grossman of blocking that and other ways of recognizing Eliezer. Grossman angrily says Eliezer has never published anything significant in his career. Uriel goes to the National Library to break the news to his father but finds him raising a toast to winning the prize with colleagues Unable to break the news to his father that Eliezer is not the recipient but rather the son Uriel is, he once again meets Grossman, asking that the prize be given to Eliezer. Grossman relents but with two conditions:

Uriel must write the committees recommendation and Uriel can never be a candidate for the prize again. Uriel agrees and writes the recommendation text, picking and choosing every word carefully. Meantime Eliezer is interviewed in Haaretz and denounces the superficial scientific and academic validity of his son's Uriel's research, when in fact the son has sacrificed his own career in honor for his father's name. In a brilliant detective hermeneutic sleuthing Eliezer does the most crucial textual reading of his life ironically in connection with this personal crisis. During the preparation for t TV interview Eliezer is struck by an uncommon Talmudic phrase in the Israel Prize's commitees recommendation. He flees the studio and returns to his study library as a place of refuge. He examines the expression, cross-checking its published uses, and realizes that the text must have actually been written by Uriel. Eliezer then reconstructs his phone conversation with the Minister of Education realizing that she had addressed him by his last name only. He concludes that the minister thought she was talking to his son when she broke the news about the Israel Prize. Comedy abounds in Eliezer's lack of familiarity with modern publicity and public relations as he does not even know what security guards are for. When Eliezer is interviewed by a reporter he shoots himself in the foot. What happens is a series of events involving academic scholarship, familial jealousy, and pride, stubbornness and poetic justice. Grossman as Shakesepare might say, is hoisted by his own petar! All of this comes together wonderfully in a complex subtle plot development that only the father and son will completely understand. On the day of the prize ceremony, Eliezer and his wife arrive at the Jerusalem International Convention Center to prepare for the ceremony, Eliezer is stressed and distracted. The movie ends a moment before the laureates are called to the stage. The son has made an ultimate sacrifice for the father in respect and honor. This is a wonderful film, that perhaps represents the old time scholarship of Eliezer who like librarians often go unrecognized and under valued while the charismatic more superficial research is all the rage of what people want now a days. However in the end it is the act of sacrifice of the son for the father that is the noble gesture, transcending petty jealousies and affirming filial devotion over vanity and fleeting fame. The film speaks to politics of academia and the desperate need for validation. The son Uriel ultimately chooses between his career advancement and his father's honor. He does not sabotage his father's glory. The sad note is that the world is full of unsung academics who toil all their lives in obsessive quest for knowledge- only to end up a footnote in someone else's career. The film transcends the father son rivalry in the Talmud department of Hebrew University in Jerusalem. The film is a meditation on the concept of the footnote and how many of our lives are like a footnote in time.[523] On another level it should be noted that Cedar the director of the film was raised with a Yeshivah background and studied the Talmud from a religious angle most of his life, so the academic making the Talmud into a text to be scientifically analyzed was something foreign to his childhood. Cedar recognizes that no other culture has created a document so vas, complex, and detailed that continues to be relevant and the text is the source not only of our culture but religious ethical behavior. Yet Talmud scholars in the film like Grossman appear to have learned little of the Talmud's ethical messages, but rather seems to be motivated by petty jealousies, academic politics, and cut throat completion, although he is recognized as a leading Talmudic academic authority. That a prize would pit father against son and ultimately each man against himself is certainly not a moral lesson taught by the true spirit of Talmudic inquiry. That a prize would cause so much strife and contention so that individuals loose their integrity is a story that needs to be told whereby jealousy, covetousness, and ayn ha-rah are the sins that bring evil into the world. While academics may spend their lives devoted to studying the intricacies of the language and history of the Talmudim as the foundation of Jewish law and culture one wonders if they have learned anything ethically from it. To learn about is an intellectual game while to learn from is a religious quest for redemption. The model of competiveness may weed out mediocrity but it can produce a world where no one is satisfied or fulfilled or certainly can see a higher mission and can loose sight of the trees for the forest. It is ironic that computer technology simulation may replace the efforts of scholars like Eliezer Skolnick. Eliezer is a taciturn and under appreciated philologist who analyzes Talmudic manuscripts in exacting detail, and is focused on the task of recreating an authentic ur text master version of that ancient collection of sacred oral texts before attempting to decipher what I all means. This is what happened when the monopoly of Harvard Dead Sea Scroll scholars who delayed in publishing their findings were beaten to the punch by a computer simulation produced by a computer scientists at Hebrew Union College in Cincinattii which forced the release of the photograph Bechtel's negatives photographed in a California library. Yet we symphathize with Eliezer's diligent hard work of old time scholarship in contrast to his son who has a gift for schmooze (played by Lior Ashkenazi) who writes popular theoretical books, eclipsing Eliezer in honors and accolades, a kind of superficiality that Eliezer loathes as a generation without memory or method. The film in part however is about the Talmud which is driven by fierece arguments over words, the tension of generations, and the tension between oral and written. Interestingly Mr. Ashkenazi did have guidance in preparing for his role from Dr. Moshe Halbertal, a professor of Jewish thought at Hebrew University, whose career trajectory may bear a passing resemblance to Uriel's although Dr. Halbertal denies any connection. The film ultimately teachers that having a life's quest in academic scholarship does not mean you are not vulnerable to petty human feelings and tensions. Academic politics are perhaps the most vicious because the stakes are so low.

Librarianship based on Technocracy (the fusion of technology and bureaucracy) favors specialization rather than the ideal of the independent autodidact scholar librarian, who never loses sight of the big picture, or seeing the forest for the trees, possessing visionary scope from the alpha to the omega, the perspective of the mental sunrise from eagle's wings as Rambam the Nesher HaGadol teaches. All of the above extraordinary 20th century Jewish scholar librarians serve as shining examples that Judaica librarianship is a mission, not merely a bourgeois professional career, punching a clock 9 to 5 pm. We learn from these scholarly librarians devoted foremost to the quest for hokmah-binah-vedaas, and in this quest for attainment of intellectual virtue, we find the fullest completion (shelemut) for which the human being was created BiTzelem Elokim. All of these scholar librarians strived ad astra for deepening Jewish knowledge, expanding the palace of Torah, by affirming that the link (kesher) between Hashem and human being is the sekel ha-poel (active intellect) which is not only redemptive, but enables the ultimate heavenly rewards, whereby one's merit is directly proportional to the cognitive virtue gained in this world (olam ha-zeh) which accrues [as the language of the Mishna notes] as `interest' in the next world and beyond etc. The example of these scholar librarians are an answer to the question- Why Judaica libraries [which are different and unique from other types of libraries], matter now more than ever? If we do not harken to the clarion call of their perfect harmonization of librarianship with scholarship, Judaica librarianship is at risk.

As addressed also in my presentation at the AJL conference in NYC titled, "reference services at LCW"[524] I demonstrate that librarians do more than show how to access information and fact check. There I write:

> *Fifty five of the Touro College LCW library guides content compiled by the speaker include more than just standard web directories, recommended databases and bibliographies. Power points,*

> *mikorot* packets of Hebrew Rabbinic primary sources, outlines-charts-exercises, book reviews, graphs, and substantive introductions pepper and spice up the library guides and make them unique resources. As Rabbi Yehudah HaNasi says in Pirke Avot: אל תסתכל בקנקן אלא במה שיש בו יש קנקן חדש מלא ישן וישן שאפילו חדש אין בו While the library guides template container may be likened to "new wine" if you explore these guides you will find "old wine. The Library Guides composed for the LCW curriculum show the increasing Interdisciplinarity of Jewish studies. Making these guides interdisciplinary shows that librarians not only teach how to "access" knowledge [and importantly serve as "fact checkers,"] but also can take an active role in organizing, interpreting commenting upon, and creatively fostering the furtherance of interdisciplinary international research.

In taking an active role in organizing, interpreting commenting upon, and creatively fostering the furtherance of interdisciplinary international research we should not forget that librarians are teachers too, and essential to any educational endeavor. Librarians to accomplish this respect should strive to be scholars too, and know what is the content of their books and journals and online resources rather than merely knowing "how to access it" in the information age[525] which poses many dangers and risks to the thriving not only of libraries but intellectual pursuits.

Bibliography

Reviews and Announcements of the Jewish Encyclopaedia and Articles and Books

Abelow, Samuel P. "An Index to the Jewish Encyclopaedia, Containing References to

Articles that Deal with the History of the Jews in the United States," in Index to the PAJHS, nos. 1-20, N.p., 1914

Ahad Ha-Am (Asher Ginzberg). Igrot Ahad Ha-Am. Vols. 2 &3. Jerusalem, 1924

AZJ, 11 September 1891, pp.434-35

AH, 1901-1905.

AI, 11 July 1901, p.1 and 18 July 1901, p.5

American Journal of Theology 6 (1902): 762-64; and 9 (1905): 521-26

Archives Israelites, 8 August 1901, pp.249-51, and 7 January 1904, pp.6-7

Athenaeum, no. 3852 (1901), pp. 246-47; no. 3907 (1902), pp. 345-46; no. 3966 (1903), p.579; no. 4007 (1904), p.209; and no. 4012 (1904), p.380

Bacher, Wilhelm. "Die Juedische Enzyklopadie." AZJ 70 (1906): 114-16.

Berger, A and Kaufman, R, "Jewish Encyclopaedias and Other Reference Books in the Last Twenty Years," Jewish Book Annual 15 (1957): 41-49.

Christian Advocate, 1 August 1901, p.1229

Christian Observer, 10 July 1901, p.667

Die Deborah. New series 1 (1901): 225-28; and 2 (1902): 226

Eisenstein, J.D. Critical Review of the Legal Articles of the Jewish Encyclopaedia

Volume I. New York, 1901

Evening Post, 2 November 1901, p.19

Friedlaender, Israel. "The Jewish Encyclopaedia." Ha-Shiloah 8 (1901): 254-61.

Hebrew Standard (New York), 28 October 1904, p.12

Jacobs, Joseph, The Jewish Encyclopaedia: A Guide to Its Contents, An Aid to Its Use, New York, 1906.

JChr, 23 February 1901, pp. 18-19; 31 May 1901; 11 July 1902, p.13; and 26 December 1902, p.18

JCom, 5 July 1901 pp.1-4; 12 July 1901, pp.1-5; and 19 July 1901, pp.2-7.

JExp, 18 January, 1901, p.8 and 19 July 1907

Krauss, Samuel. "Eine neue Encyclopaedie." Yeshurun 8 (1902): 332-34, 344-46

Launching of a Great Work: The Jewish Encyclopaedia. Publishers Announcement on the

Completion of the

First Volume. New York. 1901.

Levy, Louis. "Une Encyclopedie Juive." L'Univers Israelite, 9 August 1901, p.660-61

Menorah: A Monthly Magazine for the Jewish Home 24 (1898): 334-36; 30 (1901): 12324; 31 (1901): 123-24; 39 (1905): 113-118; and 39 (1905): 150-51.

Nation, 31 October, 1901, pp. 341-42; and 2 October 1902, p.272.

New York Times, 22 May 1901, p.9; 20 July, 1901, p.11; 16 August 1902, p.559; 2 February 1904, p.125; and 26 March 1904, p.207.

Opinions of the Press on the Jewish Encyclopaedia. [New York, 1901?].

Opinions of the World's Press on Volume I of the Funk & Wagnalls Jewish

Encyclopaedia. [New York, 1901?]

Perles, Felix, Juedische Skizzen, Leipzig, 1912.

RA, 15 June 1901, pp.555, 562-64; 27 July 1901, pp. 709-10; 7 & 14 December, 1901, pp.375-76, 399-401; and 26 March 1904, pp.113-116.

Revue des Etudes Juives 43: 291; 45: 138; 46: 282-83; and 48: 287-88.

Sun, 6 October 1901, sec. 2, p.2

Zeitschrift fuer hebraische Bibliographie 5 (1901): 115-116.

Book Reviews of the Encyclopedia Judaica

Agus, Jacob B., Conservative Judaism, Vol. 26, No.4 (Summer, 1972): 46-57.

Association for Jewish Studies Newsletter, vol. 3, No. 1 (Oct., 1972): 5-7 and No. 8 (Feb., 1973): 7-8.

(Baruch Levine reviews the Bible in EJ and Jacob Neusner reviews Talmudic Studies)

Berlin, Charles, Library Journal 97 (1972): 2562.

The Booklist 69 (1972): 209-12.

Israel Book World, No. 6 (Dec., 1971): 2-4.

Johnston, Albert H., Publishers Weekly (Feb. 28, 1972): 46-47

Raphael, Chaim, Commentary, Vol. 54, No.2 (1972): 36-44.

Rothenberg, Joshua, Zukunft 78 (Oct.1972): 332-33

Ryan, John J., Wall Street Journal (Dec. 21, 1972)

Schulman, Elias, Forward 76 (March 18, 1973): p.M2.

Silver, Daniel Jeremy, CCAR Journal, Vol. 19, No.4 (1972): 88-92.

Temkin, Sefton, Jewish Chronicle Literary Supplement (June 2, 1972), p.iii

Time (Nov. 20, 1972): 91-92

Weis-Rosmarin, Trude, Jewish Spectator, Vol. 37, No.8 (Oct., 1972): 3-6 and 30.

Zafren, Herbert C., Jewish Encyclopaedias of the Last Fifteen Years, Jewish Book Annual 31 (1973-74): 21-28.

Zeitlin, Solomon, JQR 63 (1972): 1-28.

Endnotes

1 Bemporad, Elissa. "Behavior Unbecoming a Communist: Jewish Religious Practice in Soviet Minsk". Vol 14 No.2. Jewish Social Studies New Series. Indiana University Press. Winter, 2008 .pp1-31
Ferziger, Adam S. "Outside the Shul": The American Soviet Jewry Movement and the Rise of Solidarity Orthodoxy 1964-1986". Vol 22 No.1. Religion and Culture: A Journal of Interpretation. 2012 .pp83-130
Kubicht, A. Paul. "Soviet Expansion Into Eastern Europe, 1945-1952 U.S. Policy Confronts the Issue of Religious Freedom". Vol 34 No. 1. Fides et Historia. Winter, 2002 pp73-87

2 Boyarin, Jonathan, Kinship and "Qiddushin" : genealogy and geography in b. Qiddushin iv., Talmudic Transgressions (2017) 386-406, 2017

3 Vidas, Moulie,1983, he Bavli's discussion of genealogy in "Qiddushin" IV, Antiquity in Antiquity (2008) 285-326, 2008

4 Levin, Yigal, Understanding biblical genealogies, Currents in Research: Biblical Studies 9 (2001) 11-46, 2001

5 Rendsburg, Gary, The internal consistency and historical reliability of the biblical genealogies., Vetus Testamentum 40,2 (1990) 185-206, 1990

6 Ska, Jean Louis, Le genealogie della Genesi e le risposte alle sfide della storia., Ricerche Storico Bibliche 17,1 (2005) 89-111, 2005

7 Carr, David McLain, "Biblos geneseos" revisited : a synchronic analysis of patterns in Genesis as part of the Torah, ZAW 110,2 (1998) 159-172; 3: 327-347, 1998

[8] Alexander, Thomas Desmond, Genealogies, seed and the compositional unity of Genesis, Tyndale Bulletin 44,2 (1993) 255-270, 1993

[9] Renaud, B.(Bernard), Les généalogies et la structure de l'histoire sacerdotale dans le livre de la Genèse, Revue Biblique 97,1 (1990) 5-30, 1990

[10] Schwartz, Sarah,1971, Narrative "toledot" formulae in Genesis : the case of heaven and earth, Noah, and Isaac., The Journal of Hebrew Scriptures 16 (2016) 37 pp., 2016

[11] Angel, Hayyim J., Elleh toledot" : a study of the genealogies in the Book of Genesis., Haham Gaon Memorial Volume (1997) 163-182, 1997

[12] Wallace, Howard N, The toledot of Adam, Studies in the Pentateuch (1990) 17-33, 1990

[13] Crüsemann, Frank, Human solidarity and ethnic identity : Israel's self-definition in the genealogical system of Genesis, Ethnicity and the Bible (1996) 57-76, 1996

[14] Andersen, T. David, Genealogical prominence and the structure of Genesis., Biblical Hebrew and Discourse Linguistics (1994) 242-266, 1994

[15] Hopkins, David C., The first stories of Genesis and the rhythm of the generations, The Echoes of Many Texts (1997) 25-41, 1997

[16] Hjelm, Ingrid, Tribes, genealogies and the composition of the Hebrew Bible., The Politics of Israel's Past (2013) 18-27, 2013

[17] Zadok, Ran, On the reliability of the genealogical and prosopographical lists of the Israelites in the Old Testament, Tel Aviv; Journal of the Institute of Archaeology of Tel Aviv University 25,2 (1998) 228-254, 1998

[18] Twersky, Geula,1968, Lamech's song and the Cain genealogy : an examination of Gen 4,23-24 within its narrative context., Scandinavian Journal of the Old Testament 31,2 (2017) 275-293; 2017

19 זֶה סֵפֶר, תּוֹלְדֹת אָדָם: בְּיוֹם, בְּרֹא אֱלֹהִים אָדָם, בִּדְמוּת אֱלֹהִים, עָשָׂה אֹתוֹ

20 White, Bernard, Schematized or non-schematized : the genealogies of Genesis 5 and 11., Andrews University Seminary Studies 54,2 (2016) 205-235, 2016; White, Bernard, Adam to Joshua : tracing a paragenealogy., 2016

21 Tov, Emanuel, The genealogical lists in Genesis 5 and 11 in three different versions., rom Author to Copyist (2015) 37-52, 2015; also in Textual Criticism of the Hebrew Bible, Qumran, Septuagint (2015) 221-238, 2015

22 Cohen, Jeffrey M., "Be-dorotav" : Noah's "generations" in light of antediluvian longevity, Jewish Bible Quarterly 41,3 (2013) 187-190, 2013

23 Ziemer, Benjamin, Erklärung der Zahlen von Gen 5 aus ihrem kompositionellen Zusammenhang., Zeitschrift für die Alttestamentliche Wissenschaft 121,1 (2009) 1-18, 2009

24 Hutzli, Jürg, The procreation of Seth by Adam in Gen 5:3 and the composition of Gen 5, Semitica 54 (2012) 147-162, 2012

25 Freeman, Travis R., A new look at the Genesis 5 and 11 fluidity problem, Andrews University Seminary Studies 42,2 (2004) 259-286 2004

26 אֵלֶּה, תּוֹלְדֹת נֹחַ--נֹחַ אִישׁ צַדִּיק תָּמִים הָיָה, בְּדֹרֹתָיו: אֶת-הָאֱלֹהִים, הִתְהַלֶּךְ-נֹחַ

27 Knoppers, Gary N, Shem, Ham and Japheth : the universal and the particular in the genealogy of nations, The Chronicler as Theologian (2003) 13-31, 2003

28 Gilboa, Raquel, brief note on the peoples descending from Noah (Genesis 9-10), Biblische Notizen 171 (2016) 3-12 , 2016

29 Darshan, Guy,, The biblical account of the post-diluvian generation (Gen. 9:20-10:32) in the light of Greek genealogical literature., Vetus Testamentum 63,4 (2013) 515-535, 2013

[30] וְאֵלֶּה תּוֹלְדֹת בְּנֵי־נֹחַ, שֵׁם חָם וָיָפֶת; וַיִּוָּלְדוּ לָהֶם בָּנִים, אַחַר הַמַּבּוּל

[31] Levin, Yigal, The family of man : the genre and purpose of Genesis 10, Looking at the Ancient Near East and the Bible Through the Same Eyes (2012) 291-308, 2012

[32] Lipiński, Edward, Les Sémites selon Gen 10,21-30 et 1 Chr 1,17-23, Zeitschrift für Althebraistik 6,2 (1993) 193-215, 1993

[33] Blenkinsopp, Joseph,1927, The first family : Terah and sons., ournal for the Study of the Old Testament 41,1 (2016) 3-13 2016.

[34] Mutius, Hans-Georg von, Pirke Abot V,2 als Beleg für eine bisher unbekannte Fassung von Abrahams Stammbaum in Genesis 11,10-26., Biblische Notizen 91 (1998) 16-19, 1998

[35] Hess, Richard S., Lamech in the genealogies of Genesis, Bulletin for Biblical Research 1 (1991) 21-25, 1991

[36] Northcote, Jeremy, The lifespans of the patriarchs : schematic orderings in the chrono-genealogy., Vetus Testamentum 57,2 (2007) 243-257, 2007

[37] Siegert, Folker, "Und er hob seine Augen auf, und siehe" : Abrahams Gottesvision (Gen 18) im hellenistischen Judentum., "Abraham, unser Vater" (2003) 67-85, 2003

[38] Cortese, Enzo, Patriarchal genealogies : literary, historical and theologico-political criticism, Divine Promises to the Fathers (1995) 11-27, 1995

[39] See Marx, Alfred, La généalogie d'Exode VI 14-25 : sa forme, sa function, Vetus Testamentum 45,3 (1995) 318-336, 1995

[40] Japhet, Sara, Was David a Judahite or an Ephraimite? : Light from the genealogies, Let Us Go up to Zion (2012) 297-306, 2012

[41] Knoppers, Gary N, The Davidic genealogy : some contextual considerations from the ancient Mediterranean world., Transeuphratène; recherches pluridisciplinaires sur une province de l'Empire achéménide 22 (2001) 35-50, 2001

דברי הימים א פרק ב [42]

וְרָם הוֹלִיד אֶת עַמִּינָדָב וְעַמִּינָדָב הוֹלִיד אֶת נַחְשׁוֹן נְשִׂיא בְּנֵי יְהוּדָה:
(יא) וְנַחְשׁוֹן הוֹלִיד אֶת שַׂלְמָא וְשַׂלְמָא הוֹלִיד אֶת בֹּעַז:
(יב) וּבֹעַז הוֹלִיד אֶת עוֹבֵד וְעוֹבֵד הוֹלִיד אֶת יִשָׁי:
(יג) וְאִישַׁי הוֹלִיד אֶת בְּכֹרוֹ אֶת אֱלִיאָב וַאֲבִינָדָב הַשֵּׁנִי וְשִׁמְעָא הַשְּׁלִישִׁי:
(יד) נְתַנְאֵל הָרְבִיעִי רַדַּי הַחֲמִישִׁי:
(טו) אֹצֶם הַשִּׁשִּׁי דָּוִיד הַשְּׁבִעִי:

דברי הימים א פרק ג

וְאֵלֶּה הָיוּ בְּנֵי דָוִיד אֲשֶׁר נוֹלַד לוֹ בְּחֶבְרוֹן הַבְּכוֹר אַמְנֹן לַאֲחִינֹעַם הַיִּזְרְעֵאלִית שֵׁנִי דָּנִיֵּאל לַאֲבִיגַיִל הַכַּרְמְלִית:

(ב) הַשְּׁלִשִׁי לְאַבְשָׁלוֹם בֶּן מַעֲכָה בַּת תַּלְמַי מֶלֶךְ גְּשׁוּר הָרְבִיעִי אֲדֹנִיָּה בֶן חַגִּית:

(ג) הַחֲמִישִׁי שְׁפַטְיָה לַאֲבִיטָל הַשִּׁשִּׁי יִתְרְעָם לְעֶגְלָה אִשְׁתּוֹ:

(ד) שִׁשָּׁה נוֹלַד לוֹ בְחֶבְרוֹן וַיִּמְלָךְ שָׁם שֶׁבַע שָׁנִים וְשִׁשָּׁה חֳדָשִׁים וּשְׁלֹשִׁים וְשָׁלוֹשׁ שָׁנָה מָלַךְ בִּירוּשָׁלִָם: ס

(ה) וְאֵלֶּה נוּלְּדוּ לוֹ בִּירוּשָׁלָיִם שִׁמְעָא וְשׁוֹבָב וְנָתָן וּשְׁלֹמֹה אַרְבָּעָה לְבַת שׁוּעַ בַּת עַמִּיאֵל:

(ו) וְיִבְחָר וֶאֱלִישָׁמָע וֶאֱלִיפָלֶט:

(ז) וְנֹגַהּ וְנֶפֶג וְיָפִיעַ:

(ח) וֶאֱלִישָׁמָע וְאֶלְיָדָע וֶאֱלִיפֶלֶט תִּשְׁעָה:

(ט) כֹּל בְּנֵי דָוִיד מִלְּבַד בְּנֵי פִילַגְשִׁים וְתָמָר אֲחוֹתָם: פ

(י) וּבֶן שְׁלֹמֹה רְחַבְעָם אֲבִיָּה בְנוֹ אָסָא בְנוֹ יְהוֹשָׁפָט בְּנוֹ:

(יא) יוֹרָם בְּנוֹ אֲחַזְיָהוּ בְנוֹ יוֹאָשׁ בְּנוֹ:

(יב) אֲמַצְיָהוּ בְנוֹ עֲזַרְיָה בְנוֹ יוֹתָם בְּנוֹ:

(יג) אָחָז בְּנוֹ חִזְקִיָּהוּ בְנוֹ מְנַשֶּׁה בְנוֹ:

(יד) אָמוֹן בְּנוֹ יֹאשִׁיָּהוּ בְנוֹ:

(טו) וּבְנֵי יֹאשִׁיָּהוּ הַבְּכוֹר יוֹחָנָן הַשֵּׁנִי יְהוֹיָקִים הַשְּׁלִשִׁי צִדְקִיָּהוּ הָרְבִיעִי שַׁלּוּם:

(טז) וּבְנֵי יְהוֹיָקִים יְכָנְיָה בְנוֹ צִדְקִיָּה בְנוֹ:

(יז) וּבְנֵי יְכָנְיָה אַסִּר שְׁאַלְתִּיאֵל בְּנוֹ:

(יח) וּמַלְכִּירָם וּפְדָיָה וְשֶׁנְאַצַּר יְקַמְיָה הוֹשָׁמָע וּנְדַבְיָה:

(יט) וּבְנֵי פְדָיָה זְרֻבָּבֶל וְשִׁמְעִי וּבֶן זְרֻבָּבֶל מְשֻׁלָּם וַחֲנַנְיָה וּשְׁלֹמִית אֲחוֹתָם:

(כ) וַחֲשֻׁבָה וָאֹהֶל וּבֶרֶכְיָה וַחֲסַדְיָה יוּשַׁב חֶסֶד חָמֵשׁ:

(כא) וּבֶן חֲנַנְיָה פְּלַטְיָה וִישַׁעְיָה בְּנֵי רְפָיָה בְּנֵי אַרְנָן בְּנֵי עֹבַדְיָה בְּנֵי שְׁכַנְיָה: ס

(כב) וּבְנֵי שְׁכַנְיָה שְׁמַעְיָה וּבְנֵי שְׁמַעְיָה חַטּוּשׁ וְיִגְאָל וּבָרִיחַ וּנְעַרְיָה וְשָׁפָט שִׁשָּׁה:

(כג) וּבֶן נְעַרְיָה אֶלְיוֹעֵינַי וְחִזְקִיָּה וְעַזְרִיקָם שְׁלֹשָׁה:

(כד) וּבְנֵי אֶלְיוֹעֵינַי הדיוהו הוֹדַוְיָהוּ וְאֶלְיָשִׁיב וּפְלָיָה וְעַקּוּב וְיוֹחָנָן וּדְלָיָה וַעֲנָנִי שִׁבְעָה: ס

[44] Barrick, W. Boyd,, Genealogical notes on the 'House of David' and the 'House of Zadok,
Journal for the Study of the Old Testament 96 (2001) 29-58
, 2001

דברי הימים א פרק ה [45]

וּבְנֵי קְהָת עַמְרָם יִצְהָר וְחֶבְרוֹן וְעֻזִּיאֵל: ס
(כט) וּבְנֵי עַמְרָם אַהֲרֹן וּמֹשֶׁה וּמִרְיָם ס וּבְנֵי אַהֲרֹן נָדָב וַאֲבִיהוּא אֶלְעָזָר וְאִיתָמָר: ס
(ל) אֶלְעָזָר הוֹלִיד אֶת פִּינְחָס פִּינְחָס הֹלִיד אֶת אֲבִישׁוּעַ:
(לא) וַאֲבִישׁוּעַ הוֹלִיד אֶת בֻּקִּי וּבֻקִּי הוֹלִיד אֶת עֻזִּי:
(לב) וְעֻזִּי הוֹלִיד אֶת זְרַחְיָה וּזְרַחְיָה הוֹלִיד אֶת מְרָיוֹת:
(לג) מְרָיוֹת הוֹלִיד אֶת אֲמַרְיָה וַאֲמַרְיָה הוֹלִיד אֶת אֲחִיטוּב:
(לד) וַאֲחִיטוּב הוֹלִיד אֶת צָדוֹק וְצָדוֹק הוֹלִיד אֶת אֲחִימַעַץ:
(לה) וַאֲחִימַעַץ הוֹלִיד אֶת עֲזַרְיָה וַעֲזַרְיָה הוֹלִיד אֶת יוֹחָנָן:
(לו) וְיוֹחָנָן הוֹלִיד אֶת עֲזַרְיָה הוּא אֲשֶׁר כִּהֵן בַּבַּיִת אֲשֶׁר בָּנָה שְׁלֹמֹה בִּירוּשָׁלִָם:
(לז) וַיּוֹלֶד עֲזַרְיָה אֶת אֲמַרְיָה וַאֲמַרְיָה הוֹלִיד אֶת אֲחִיטוּב:
(לח) וַאֲחִיטוּב הוֹלִיד אֶת צָדוֹק וְצָדוֹק הוֹלִיד אֶת שַׁלּוּם:
(לט) וְשַׁלּוּם הוֹלִיד אֶת חִלְקִיָּה וְחִלְקִיָּה הוֹלִיד אֶת עֲזַרְיָה:
(מ) וַעֲזַרְיָה הוֹלִיד אֶת שְׂרָיָה וּשְׂרָיָה הוֹלִיד אֶת יְהוֹצָדָק:
(מא) וִיהוֹצָדָק הָלַךְ בְּהַגְלוֹת יְקֹוָק אֶת יְהוּדָה וִירוּשָׁלִָם בְּיַד נְבֻכַדְנֶאצַּר

מלכים ב פרק כב [46]

וַיְהִי בִּשְׁמֹנֶה עֶשְׂרֵה שָׁנָה לַמֶּלֶךְ יֹאשִׁיָּהוּ שָׁלַח הַמֶּלֶךְ אֶת שָׁפָן בֶּן אֲצַלְיָהוּ בֶן מְשֻׁלָּם הַסֹּפֵר בֵּית יְקֹוָק לֵאמֹר

ירמיהו פרק לו [47]

וַיִּשְׁלְחוּ כָל הַשָּׂרִים אֶל בָּרוּךְ אֶת יְהוּדִי בֶן נְתַנְיָהוּ בֶּן שֶׁלֶמְיָהוּ בֶן כּוּשִׁי לֵאמֹר הַמְּגִלָּה אֲשֶׁר קָרָאתָ בָּהּ בְּאָזְנֵי הָעָם קָחֶנָּה בְיָדְךָ וָלֵךְ וַיִּקַּח בָּרוּךְ בֶּן נֵרִיָּהוּ אֶת הַמְּגִלָּה בְּיָדוֹ וַיָּבֹא אֲלֵיהֶם

[48] Stone, Michael E, The genealogy of Bilhah., Dead Sea Discoveries 3,1 (1996) 20-36, 1996

וַיִּתֵּן אֱלֹהַי אֶל-לִבִּי, וָאֶקְבְּצָה אֶת-הַחֹרִים וְאֶת-הַסְּגָנִים וְאֶת-הָעָם [49] לְהִתְיַחֵשׂ; וָאֶמְצָא, סֵפֶר הַיַּחַשׂ הָעוֹלִים בָּרִאשׁוֹנָה, וָאֶמְצָא, כָּתוּב בּוֹ

[50] Ron, Zv, the genealogy of Moses and Aaron., Jewish Bible Quarterly 31,3 (2003) 190-194, 2003

[51] וְאֶחָיו, לְמִשְׁפְּחֹתָיו, בְּהִתְיַחֵשׂ, לְתֹלְדוֹתָם--הָרֹאשׁ יְעִיאֵל, וּזְכַרְיָהוּ

[52] אִישׁ יְהוּדִי, הָיָה בְּשׁוּשַׁן הַבִּירָה; וּשְׁמוֹ מָרְדֳּכַי, בֶּן יָאִיר בֶּן-שִׁמְעִי בֶּן-קִישׁ--אִישׁ יְמִינִי

[53] Hutzli, Jürg,1963, Role and significance of ancestors in the Books of Samuel, The Books of Samuel (2016) 423-437, 2016.

[54] וַיְהִי-אִישׁ מבן ימין (מִבִּנְיָמִין), וּשְׁמוֹ קִישׁ בֶּן-אֲבִיאֵל בֶּן-צְרוֹר בֶּן-בְּכוֹרַת בֶּן-אֲפִיחַ--בֶּן-אִישׁ יְמִינִי: גִּבּוֹר, חָיִל

[55] Tetley, M. Christine, The genealogy of Samuel the levite, Buried History 33,1 (1997) 20-30; 33,2: 39-51, 1997

[56] וּמִשְׁפְּחוֹת סֹפְרִים ישבו (יֹשְׁבֵי) יַעְבֵּץ, תִּרְעָתִים שִׁמְעָתִים שׂוּכָתִים; הֵמָּה הַקִּינִים הַבָּאִים, מֵחַמַּת אֲבִי בֵית-רֵכָב

[57] דברי הימים א פרק ב
וּבְנֵי כָלֵב אֲחִי יְרַחְמְאֵל מֵישָׁע בְּכֹרוֹ הוּא אֲבִי זִיף וּבְנֵי מָרֵשָׁה אֲבִי חֶבְרוֹן:
(מג) וּבְנֵי חֶבְרוֹן קֹרַח וְתַפֻּחַ וְרֶקֶם וָשָׁמַע:
(מד) וְשֶׁמַע הוֹלִיד אֶת רַחַם אֲבִי יָרְקֳעָם וְרֶקֶם הוֹלִיד אֶת שַׁמָּי:
(מה) וּבֶן שַׁמַּי מָעוֹן וּמָעוֹן אֲבִי בֵית צוּר:
(מו) וְעֵיפָה פִּילֶגֶשׁ כָּלֵב יָלְדָה אֶת חָרָן וְאֶת מוֹצָא וְאֶת גָּזֵז וְחָרָן הֹלִיד אֶת גָּזֵז: ס
(מז) וּבְנֵי יָהְדָּי רֶגֶם וְיוֹתָם וְגֵישָׁן וָפֶלֶט וְעֵיפָה וָשָׁעַף:
(מח) פִּלֶגֶשׁ כָּלֵב מַעֲכָה יָלַד שֶׁבֶר וְאֶת תִּרְחֲנָה

[58] Gosse, Bernard, Subversion de la législation du Pentateuque et symboliques respectives des lignées de David et de Saül dans les livre de Samuel et de Ruth., ZAW 110,1 (1998) 34-49, 1998

[59] Sakenfeld, Katharine Doob, Why Perez? Reflections on David's genealogy in biblical tradition, David and Zion (2004) 405-416, 2004

[60] Janzen, David,1968, A monument and a name : the primary purpose of Chronicles' genealogies., Journal for the Study of the Old Testament 43,1 (2018) 45-66, 2018 ; the absence of women in genealogies of chronciles is the subject of the essay: Löwisch, Ingeborg, Miriam Ben Amram, or : How to make sense of the absence of women in the genealogies of Levi (1 Chronicles 5:27-6:66)., he Bible and Feminism (2017) 355-370; 2017 ; Löwisch, Ingeborg, Gendered genealogies in response to fractured pasts : inquiring processes of othering in 1 Chronicles 1-9 from a German perspective., Samuel, Kings and Chronicles (2017) 95-111, 2017; Klein, Neriah, Between genealogy and historiography : Er, Achar and Saul in the Book of Chronicles., Vetus Testamentum 66,2 (2016) 217-244, 2016; obolowsky, Andrew, Reading Genesis through Chronicles : the creation of the sons of Jacob, Journal of Ancient Judaism 7,2 (2016) 138-168; 2016. ; Glatt-Gilad, David A, Genealogy lists as window to historiographic periodization in the Book of Chronicles., Maarav; a Journal for the Study of the Northwest Semitic Languages and Literatures 21,1-2 (2014) 71-79, 2014; Bodner, Keith,1967-, Reading the lists : several recent studies of the Chronicler's genealogies., Chronicling the Chronicler (2013) 29-41, 2013; Schweitzer, Steven James, The genealogies of 1 Chronicles 1-9 : purposes, forms, and the utopian identity of Israel., Chronicling the Chronicler (2013) 9-27, 2013; Finkelstein, Israel, The historical reality behind the genealogical lists in 1 Chronicles, Journal of Biblical Literature 131,1 (2012) 65-83, 2012; Jonker, Louis C, Reading the Pentateuch's genealogies after the exile : the chronicler's usage of Genesis 1-11 in negotiating an all-Israelite identity., Old Testament Essays 25,2 (2012) 316-333, 2012; Schweitzer, Steven James, Judging a book by its citations : sources and authority in Chronicles., What Was Authoritative for Chronicles? (2011) 37-65, 2011; Löwisch, Ingeborg, Genealogies, gender, and the politics of memory : 1 Chronicles 1-9 and the documentary film "Mein Leben Teil 2"., Performing Memory in Biblical Narrative and Beyond (2009) 228-256, 2009; Gardner, Anne Elizabeth, 1 Chronicles 8:28-32; 9:35-38 : complementary or contrasting genealogies?, Australian Biblical Review 55 (2007) 13-28, 2007; Assis, Eliyahu, From Adam to Esau and Israel : an anti-Edomite ideology in 1 Chronicles I, Vetus Testamentum 56,3 (2006) 287-302, 2006; Levin, Yigal, From lists to history : chronological aspects of the Chronicler's genealogies., ournal of Biblical Literature 123,4 (2004) 601-636, 2004 ; Snyman, Gerrie, A possible world of text production for the genealogy in 1 Chronicles 2.3-4.23, The Chronicler as Theologian (2003) 32-60, 2003; Gillet-Didier, Véronique, Passé généalogique et passé électif : usage comparé des généalogies dans les livres des Chroniques et le "Livre des antiquités bibliques" du Pseudo-Philon., Revue des Etudes Juives 161,3-4 (2002) 357-392, 2002; Braun, Roddy L., 1 Chronicles 1-9 and the reconstruction of the history of Israel : thoughts on the use of genealogical data in Chronicles in the reconstruction of the history of Israel, The Chronicler as Historian (1997) 92-105, 1997; Galil, Gershon, The Chronicler's genealogies of Ephraim, Biblische Notizen 56 (1991) 11-14, 1991; Na'aman, Nadav, Sources and redaction in the Chronicler's genealogies of Asher and Ephraim., Journal for the Study of the Old Testament 49 (1991) 99-111, 1991; Williamson, H. G. M.(Hugh Godfrey Maturin),, Sources and redaction in the Chronicler's genealogy of Judah., Journal of Biblical Literature 98,3 (1979) 351-359, 1979; Demsky, Aaron, The genealogy of Gibeon (1 Chron 9:35-44) : biblical and epigraphic considerations., BASOR 202 (1972) 16-23, 1972

[61] Demsky, Aaron, Abbaye's family origins : a study in rabbinic genealogy., "Follow the Wise" (2010) 235-240, 2010

[62] See David B Levy unedited Review in Jewish Press: Jewish Identity: *Who is a Jew?: Modern responses and opinions on the registration of children of mixed marriage*: Baruch Litvin; edited by Sidney B Hoenig Publisher: Ktav Publishing House; . Published originally in 1965, this reissue of a classic is now more relevant than ever. Jewish law legislates that a child is Jewish if the mother is Jewish, or one who had converted to Judaism according to specific halachic requirements. Jewish identity is thus not merely sociological and demographic (if Jews live in the land of Israel) nor ethnic (differences in customs, folkways, and liturgy and practice of Ashkenazi Jews vs. Sephardic Jews), but rather determined by a maternal hereditary religious blood covenant. The rabbis and the Talmud trace the determination of Jewish status through the mother from Deuteronomy 7:3-4. The paradigm of legitimate conversion to Judaism is Ruth who tells her mother-in-law Naomi, "Your people will be my people, where you go I will go, etc.," and it is from Ruth and Boaz that the messiah is traced back to Judah and Tamar. The convert in Jewish law engages in (1) ritual immersion for purification in a *mikveh*, (2) circumcision for males, (3) acceptance of the *mitzvot*, and (4) offering a sacrifice, when the Temple stood, and will be rebuilt. Tractate Demai requires a convert's substantive acceptance of the *mitzvoth* – *kabbalat ha-mitzvot*. The Chazon Ish understands the acceptance of the *mitzvot* in its theological rather than practical sense, a convert must accept the chosen uniqueness of the Jewish people as it relates to our role in the world. This acceptance must be acknowledged *al da'at bet din*. Rav Joseph B. Soloveitchik holds the halachic principle of *kibush* which would allow for a *beit din* and parents to convert a child without asking and rear the child in their own faith; thus the *ger katan* program. Rabbi Chaim Ozer Grodzinski is of the position that *kabbalat ha-mitzvot* need not be accompanied by full and complete observance but needs to be accompanied by observance of significant basics such as Shabbos observance, *kashrut*, and *taharat ha-mishpaha*. The details of this process are complex, with nuanced disputes among *Rishonim* and later *Achronim*, and clarified in codes such as the *Tur, Mishneh Torah*, and *Shulchan Aruch*.

In 1950 the state of Israel passed the Law of Return, by which "every Jew has the right to come to the country as an *oleh*" which was amended in 1970 to include anyone with a Jewish grandparent and their spouses, unless they have *voluntarily* renounced Judaism.

The question of Jews who are forcibly converted to Christianity and wish to return to Judaism is addressed by the 13th century Rabbi Meir of Rothenburg [1215-1295]. While Rambam holds Christianity to be a form of heretical idolatry while Islam is monotheistic, Maimonides [1135-1204] advised the Jews of Yemen living in a Islamic culture to commit martyrdom only in order to avoid the three cardinal sins: idolatry, sexual improprieties, or murder. A further question arises about 16th and 17th Century Jewish Conversos/Maranos who were forced to convert to Christianity by the Inquisition. More recently Rabbi Yitzhak Herzog retrieved and brought to Israel children hidden in Catholic monasteries during the Holocaust. Rabbi Ephraim Oshry deals with the halachic status of these children and many more in his work *She'eilos Uteshuvos Mima'amakim*.

[63] Hayes, Christine Elizabeth, Genealogy, illegitimacy, and personal status : the Yerushalmi in comparative perspective, The Talmud Yerushalmi and Graeco-Roman Culture III (2002) 73-89, 2002

64 Ronn, Michoel, Chabad-Lubavitch literature as a genealogical source, Avotaynu; the International Review of Jewish Genealogy 8,3 (1992) 40-44, 1992

65 Tsoulos, Jeannette, The many facets of Jewish genealogy., Australian Jewish Historical Society Journal 21,2 (2013) 195-207, 2013

66 Rosenstein, Neil,1944-, Difficulties in rabbinic genealogy : the case study of Reb Meilich and Reb Zusha., Avotaynu; the International Review of Jewish Genealogy 30,4 (2014) 50-53, 2014

67 Wagner, Hanoch Daniel, Tracing pre-1700 Jewish ancestors using metrical and rabbinical records., Avotaynu; the International Review of Jewish Genealogy 34,2 (2018) 15-19, 2018

68 Wunder, Meir, Genealogical research in the Haredi (ultra-Orthodox) community., Avotaynu; the International Review of Jewish Genealogy 31,3 (2015) 21-22, 2016

69 Wunder, Meir, The reliability of genealogical research in modern rabbinic literature, Avotaynu; the International Review of Jewish Genealogy 11,4 (1995) 31-36, 1995

70 Tauber, Laurence S, Genealogical information in rabbinical texts : an examination of "Ohr Olam", Avotaynu; the International Review of Jewish Genealogy 18,2 (2002) 43-45, 2002

71 Honey, Michael, A method for depicting interconnected rabbinical families simultaneously : the Jewish historical clock, Avotaynu; the International Review of Jewish Genealogy 17,3 (2001) 10-15, 2001

72 NYPL Yizkor books at https://digitalcollections.nypl.org/collections/yizkor-book-collection by town

73 Baker, Zachary M., Bibliography of Eastern European memorial books, updated and revised, Toledot; the Journal of Jewish Genealogy 3, 2-3 (1980) 7-22, 1980

74 Klarsfeld, Serge, Des fichiers au mémorial : la publication des archives de la Shoah en France - réalisation, projets, obstacles., International Seminar on Jewish Genealogy (5th, 1997, Paris) (1998) 119-130, 1998

75 Jablon, Rachel Leah, Going online to go 'home" : Yizkor books, cyber-shtetls, and communities of location., Connected Jews; Expressions of Community in Analogue and Digital Culture. (2018) 215-233 2018

76 Berkovitz, Jay R.,1951-, The Pinkas of the Metz Beit Din (1771-1789) : communal registers as a new genealogical resources., Avotaynu; the International Review of Jewish Genealogy 31,3 (2015) 46-48, 2016

77 Putík, Alexandr, Inscriptions on circumcision binders as a genealogical source., May God Let Him Grow (2009) 74-103, 2009Genealogical resources at Yad Vashem, Avotaynu; the International Review of Jewish Genealogy 19,3 (2003) 10-13, 2003

78 Baird, Carol Davidson, Frielendorf, Hessen : early 19th century census and marriage records., Stammbaum; the Journal of German-Jewish Genealogy 22 (2003) 40-45, 2003

79 Boonin, Harry D, The pinkas of the chevra kadisha of Slutsk / Harry D. Boonin [et al.], Avotaynu; the International Review of Jewish Genealogy 13,2 (1997) 28-33, 1997

80 Sela, Shulamit, The genealogy of Sefo ben Elifaz : the importance of a Genizah fragment for Josippon's history., Genizah Research after Ninety Years (1992) 138-143,1992

81 Avram, Alexander,

82 Lewis, Megan, Finding information in postwar resources at the United States Holocaust Memorial Museum., Avotaynu; the International Review of Jewish Genealogy 29,2 (2013) 33-36, 2013

[83] Altskan, Vadim, New acquisitions at the United States Holocaust Memorial Museum offer riches for genealogists, Avotaynu; the International Review of Jewish Genealogy 31,1 (2015) 6-9, 2016;

[84] Albrecht, Joachim, The children's transport from the Bialystok Ghetto to Theresienstadt and Auschwitz : analysis of names on deportation lists.; Avotaynu; the International Review of Jewish Genealogy 31,1 (2015) 35-37, 2016

[85] Fürth, Thomas, Refugee files in the Swedish National Archives., Avotaynu; the International Review of Jewish Genealogy 31,4 (2015) 48-50, 2015

[86] Amdur Sack, Sallyann, International Tracing Service : mother lode of Holocaust information, Avotaynu; the International Review of Jewish Genealogy 16,4 (2000) 11-15, 2000

[87] Lerer Cohen, Rose, Remembering Lithuanian Shoah victims : a research project, Avotaynu; the International Review of Jewish Genealogy 15,1 (1999) 21-25, 1999

[88] Ben Ya'akov, Michal,1950-, European Jewish refugees in Morocco during World War II., Avotaynu; the International Review of Jewish Genealogy 31,2 (2015) 41-45; 2016

[89] Figueiroa-Rego, João, From the House of David to the tribe of Levi : the concept of nobility among communities of Sephardic origin., In the Iberian Peninsula and Beyond I (2015) 211-227, 2015

[90] Nelson, Greg, Jewish records of East Europe on FamilySearch and in the family history library., Avotaynu; the International Review of Jewish Genealogy 33,1 (2017) 15-17; 2017

[91] Diamond, Stanley,1922-, Update on Jewish records indexing-Poland : phase three., Avotaynu; the International Review of Jewish Genealogy 32,3 (2016) 11-16, 2016

[92] Strausfeld, Dave, sing U.S. records to find an ancestor's town of origin, Avotaynu; the International Review of Jewish Genealogy 31,2 (2015) 21-23, 2015

[93] Barth, Naomi, "The Joint" archives : major online treasures for Jewish genealogists, Avotaynu; the International Review of Jewish Genealogy 28,2 (2012) 3-12, 2012

[94] Boonin, Harry D., Vital statistics in Czarist Russia, Avotaynu; the International Review of Jewish Genealogy 5,3 (1989) 6-12, 1989

[95] Bronstein, Shalom, Central Zionist Archives, Jerusalem, Israel., Avotaynu; the International Review of Jewish Genealogy 24,1 (2008) 13-16, 2008

[96] Gircyte, Vitalija, Jewish genealogical resources at the Kaunas State Archives, Avotaynu; the International Review of Jewish Genealogy 14,3 (1998) 29-31, 1998

[97] Friedlander, Alex E., Jewish vital statistic records in Lithuanian archives, Avotaynu; the International Review of Jewish Genealogy 6,4 (1990) 4-12, 1990

[98] Melamed, E. I.(Efim Iosifovich), Information for Jewish genealogists in the State Archive of Zhitomir Oblast, Avotaynu; the International Review of Jewish Genealogy 12,1 (1996) 14-18, 1996

[99] Rickman, Gregg, Swiss banks and the name lists, Avotaynu; the International Review of Jewish Genealogy 14,2 (1998) 4-8, 1998

[100] Rhode, Harold, What may be learned from 19th-century Czarist Jewish birth records and revision lists, Avotaynu; the International Review of Jewish Genealogy 10,3 (1994) 3-7, 1994

[101] Volovici, Hanna, Polish sources at the Central Archives for the History of the Jewish People, Avotaynu; the International Review of Jewish Genealogy 10,2 (1994) 21-22, 1994

[102] Boonin, Harry D., Russian business directories, Avotaynu; the International Review of Jewish Genealogy 6,4 (1990) 23-31; 7,3 (1991) 13-15, 1990

[103] Luft, Edward David, Newspaper and magazine websites valuable for genealogical research., Avotaynu; the International Review of Jewish Genealogy 24,3 (2008) 15-17, 2008

[104] Gaffin, Stephen L, Jewish newspapers as a genealogical resource, Avotaynu; the International Review of Jewish Genealogy 21,2 (2005) 27-31, 2005

[105] Matras, Hagit, The genealogical treasures in the Yeda-Am collection at the Jewish National and University Library in Jerusalem., Sharsheret Hadorot 22,3-4 (2008) xi-xiv, 2008

[106] Tahan, Ilana, Genealogical resources in the British Library Hebrew collection, Avotaynu; the International Review of Jewish Genealogy 18,1 (2002) 39-44, 2002

[107] Murphy, Ellen R., Jewish genealogical materials in the Library of Congress : an introductory checklist with annotations, Toledot; the Journal of Jewish Genealogy 4,3 (1982) 3-15, 1982

[108] Endelman, Judith E, Genealogical resources at the Jewish Theological Seminary, Toledot; the Journal of Jewish Genealogy 2,4 (1979) 5-8, 1979

[109] Belousova, Lilia Grigorevna, Jewish history as reflected in the documents of the State Archives of Odessa region, Avotaynu; the International Review of Jewish Genealogy 23,3 (2007) 41-51, 2007

[110] Frojimovics, Kinga, Documents of the Hungarian Jewish Archives, Avotaynu; the International Review of Jewish Genealogy 19,4 (2003) 13-18, 2003

[111] Solit, Roberta, U.S. National Archives II highlights, Avotaynu; the International Review of Jewish Genealogy 18,4 (2002) 17-21, 2002

[112] Lamdan, Neville, International Institute for Jewish Genealogy opens its doors, Avotaynu; the International Review of Jewish Genealogy 21,4 (2005) 3-5, 2005

[113] Baker, Zachary M., Chester G. Cohen, "Shtetl Finder; Jewish Communities in the 19th and Early 20th Centuries in the Pale of Settlement of Russia and Poland, and in Lithuania, Latvia, Galicia and Bukovina, with Names of Residents" (1980)., Toledot; the Journal of Jewish Genealogy 4,1-2 (1981) 13-17, 1981

[114] Sarna, Jonathan D, Arthur Kurzweil, "From Generation to Generation; How To Trace Your Jewish Genealogy and Personal History, Commentary 70,1 (1980) 69-71, 1980

[115] Baker, Zachary M., Resources on the genealogy of Eastern European Jews, Slavic & East European Information Resources 4,2-3 (2003) 169-184, 2003

[116] Vandor, Karoly (Karesz), Hungarian Jewish genealogy : historical background and resources, Avotaynu; the International Review of Jewish Genealogy 30,2 (2014) 36-37, 2014

[117] Pelts, Diana, Sources de la généalogie juive du XVIIIe au XIXe siècles dans les fonds des Archives Historiques Centrales d'Etat de l'Ukraine et de la ville de Lviv, International Seminar on Jewish Genealogy (5th, 1997, Paris) (1998) 237-242, 1998

[118] Lozytsky, Volodymyr, Sources for Jewish genealogy in the Ukrainian archives, Avotaynu; the International Review of Jewish Genealogy 10,2 (1994) 9-14, 1994

[119] Valdin, Anton, Report on Ukrainian and Latvian archives, Avotaynu; the International Review of Jewish Genealogy 9,3 (1993) 8-9, 1993

[120] Weiss, Robert, Research in Eastern European archives, nternational Seminar on Jewish Genealogy (5th, 1997, Paris) (1998) 217-234, 1998

[121] Friedlander, Alex E., New sources for Jewish genealogists in Polish archives., Avotaynu; the International Review of Jewish Genealogy 29,2 (2013) 11-20, 2013

[122] For genealogical research of records in rural areas of Minsk see Ḳaliḳ, Yehudit, Researching the rural Jewish population of Minsk Guberniya, 1795-1914., Avotaynu; the International Review of Jewish Genealogy 29,2 (2013) 47-49, 2013 ; Lamdan, Neville, Village Jews in imperial Russia's nineteenth-century Minsk Guberniya viewed through a genealogical lens., Avotaynu; the International Review of Jewish Genealogy 29,2 (2013) 50-56, 2013

[123] Fel'dman, D. Z.(Dmitriĭ Zakharovich), Archival sources for the genealogy of Jewish colonists in southern Russia in the 19th century, Avotaynu; the International Review of Jewish Genealogy 15,2 (1999) 14-17, 1999

[124] Weisberger, Pamela A., Galician genealogy : researching your roots with Gesher Galicia, Sharsheret Hadorot 26,2 (2012) 16-27, 2012

[125] Malka, Jeffrey S, Jews of Cervera : example of the rich genealogical resources in Spain., Avotaynu; the International Review of Jewish Genealogy 27,1 (2011) 47-49, 2011

[126] Graner, Georges, Les Juifs en Hongrie : histoire et recherches généalogiques, Revue du Cercle de Généalogie Juive 101 (2010) 4-11, 2010

[127] Vogel, Carole Garbuny, Constructing a town-wide genealogy : Jewish Mattersdorf, Hungary, 1698-1939., Avotaynu; the International Review of Jewish Genealogy 23,1 (2007) 30-39, 2007

[128] Gyemant, Ladislau, The perspectives of the Jewish genealogical research in the Askenazi world from Central and Eastern Europe., Noi perspective în istoriografia evreilor din România (2010) 28-41, 2010

[129] Spaans-van der Bijl, T., Handleiding voor joods-genealogisch onderzoek in Nederland., Misjpoge 10,4A (1997) 1-101, 1997

[130] Kallmann, Ernest, L'état actuel de la généalogie juive en Allemagne., Revue du Cercle de Généalogie Juive 101 (2010) 18-26, 2010

[131] Sielemann, Jürgen, Jewish genealogy in Germany, Avotaynu; the International Review of Jewish Genealogy 20,2 (2004) 26-30, 2004

[132] Taranto, Leon, History and genealogy of the Jews of Rhodes and their diaspora, Avotaynu; the International Review of Jewish Genealogy 25,1 (2009) 22-28

[133] Mayer-Crémieux, Michel, Recherches généalogiques chez les Juifs de Provence, nternational Seminar on Jewish Genealogy (5th, 1997, Paris) (1998) 435-444, 1998

[134] Katz, Pierre, La recherche généalogique juive en Alsace, Revue du Cercle de Généalogie Juive 36 (1993) 8-12, , 1993

[135] Matušíková, Lenka, Czech archival sources : history of the Jews in the Czech Lands., Avotaynu; the International Review of Jewish Genealogy 24,2 (2008) 19-22, 2008

[136] Wollmershäuser, Friedrich R., Genealogical sources for the Jews of southern Germany during the pre-emancipation period., Avotaynu; the International Review of Jewish Genealogy 24,3 (2008) 31-34, 2008

[137] Klauzińska, Kamila, A modern approach to the genealogy of Polish Jews : Zduńska Wola as a test case, cripta Judaica Cracoviensia 5 (2007) 39-51,2007

[138] Lyon-Caen, Bernard, Juifs d'Italie et recherches généalogiques., Revue du Cercle de Généalogie Juive 90 (2007) 27-30, 2007

[139] Voghera Luzzatto, Laura, La ricostruzione storica delle memorie familiari ebraiche e delle genealogie : proposte metodologiche, Le Comunità ebraiche a Modena e a Carpi (1999) 167-175, 1999

[140] Colletta, John Philip, Jewish genealogical research in Italy, Avotaynu; the International Review of Jewish Genealogy 8,1 (1992) 20-27, 1992

[141] Naar, Devin E., "Bushkando muestros nonos i nonas" : family history research on Sephardic Jewry through the Ladino language archives of the Jewish community of Salonika., Avotaynu; the International Review of Jewish Genealogy 23,1 (2007) 40-49, 2007

[142] Isaacs, Nigel, Finding Jewish ancestors in New Zealand, Shemot; the Jewish Genealogical Society of Great Britain 13,1 (2005) 22-24, 2005

[143] Taranto, Leon, Sources for Ottoman Sephardic genealogy : Turkey and Rhodes, Avotaynu; the International Review of Jewish Genealogy 21,3 (2005) 35-42, 2005

[144] Dunai, Alexander, Jewish genealogical resources in Transcarpathia, Avotaynu; the International Review of Jewish Genealogy 19,2 (2003) 6-10, 2003

[145] Hoffman, David B., 18th-century records from the former Commonwealth of the Grand Duchy of Lithuania and the Kingdom of Poland, Avotaynu; the International Review of Jewish Genealogy 19,3 (2003) 21-24, 2003

[146] Kaplan, Harvey L, Jewish genealogical research in Scotland, Avotaynu; the International Review of Jewish Genealogy 19,1 (2003) 25-28, 203

[147] Gyemant, Ladislau, Sources of Jewish genealogical research in Romania (18th-20th centuries), International Seminar on Jewish Genealogy (5th, 1997, Paris) (1998) 257-265, 1998; Sources of Jewish genealogical research in the Romanian archival system, Avotaynu; the International Review of Jewish Genealogy 14,3 (1998) 22-28, 1998

[148] Assouline, Hadassah, Documentation of Byelorussian Jewish history at the Central Archives for the History of the Jewish People, Avotaynu; the International Review of Jewish Genealogy 18,2 (2002) 17-18, 2002

[149] Boonin, Harry D, What we know about genealogical records in Belarus, Avotaynu; the International Review of Jewish Genealogy 9,4 (1993) 6-8, 1993

[150] Amdur Sack, Sallyann, Genealogy in Israel, May 1999, Avotaynu; the International Review of Jewish Genealogy 15,2 (1999) 9-13, 1999

[151] Ostrer, Harry, The genetic origins of Ashkenazi Jews., Avotaynu; the International Review of Jewish Genealogy 33,2 (2017) 3-5, 2017

[152] Greenspan, Bennett, Genetic genealogy : history and current issues, Avotaynu; the International Review of Jewish Genealogy 30,2 (2014) 15-16, 2014

[153] Paull, Jeffrey Mark,1951-, Connecting to the Wertheim-Giterman rabbinical lineage through Y-DNA., Avotaynu; the International Review of Jewish Genealogy 30,3 (2014) 46-53,2014; Paull, Jeffrey Mark,1951, Why autosomal DNA test results are significantly different for Ashkenazi Jews., Avotaynu; the International Review of Jewish Genealogy 30,1 (2014) 12-18, 2014;

[154] Sachs, Sidney, Understanding and using genetic (DNA) testing results., Avotaynu; the International Review of Jewish Genealogy 29,2 (2013) 25-30, 2013

155 Akaha, Janet Billstein,1953, Is a Rabbi hiding in your family tree? : Lessons from genetic genealogy for traditional genealogists.; Avotaynu; the International Review of Jewish Genealogy 31,3 (2015) 15-20, 2016

156 Reisman, Samuel, Hemophilia in Jewish traditions and genomes., B'Or Ha'Torah 23 (2014-2015) 71-83; Nodah beYehudah's niece has a bleeding problem which raised a problem how to consummate relations on wedding night as a nidah?

157 Imhoff, Sarah, Lost, hidden, discovered : theologies of DNA in North American Judaism and messianic Judaism., Mishpachah (2016) 111-133, 2016

158 Unkefer, Rachel, Y-DNA evidence for an Ashkenazi lineage's Iberian origin., Avotaynu; the International Review of Jewish Genealogy 32,1 (2016) 23-26; 2016

159 Unkefer, Rachel, Y-DNA and documentary research collaboration reveals ancestral origins., Avotaynu; the International Review of Jewish Genealogy 30,1 (2014) 6-11, 2014

160 Paull, Jeffrey Mark, Connecting to the great rabbinic families through Y-DNA : a case study of the Polonsky rabbinical lineage., Avotaynu; the International Review of Jewish Genealogy 29,3 (2013) 17-24, 2013

161 Paull, Jeffrey Mark, Using autosomal DNA analysis to connect rabbinical lineages : a case study of the Wertheimer and Wertheim dynasties., Avotaynu; the International Review of Jewish Genealogy 28,4 (2012) 59-69, 2012

162 Lavender, Abraham D., DNA origins and current consequences for Sephardi, Mizrahi, and Ashkenazi males and females : latest results from medical, genealogical-familial, and national-ethnic research., Journal for the Study of Sephardic and Mizrahi Jewry (2008-2009) 99-129, 2008

[163] Farhi, Alain, Preliminary results of Sephardic DNA testing., Avotaynu; the International Review of Jewish Genealogy 23,2 (2007) 9-12, 2007

[164] Huebscher, Herbert, DNA and Jewish genealogy join forces., Avotaynu; the International Review of Jewish Genealogy 23,2 (2007) 4-8, 2007

[165] Wahrman, Miryam Z., DNA markers that illuminate Israelite/Jewish migration., B'Or Ha'Torah 17 (2007) 97-112, 2007

[166] Sutton, Wesley K., "Jewish genes" : ancient priests and modern Jewish identity., Who Is a Jew? (2014) 105-115, 2014

[167] Stein, Wilfred D., The Rolnick chromosome : its origin and evolution., Avotaynu; the International Review of Jewish Genealogy 28,2 (2012) 21-28, 2012

[168] Gelles, Edward, Chief rabbis in the genes, Manna; the Forum for Progressive Judaism 69 (2000) 34-36, 2000

[169] Both, Hélène, Mise en forme et édition du corpus des tombes et présentation de quelques sources documentaires utilisées lors de recherches généalogiques., 2012

[170] Wagner, Daniel, Tombstone identification through database merging., Avotaynu; the International Review of Jewish Genealogy 24,1 (2008) 8-10, 2008

[171] Herschmann Rechtschafner, Esther, From Rachel's Tomb to BillionGraves : inscriptions on Jewish tombstones, Avotaynu; the International Review of Jewish Genealogy 32,3 (2016) 42-46, 2016

[172] Wrzosiński, Witold, Hebrew epitaphs as a unique source for the study of Jewish history and genealogy, Avotaynu; the International Review of Jewish Genealogy 31,3 (2015) 3-6, 2016

[173] Elyasaf, Immanuel, Decoding civil registry and mapping the Brody community cemetery,, Sharsheret Hadorot 26,2 (2012) 37-50, 2012

[174] Greenblatt, Ada, Jewish burial societies in the New York metropolitan area : some pointers about landsmanshaftn plots., Avotaynu; the International Review of Jewish Genealogy 17,3 (2001) 40-42,2001

[175] Bernard, Jean-Pierre, Les cimetières juifs en France, International Seminar on Jewish Genealogy (5th, 1997, Paris) (1998) 367-372, 1998

[176] Rozen, Minna, Turkish-Jewish cemeteries of the Ottoman period, Avotaynu; the International Review of Jewish Genealogy 8,3 (1992) 45-47, 1992

[177] Sárraga, Marian, The Sephardim of the Altona cemetery, Avotaynu; the International Review of Jewish Genealogy 8,1 (1992) 14-17, 1992

[178] Lewin, Harold, Older London burial records and sites, Avotaynu; the International Review of Jewish Genealogy 7,3 (1991) 24-27, 1991

[179] Link, Ury, Burial books of Ashkenazic Jews of Amsterdam, 1872-1935, Avotaynu; the International Review of Jewish Genealogy 20,3 (2004) 32-36, 2004

[180] Japhet, Gilad, Eight unique technologies for genealogical discoveries., Avotaynu; the International Review of Jewish Genealogy 32,1 (2016) 3-8, 2016

[181] Luft, Edward David, Online research in the Austro-Hungarian Empire and nearby, Avotaynu; the International Review of Jewish Genealogy 32,3 (2016) 29-35, 2016

[182] Kahn, Vivian, JewishGen's Hungary database, Avotaynu; the International Review of Jewish Genealogy 32,3 (2016) 17-20, 2016

[183] Lande, Peter W., How 85,000 became 7 million : databases at the United States Holocaust Memorial Museum., Avotaynu; the International Review of Jewish Genealogy 27,4 (2011) 19-22, 2011

[184] Bronstein, Shalom, Using the pages of testimony computerized database, Avotaynu; the International Review of Jewish Genealogy 17,1 (2001) 15-17, 2001

[185] Lamdan, Neville, The Ellis Island Database from the micro to the macro level : the cases of Lechovich and Baranovich., Avotaynu; the International Review of Jewish Genealogy 17,4 (2001) 8-10, 2001

[186] Mokotoff, Gary, Strategies for using the Ellis Island database, Avotaynu; the International Review of Jewish Genealogy 17,2 (2001) 3-6, 2001

[187] Lande, Peter W., Databases of German/Austrian Holocaust victims currently available on the web, Stammbaum; the Journal of German-Jewish Genealogy 16 (2000) 5-7, 2000

[188] Altskan, Vadim, The NAME SEARCH database at the U.S. Holocaust Memorial Museum, Avotaynu; the International Review of Jewish Genealogy 15,4 (1999) 15-16, 1999

[189] Shull, Benjamin, Uprooted - the story of a tree, a family, the internet and the Jews, Avotaynu; the International Review of Jewish Genealogy 30,2 (2014) 42-45, 2014

[190] Harris, Laurence, New Internet resources for research in the United Kingdom, Avotaynu; the International Review of Jewish Genealogy 20,1 (2004) 26-28, 2004

[191] See CJH catalog http://search.cjh.org by town or region for material you can see here or digitized online.

[192] Brown, Adam R., The coming "big bang" in genealogical research : automated matching of databases and family trees., Avotaynu; the International Review of Jewish Genealogy 29,2 (2013) 3-6, 2013

[193] Blumberg, Henry, Jewish genealogical search engines, databases and social interaction networks., Avotaynu; the International Review of Jewish Genealogy 24,3 (2008) 35-39, 2008

[194] Arons, Ron, Using CD-ROM databases and the Internet to research England from afar, Avotaynu; the International Review of Jewish Genealogy 16,1 (2000) 25-28, 2000

[195] Humphrey, Marlis Glaser, Jewish genealogy 2015 : trends, breakthrough and tragectory reflections on the evolution of Jewish genealogy. Avotaynu; the International Review of Jewish Genealogy 31,1 (2015) 11-17, 2015

[196] Pascal, Paul Micheikin, How and why I created a shtetl map, Avotaynu; the International Review of Jewish Genealogy 13,2 (1997) 34-39, 1997

[197] For more information by town, we recommend https://www.jewishgen.org/Communities/Search.asp which provides a bibliography relevant to towns in the database.

[198] The 1000 Towns database is free with a registration and includes photos by town names.
See: http://yivo1000towns.cjh.org/default.asp ; There may be more photographs in the YIVO Photo Archive here at Center for Jewish History. Those not in the catalog can be seen only by appointment. Check the website https://yivo.org/photographs and write to photofilm@yivo.cjh.org for more information.

[199] Baker, Zachary M, Eastern European "Jewish geography" : some problems and suggestions, Toledot; the Journal of Jewish Genealogy 2,3 (1978-1979) 9-14, 1978

[200] Hershkovitz, Arnon, In Ben-Yehuda Straße with Apfelstrudel : the beginnings of organized Jewish genealogy in Germany and in Israel., Sharsheret Hadorot 25,2 (2011) 6-15, 2011.; Early Jewish genealogy organizations in Berlin and Jerusalem, Avotaynu; the International Review of Jewish Genealogy 27,2 (2011) 23-26, 2011

[201] Klein, Birgit E, Herkunft, Ehe und Vererbung : die Bedeutung von Familie und Genealogie in der jüdischen Kultur., Jüdische Genealogie im Archiv, in der Forschung und digital (2011) 19-36, 2011

[202] Dwoskin, Beth, Genealogy in the Jewish library : an update., Judaica Librarianship 15 (2009) 13-24, 2009

[203] Lamdan, Neville, Jewish genealogy : moving towards recognition as a sub-branch of Jewish studies., Avotaynu; the International Review of Jewish Genealogy 25,2 (2009) 3-8, 2009

[204] Wagner, Hanoch Daniel, Genealogy as an academic discipline, Avotaynu; the International Review of Jewish Genealogy 22,1 (2006) 3-11, 2006

[205] Creveld, Isaac Bernard van, Joodse genealogie in de praktijk, Gids voor onderzoek naar de geschiedenis van de joden in Nederland (2000) 180-184, 2000

[206] Baker, Zachary M., What we owe the genealogists : genealogy and the Judaica reference librarian, Judaica Librarianship 6,1-2 (1991-1992) 43-46, 48, 1991

[207] Schafler, Sara, Jewish genealogy, Encyclopaedia Judaica Year Book 1983-5 (1985) 68-76, 1985

[208] See Heschel. J. Abraham, *"Renunication and Fulfilment"*, Maimonides, Image Books, 209.

[209] Rambam does advocate departure from the Aristotelian mean (*yesh deot sheasor liAdam linhog bahen beyonit*) with regards to humility and not getting angry. We are bidden to go to the extreme in humility because in *BaMidbar* we read, *"l'eHaEish Moshe ana miod mikol haAdam asher al penai HaAdamah"*. Rambam also recognizes that the Hasid will depart from the mean when he writes, *"Mi shehu medakdek al azmo biyoter veyitrachak mideah beyonit meat letzad zeh olit-ad-zeh nekrah Hasid (Mishneh Torah. 47b, lines 17-18).*

210 Aristotle teaches that there are four causes: (1) the *causa materialis*; (2) *the causa formalis*; (3) the *causa finalis*; and (4) *causa efficiens*. HaShem can be thought to be the *causa efficiens* in the creation of everything that exsists. The teleological or *causa finalis* of the world is the messianic age when according to the Book of Judges of the *Yad hazakah* the following contingencies will obtain: (1) no war, (2) no famine, (3) no jealousy, (4) no strife, (5) blessings will be abundant (scholars will be able to study full time without financial burdens), (6) the Levitical priesthood will be reinstated in a rebuilt Temple complex, (7) Jews will not be persecuted (i.e. the land (Jews), will dwell with the wolf (other nations that persecute us), (8) the one preoccupation of the world will be to know HaShem, for according to Isaiah, "For the earth shall be full of the knowledge of HaShem, as the waters cover the sea (11:9)."

211 See *Moreh Nekuvim* III, 8-24.

212 Strauss, Leo, Persecution and the Art of Writing, Chicago; Univ. of Chicago Press, 1980, 19

213 Weinberger, Moshe c., *Censorship and Freedom of Expression in Jewish History*, Yeshivah University Press, 32.

214 Zeitlin, Solomon, "Mishne Torah-Jewish Constitution" Maimonides, Bloch Publishing CO., 80.

215 See Sefer HaMadah, Hilkot Teshuvah, 84b III, 7

216 See Sefer HaMadah, Hilkot Teshuvah, 90a, VIII, 2

217 Touati, "Les ConjlitsAutour de Maimonide", in Juifs et Judaismer de Languedoc. Cathiers de Fanjeux, 176; also see Zinberg, Israel, Die geshikhte fun der literature bay yidn, Vilna, volume 3.

218 Touati, "*les Deux Conflicts Autour de Maimonide et des Etudes Philosophiques*". In Juifs et Judaisme de Languedoc. Edouard Privat editeur, Cahiers de Fanjeaux, 174.

[219] See *Moreh Nevukim* III, 51; Rambam writes, "Among them there (present in the ruler's council) is he who beacause os the greatness of his apprehension and his renouncing everything that is other than HaShem, may He be exalted, has attained such a degree that it is said of him, 'And he was there with HaShem (EX.34:28), putting questions and receiving answers, speaking and being spoken to, in that holy place". This is Platonic in that, "Questioning is the piety if thought".

[220] Touati, "*Les Deux Conflicts autour de Maimonide et des Etudes Philosophiques*", Juifs et Judaisme de Languedoc, 179

[221] For Example, "What is the nature of light on the first day of creation, if the sun, moon, and the starts (light giving bodies), are not hung up on the firmament until the fourth day? Rashi remarks that "the light created on the first day in the light stored up fpr the righteous in *Olam HaBah*"? What is the nature of such stored up hidden light? See Rambam's commentary on Bereshit.

[222] See *Moreh Nevukim* II, 32-48

[223] See *Moreh Nevukim* II 3-12

[224] It is a matter of debate whether the Rabbinic tradition (see TB Hagigah13a) may link ma'aseh merkavah and ma'aseh bereishit together based on the following passage from seder Olam Rabbah (ed Milkovsky p. 445) where we read, "He reveals the deep and secret things (Dan 2:22) deep that is the depths of the merkavah and secret that is the secrets of ma'aseh bereishit.

[225] See Sefer HaMadah, Hilkot Teshuvah, 90a, VIII, 2

[226] See Sefer HaMadah, Hilkot Teshuvah, 90a, VIII, 2

[227] Merkavah is also found in Mishneh: Megillah 4:10; Toseftta: Meg 3(4):28, 34, BT: Ber. 21b, Shabb 80b, Sukk 28a (BB134a), Meg 24b, 31a.

[228] Gitten 60b reads, "Devarim shebal'peh e atah rashaey lekatvatan mekan atah lemad shehatalmud lo netan lektov eleh mepeneai shehatorah meshtakchat.

Endnotes 223

[229] Strauss, Leo, Persecution and the Art of Writing 45, and "Jerusalem and Athens, in Studies in Platonic Political Philosophy, Univ. Chicago Press, 1983, 154, see Gitten 60b and Berachot 54a

[230] See Halperin, David, The Merkavah in Rabbinic Literature, the American Orientatl Society, New Haven, 1980

[231] Dubnov, Simon, "Die Maimonisten und Ihre Gegner," Weltsges Des Judischen Volkes, 109; Touati puts it this way, *"Vers 1230, un eminent rabbin de Montpellier, Solomon ben Abraham et ses deux eleves Rabbi Yonah Geronid and Rabbi David ben Saul, se decident a passer a l'action et a barrer la route a la speculation philosophique en interdisant sous peine d'excommunication, l'etude de Sefer Ha-Mada, l'introduction philosophique au code de Maimonides, celle du Guide et des sciences generals (175).*

[232] Graetz, Heinrich, "Maimuni's Schriften und die Inquisition", Geschichte Des Juden vol 7, 66.

[233] Dubnov, Simon, "Die Maimonisten und Ihre Gegner," Weltgeschichte des Judischen Volkes, 113

[234] See Cohen, Jeremy, "The Actual Controversy," in The Friars and the Jews, Cornell University Press, 153; Cohen notes that the biases against the Talmud that fueled its being burned by the Church included: (1) parts of it were considered blasphemous against Christians, (2) the argument that without the Talmud the Jews would be more likely to convert to Christianity, and (3) it could injure Chrisitan faith. Cohen's thesis is that it is not until after the 1232 burning of Maimonides writings that the friars systematically undertook the study of Hebrew and the Aramaic of Talmudic texts to conduct disputations in order to beat the Jews at their own hermeneutic game of interpretations of rabbinic texts, now used by the friars to attempt to prove the truth of Christianity. 32. Dubnov, Simon, "Die Maimonisten und Ihre Gegner " in Weltgeschichte Des Judischen Volkes, 67. These games were not child's play but rather much Jewish blood was spilt over matters of interpretations, no mere hermeneutical gymnastics.

[235] Agus, Jacob, "The Encyclopaedia Judaica," Conservative Judaism 26, (1971), 46

[236] Choice (October 1972), 449.

[237] Library Journal, (August 1972), 2562.

[238] Catholic Library World, (October 1972), 163.

[239] Zeitlin, Solomon, JQR 63 (1972-1973), 1-28.

[240] American Israelite (11 July, 1901): 1.

[241] A Historic Jewish Banquet in the City of New York (tendered to the Editors and Publishers of the Jewish Encyclopaedia) (New York, 1901), 15; Kohler wrote, "The Jewish Encyclopaedia goes forth as a peacemaker and friendly intermediary between all shades of opinion among the Jews, between Orthodoxy and Reform, Radicalism and Conservatism, Nationalist and Cosmopolitan, as well as between Jew and nonJew." Kohler in an appeal to Jewish unity later wrote, "Let all differences of opinion be waived. Let all wrangling and bickering between Reform and Orthodoxy, between Conservative and Radical, between East and West, in pulpit and press, cease once and for all! Mark well! There is no plural in the verb Sh'ma- hear; no plural to the noun Israel. I am the very last to deprecate Orthodoxy. It is the soil out of which we have drawn sap and marrow" (Kaufmann, Kohler, A Living Faith: Selected Sermons and Addresses from the Literary6 Remains of Dr. Kaufmann Kohler, ed. Samuel S. Cohon (Cincinnati, 1948), 8-18.).

[242] Presbyterian Banner (Pittsburgh), (18 June 1901) and St. Paul Dispatch (20 July 1901), in Opinions of the Worlds Press, 13-14, 21-22.

[243] Hirsch, Emil G., Athenaeum, no.3907 (13 Sept 1902), 346.

[244] Eisenstein, Judah David, Critical Review of the Legal Articles of the Jewish Encyclopaedia Volume 1 (including discussion with Lewis N. Dembitz and S. Mendelsohn) (New York, 1901), 1-13; idem Otsar zikhronotai: (New York, 1929), 320-29.

[245] Both Steinschneider and Ahad Ha-Am came to acknowledge the importance of the JE. Ahad Ha-Am corresponded with Singer concerning the possibility of issuing a Hebrew translation and Steinschneider too changed his mind about its value. See: George Alexander Kohut, "Steinschneideriana," Studies in Jewish Bibliography and Related Subjects in the memory of Abraham S. Freidus 1867-1923 (New York, 1929), 84-85, 107-108; Ahad Ha-Am, *Igrot Ahad Ha-Am* (Jerusalem, 1924), 3: 19-20, 23-35.

[246] In Rabbinic theology the Talmud is a co-terminous revelation with the Torah on Har Sinai because Pirke Avot reads, "*Moshe Kebel Torah MiSinai*" and since the text does not say "*ha-Torah*" but "*Torah*" in general it refers to the *oral law* as well as the *written law*.

[247] Schwartz, Shuly Rubin, The Emergence of Jewish Scholarship in America: The Publication of the Jewish Encyclopaedia, Cincinnati: Hebrew Union College Press, 1991, 130.

[248] Schwartz, Shuly Rubin, The Emergence of Jewish Scholarship in America: The Publication of the Jewish Encyclopaedia, Cincinnati: Hebrew Union College Press, 1991, 165.

[249] Ibid., 108.

[250] Jewish Encyclopaedia, Preface, p.xiii.

251 Eisenstein's critique of the sympathies of the JE for Higher Biblical criticism must be tempered with the fact that Joseph Jacobs as later head of Biblical entries sought to attempt to present what was felt to be the proper Jewish attitude toward higher biblical criticism. Schwartz writes, "There is a definite though somewhat uneven movement away from the conscious embrace of both non-Jewish collaboration and the results of higher biblical criticism toward a more conservative Jewish stance that still remains grounded in scientific critical methods" (145). The tension between reform and conservative elements of the JE, but their shared commonality is seen in the following remark by Schwartz, "... though Lauterbach and his fellow traditionalist collaborators differed from their more liberal counterparts in their commitment to Jewish peoplehood, their personal observance of the *mitsvot*, and their uneasiness with Reform, all shared with their Reform collaborators a modern, historical conception of Judaism and were united by their commitment to strengthening Jewish life and *Wissenschaft des Judentums* in America" (163).

252 Hirsch praises Zunz as the founder of the modern scientific study of Judaism. Zacharias Frankel's *Darkhe ha-mishnah* is called one of the most valuable attempts at systematic exposition of the history of rabbinic literature and theology. The history of *halakhah, Dor dor ve-Dorshav* by Isaac Hirsch Weiss is termed "stupendous."

253 Schwartz, Shuly Rubin, The Emergence of Jewish Scholarship in America: The publication of the Jewish Encyclopaedia, Cincinnati: HUC Press, 1991, 119.

254 Trachtenberg, Joshua, "American Jewish Scholarship," in the Jewish People Past and Present, vol. 4, N.Y., 1955, 415, 417.

255 Baron, Solo W., Steeled By Adversity, Essays and Addresses on American Jewish Life, Philadelphia, 1971, 397-401

256 Brisman, Shimeon, A History and Guide to Judaic Encyclopaedias and Lexicons, Cincinnati, 1987, 32

[257] Schwartz, Shuly Rubin, The Emergence of Jewish Scholarship in America: The Publication of the Jewish Encyclopaedia, Cincinnati: Hebrew Union College Press, 1991, 166.

[258] Previous motions for publishing Jewish Encyclopaedias can be noted. Isaak Jost in 1840 called on scholars to join in compiling an *"Encyclopadie der Judische-Theologischen und literarischen Kentnisse*. David Cassel and Moritz Steinschneider published a prospectus for a similar work in 1844. In 1837 Ludwig Philipson had proposed a *Real Encyclopadie oder eine Konversations-Lexikon des Judenthums*. In Eastern Europe during the same time Singer was promoting the idea of the JE, Ahad Ha-Am was simultaneously issuing a proposal in 1894 for a Jewish Encyclopaedia in Hebrew to be called, *Otsar Hayahadut*. The tradition of compiling Encyclopaedias can be said to stem from the 18th century where Diderot published his *Encyclopedie* between 1751-1757 to which D'Alembert, Voltaire, Rousseau, and Montesquieu contributed. The perspective of Diderot's Encyclopaedia was the Enlightenment which was very critical of superstitious religion and belief. *The Encyclopaedia Britannica* was published in 1771. La Grande Encyclopedie between 1882-1902 saw publication. *The Brockhaus Konversationslexikon, Chambers Encyclopaedia, The New American Cyclopedia* (1858), *Hastings Dictionary of The Bible* (1899-1902), and *Encyclopaedia Biblica* (1829-1903) followed.

[259] The sixteen volume Russian Jewish Encyclopaedia, *Evreiskaia Entsiklopedaia* came out in St. Petersburg with contributors such as Zalman Shazar. This work tended to be particularly strong in East European Subjects. According to Solomon Zeitlin, this work is the best Jewish Encyclopaedia of all the Jewish Encyclopaedias (Zeitlin, Solomon, "Encyclopaedia Judaica: The Status of Jewish Scholarship," JQR 63 (1972-73), 28.

[260] There have also been a series of one-volume Jewish Encyclopedias that have appeared since 1958 including: (1) *The Encyclopaedia of the Jewish Religion* (Jerusalem-Tel Aviv, Massada-P.E.C. Press, 1966) edited by R.J.Z. Werblowsky and Geoffrey Wigoder; (2) *A Book of Jewish Concepts* by Philip Birnbaum (N.Y., Hebrew Publishing, 1964); (3) *The Book of Jewish Knowledge* by Nathan Ausubel (N.Y., Crown, 1964); (4) *The New Standard Jewish Encyclopaedia* (Garden City, Doubleday, 1970) edited by Cecil Roth and Geoffrey Wigoder; (5) *The Junior Jewish Encyclopaedia* (7th rev. ed., N.Y., Shengold, 1970); (6) Two volumes on Holocaust have appeared in Yiddish *Algemayne Entsiklopedye* as volumes 6 and 7 of Yidn (N.Y., Dubnov Fund and Encyclopaedia Committee, 1963 and 1966); (7) *Haentsiklopedyah Haivrit* (Jerusalem, Massada and Encyclopaedia Publishing Co., 1949-).

[261] Silver, Daniel, J., "Book Review," CCAR Journal, Vol. 19, no.4 (1972): 89.

[262] American Zionist 62, (1971-72), 32.

[263] We read in Ariel, "experts were so wrapped up in teaching and in their own writings that they could not undertake an entry within our timetable" (109).

[264] Wigoder, Geoffrey, "Making The Encyclopaedia Judaica," Jewish Digest, (1972), 46.

[265] American Zionist 62 (1971-72): 32.

[266] "The New Encyclopaedia Judaica," Ariel, no.30-34, 1972-73, 108.

[267] Introduction to Encyclopaedia Judaica, 4.

268 Reinhold Scholem on January 5, 1973 wrote to Gershom notifying him, "*Time* (the issue of November 20, 1972) ran a story on Keter Publishing House's Jewish Encyclopedia and called your eighty-three-page article "the most lucid treatment of this complex subject. My copy of your article on the Kabbalah from the *Judisches Lexikon* has only fifty-one pages" (see: Gershom Scholem: A Life in Letters 1914-1982, edited by Anthony David Skinner, Cambridge, Mass.: Harvard University Press, 2002, p. 448). Scholem responded from Jerusalem on January 30, 1973, "Its no wonder my present article on the Kabbalah is at least twice as long as the earlier essay in the first German language *Encylopedia Judaica*, volume 9, 1932 (and not the *Judisches Lexicon*, to which I didn't contribute). In reality, it's even much longer. For it's a summary of forty years of additional research. I wrote the first text in 1931; the other in 1970. Moreover, these articles on Jewish mysticism will appear in a special book, which should be at least four or five hundred pages" (450).

269 Raphael, Chaim, "Encyclopaedia Judaica," Commentary, (August 1972), 36.

270 Catholic Library World, (October 1972), 162.

271 Raphael, Chaim, "Encyclopaedia Judaica," Commentary (August 1972), 38.

272 For example *Bereshit* can be compared to Babylonian *Enuma Elish*; the Joseph/Potiphar episode can be compared to *Egyptian Story of Two Brothers*; Torah law can be compared with case law in the Code of Hammurabi (1792 B.C.E.) i.e. the goring ox (Ex. 21:28-36), false accusation (Deut.5:20; 19:16-21;
Ex.23:1-3), kidnapping (Ex. 21:16; Deut.24:7), sharecropping (Lev. 19:23-25, adultery (Deut. 22:22), rape (Deut. 22:23-27), incest (Lev. 18:6-18; 20:10-21), strike parent (Ex.21:15), two men fight and cause miscarriage in women (Ex.21:22-25)

[273] For example *Cherubim* and winged lions are also found in Assyrian culture. Further the term *Tzelem* in *Bereshit* has proven to be a physical object. Archeologists have found in the city of Assur in the 1930s a monument/stele/ statue called *Tzelem* which served as a substitute representative for individuals i.e. this is the Tzelem of so and so.

[274] For example Kutscher authored a work on loan words in the *Tanakh* i.e. the Egyptian loan word *"sack"* makes its way into the Joseph *novella*, the Akkadian loan word *"rakiah"* means copper beaten dome and finds its way into the creation account of the *firmament*, and *"Pardes"* is a loan word from Persian. Shmuel Krauss authored a dictionary of Greek and Latin loan words into the Talmud.

[275] The documentary hypothesis can point to the fact that in some cases Sinai is called Horeb, Jethro is called Hobab, etc to suggest different editorial schools. Further the fact that the manna and quail and Moshe striking the rock is mentioned two times is used to suggest two different editorial schools. Likewise three sets of the ten commandments in Exodus 20 (*Zakor et Yom HaShabat*) and Deuteronomy 5 *(Shamoor Et Yom HaShabat)* suggest different editorial schools. Modern critics of the Bible argue that the ten commandments in Exodus 34 are the product of an organized agricultural society for it says, "Six days you shall work, but on the seventh day you shall cease from labor, you shall cease from labor even at plowing time and harvest time..." Traditionalists can claim that such claims have already been treated in the *gemara* for example which mentions that Jethro had seven names. The conclusions traditionalists draw from this evidence is radically different than the Documentary hypothesis.

276 Introduction to *Encyclopaedia Judaica*, p.9; It should be noted in some cases the EJ is closer to the traditional view than the JE. For example the critical section of the JE suggest that the biography of Abraham in Genesis is probably to be regarded as legendary, while the EJ remarks that the evidence of sociological and onomastic nature that has been accumulated since the discoveries of Nuzi and Mari tends to show that Abrahamic traditions are more likely to be authentic reflections of a true historical situation rather than retrojections from a later period.

277 Raphael, Chaim, Commentary (August 1972), 38.

278 The following literal translation from the German 1920s EJ is by David B. Levy.

279 Leo Strauss writes of Germany's liberal democracy that offered German Jews assimilation but through this process had locked them off from their Hebrew traditions. In some sense Hermann Cohen's Die *Religion Der Vernunft* in the spirit of Kantian *Aufklarung* was an attempt to lead Wissenschaft des Judentums Jews back to the roots of the prophetic tradition. (see: *Die Religionskritik Spinozas als
Grundlage seiner Bibelwissenschaft Untersuchungen zu Spinozas Theologisch-Politischen Traktat*, "Vorwort," Akademie-Verlag, Berlin 1930.)

280 Ariel, no.30-34, 1972-73, 107.

281 Booklist, (November 1, 1972), 212.

282 Silver, Daniel J., CCAR Journal, vol. 19, no.4 (1972): 89; Silver further remarks, "The EJ was not only edited in Israel, but is to a large degree about Israel. Sections on the great archeological sites, coins and currency, immigration and absorption, modern Hebrew writing and art, are remarkably full and complete" (90).

283 Berlin, Charles, Library Journal 97 (1972): 2562.

284 Ibid.

285 Ibid.

[286] Silver however contends that "The EJ is not without faults. Many of the assigned articles were rewritten by unseen hands, in many cases by men for whom English obviously was not a native tongue. Some effectively written pieces were turned into prosaic Encyclopaediaese. Each article is signed, but the sense of a single rather prosaic style permeates" (90).

[287] Silver, Daniel J., "Book Review," CCAR Journal vol. 19, No.4 (1972): 88.

[288] Ibid., 92.

[289] However *Time* is critical that the treatment of the Arab refugee question is not very successful in its attempt to present the Arab side. Further it notes that there is no treatment of Jewish humor beyond Hebrew parody- because say the editors, they could not find a suitable author" (Time (Nov.20, 1972): 92.

[290] Time (Nov. 20, 1972): 91.

[291] Ibid.

[292] See endnote #35

[293] Zeitlin, Solomon, "The Encyclopaedia Judaica: The Status of Jewish Scholarship," JQR, 1972-73, 27.

[294] Agus, Jacob, "The Encyclopaedia Judaica: A Review Essay," Conservative Judaism 26, 1971-72, 55.

[295] Ibid.

[296] Weis-Rosmarin, Trude, Jewish Spectator, October 1972, 6.

[297] Zeitlin also questions editorial choice when he objects, "the inclusion of gangsters and the exclusion of Jewish scholars is an affront to learning and Jewish scholarship. It has a touch of vulgarism" (JQR 64 (July 1973): 81.

[298] See Israel Abrahams, Hebrew Ethical Wills, (Phil, 1926) 1:63-64, n.23

[299] For commentary see see Raymond P. Scheindlin, "The Song of the Silent Dove: the Pilgrimage of Judah Halevi," in Bringing the Hidden to Light: the Process of Interpretation, edited by Kravitz, Sharon, and Geller, p. 230

[300] Assaf, Be'oholei Yakov,; see Emanuel Fragments of Tables: Lost books of the Tosaphists, Jerusalem, 2006, p.198

[301] Israel Abrahams, Hebrew Ethical Wills, (Phil 1926) 1:64

[302] Assaf, Meqorot, vol.4, p.17; ad loc also p. 61 documents of 2 latin texts from Spain (Aragon dated 1328 and Seville 1332) testifying about private individual bequeathing and financing thei purchase of books for students in a Beit Midrash who were poor.

[303] See Musar ha-Sekhel, par 128, a rhymed ethical treatise consisting of counsel for guidance in life where the Hai Gaon admonishes, "If children thou shoulds't bear at length/ Reprove them but with tender thought/ Purchase them books with all thy strength (bikol modekhah)/ and by skilled teachers have them taught..

[304] See Hacker, Joseph, "Jewish Book Ownders and Their Libraries in the Iberian Peninsula, Fourteenth-Fifteenth Centureis, in The Late Medieval Hebrew Book in the Western Mediterranean: Hebrew manuscripts and incunabula in context, Leiden: Brill, 2015.

[305] He-Hafetz Hayyim ha-Yov u-Fealav, vol. 1, ch.4; also see Kukis, "Be-Maalot ha-Sefer ha-Ivri"

[306] Mahanayim, vol 106 (1966) by Menachem Ha-Kohen: Avraham Arazi, 'Ha-Sefer ve-ha-Sofer be- einei Hazal", 14-21; Avraham Broides, "Devarim al ha-Sefer", 58-61; Yosef Nedavah, "Gezerot al Sefarim Ivriyim", 84-87; Mordechai Kurkis, "Be-Maalot ha-Sefer ha-Ivri" 84-87; G. Kresel, "Otzarot Sifrei Yisrael ba-Olam", 62-71

[307] Yoreah Deah 277; Sefer Hasidim 754

[308] Massekhet Soferim 83

[309] Likutei Mahril 118

[310] Israel, Goldman M. The Life and Times of Rabbi David ibn abi Zimra, NY. 1970, p.32; also Federbush, Hikrei Yahadut, p.28; An opinion in the Talmud is that "for the study of scripture or Midrash or Mishnah or Talmud a benediction is required and the sage Rabbi Hiyya bar Ashi said, "Many times did I stand before Rab to repeat our section of Sifra in the School of Rab, and he used to first wash his hands and say a blessing and then go over our section with us" see T. Berachot 11b.

[311] Assaf, Beoholei Ya'akov p.3-6

[312] Responsa Vilnius edition 1885, Kelal 6, par. 25

[313] R Judah ha-Kohen; see A. Grossman, "Rabbi Yehudah ha-kohen and his sefer ha-Dinim", Alei Sefer 1 (1975, p.33

[314] Responsa R.'Zerahya ha-Levi cited in Responsa by Rashba, Livorno edition 1825, par. 166 (fol 34v); Cited in N. Morris, A History of Jewish Education, vol2/1 Jersualem 1977, p.146

[315] A Neubauer, Catalogue of the Hebrew Manuscripts in the Bodleian Library and in the College Libraries of Oxford, vol 1, Oxford 1886, n. 1025; see Catalogue of the Hebrew Ms in the Bodleian Library: Supplement of Addenda and Corrigenda to Vol 1 (A. Neubauer's Catalogue), compiled by the Institute of Microfilemd Hebrew MS at the JNUL in Jerusalem. This early public commissioned siddur is catalogued as Mich. 436. The siddur is vocalized by Sofer Yakov in the interest of correct standard pronunciation for public prayer.

[316] See M Beit Arie, "the Worms Mahzor: its history and its palaeographic and codicological characteristics" in M Beit Arie (ed.) Worms Mahzor, MS Jewish Natiaorila nd University Library: Introductory Volume (of a facsimile eiditon), Vaduz and Jerusalem, 1985, p.13-25

[317] Ms Lonon, Valmadonna Trust Library 10; see B Richler (ed) The Hebrew Manuscripts in the Valmadonna Trust Library, London, 1998, n. 103, p. 61-63

[318] See M. Glatzer and C Sirat, Manuscripts medievaux en caracteres hebraiques portant des indications de date jusqu'a 1540, III, Paris, 1986, no.112; the private commissioner of the book is named (MS Jerualem, Private collection of Prof. M Benyahu; see Glatzer, no. 118; In another non-liturgical book (Rambam's pirush al ha Mishnah in Judeo-Arabic) the name of the scribe and commissioner are not named and only a short colophon indicates that the copy was completed in 1496 for the synagogue.

[319] See Beit Arie, Malachi, Commissioned and Owner Produced Manuscripts in the Sephardic Zone and Italy in the 13th to 15th centuries, in the Late Medieval Hebrew book in the Western Mediterranean: Hebrew manuscripts and incunabula in context, Leinden: Brill, 2015, p.20

[320] See Israel Zvi Feintuch, Masorot u-mehqarim ba-talmud (Ramat Gan: Bar Ilan Univ. Press, 1985), 65-85 and Israel M. Ta-Shma, "sefer halakhot italqi qadmon," Qovets al yad, New Series 15 (2008), 180, n. 58; cited by Beit Arie, Malachi, "Commissioned and Owner Produced manuscripts in the Sephardic Zone and Italy in the 13th to 15th Centuries", p. 20

[321] See Pasternak, Nurit, "The Judeo-Italian translation of the Song of Songs and Ya'aqov da Corinaldo," Materia giudaica 10 (2005), 275; Pasternak, "Together and Apart: Hebrew Manuscripts as Testimonies to Encounters of Jews and Chrisitans in 15th Century Florence- the Makings, the Clients, Censorship' (PhD Diss., HUJ, 2009), 89-94

[322] See Beit-Arie, Malachi, "Publication and Reproduction of Literary Texts in Jewish Medieval Civilization: Jewish Scribality and Its Impact on the Texts Transmitted," in Transmitting Jewish Traditions: Orality, Textuality, and Cultural Diffusion, eds. Elman, Yaakov and Gershoni, Israel,, (New Haven: Yale Univ. Press, 2000), 225-47.

[323] See: Beit Arie, Malachi, "The individual nature of Hebrew book production and consumption" in Manuscrits hebreux et arabes: melanges en l'honneur de Colette Sirat, De Lange, N.R. M. ; Olszowy-Schlander, Judith (eds), Brepols, p.17; Beit Arie notes further that the response attest to few Jewish estabalishemnts such as batei midrash, yeshivot, synagogues, or community authorities that instigated and financed the production of Hebrew ms or administred the selection and the versions of texts to be copied. Neither did they often assemble and preserve them in communal or in academic collections, so that Jewish medieval books functionted mostly in the domain of private individual collectors. Beit Arie identifies that it was with the Renaissance in Italy that princely initiative under Humanistic influence established state libraries which are the precursors of public and state libraries today. However for much of the early Middle Ages the making of Hebrew books was the outcome of private enterprise motivated by personel need and aimed at private use (p.18). There is mention of Italian Deeds of sale in the renaissance inscribed at the end of manuscripts, however often books where inherited as yerushah in Ethical wills.

[324] See Assaf, S. "Am haSefer ve-haSefer", Reshumot 1 (1916/17), p.292-316

[325] See J-P Rothschild, "Les listes de libres reflet de la culture des juis en Italie du nord au XV et XVI siècle," in G. Tamani and A Vivian (eds.) Manoscritti framenti e libri ebraici nell Italia de secoli XV-XVI: Atti del VII Congresso internazionale del AISG S. Miniato, 7,8,9, novembre 1988, Roma, 1991, p.163-193; R. Bonfil The Rabbinate in Renaissance Italy, Jerusalem, 1969, Appendix 2, p 295-298 listed 41 Italian book lists, partly published and partly unpublished ; Lists are characterized by owners listing titles, sometimes codicological information or even palaeographical information such as the writing material, the kind of binding and the type of script (Bet Arie, Hebrew Ms. Of East and West, p.33) In the middle east evidence exists of lists by book dealers recovered from the Cairo Geniza.

326 See Allony, N., published many Geniza lists published posthumously by M. Frenkel and H. Ben-Shammai, Jewish Library in the Middle Ages, Book Lists from the Cairo Geniza, Jerusalem, 2006; see Bibliography of Allony, N. and A. Scheiberg, "An autograph of R. Josef Rosh Haseder", Kirjath Sepher 48, 1972-2973, p. 152-172 nand N. Allony "An 11th century Book list", Alei Sefer 6-7 (1979), p. 28-49. Book lists found in the Cairo Geniza testify to book dealers sale catalogues and inventories (M Frenkel "Book lists from the Geniza as a source for the cultural history of the Jews in the Mediterarean Society", Te'udo 15, 1999, p.333-349. Of course the pioneering work of SD Goiten author of A Mediterranean Society: The Jewish Commnities of the Arab World as Portrayed in the Documents of the Cario Geniza, 5 vols, Berkeley and LA 1967-1988, cannot not be mentioned as well as many of Goitein's hundreds of specialized journal articles in this area. A letter from the Cairo Geniza reveals that 230 biblical books, 100 small codices, and 8 sifrei Tora all looted from the foundations of the Jewish community in Jerusalem by Crusaders when they conquered the city in 1099, were redeemed in the summer of 1100 (see Goitein, SD, "New sources on the fate of the Jews during the Crusaders conquest of Jerusalem," Zion 17, 1952 p.132, 137, 141-142

327 Langermann, Y.Ts, "The scientific writing of Mordecai Finzi, Italia 7 (1988), p. 7-44; see Beit Arie, "Mordecai Finzi's copy of a work by Averroes" in AK. Offenberg, E.G.L. Schruver, FJ Hoogewould (eds.), Bibliotheca Rosenthaliana Treasures of Jewish Booklore, Amsterday, 1994, 8.; many medical books are in the Finizi family library as the family included many physicians including Shelomoth Finzi. According to a legeal document 1454 in the archives of Bologna the Finzi library had 226 books (C. Bernheimer, "Una collezione private di duecento manoscritti ebraici net xv secolo", La Bibliofillia 26, 1924-25, p.1-26.

[328] See J.N. Hillgarth, Readers ad books in Majorca, 1229-1550, vo..2 Paris 1991 p. 434-442 and inventory of books by Raphael Dayyan from Majorca dated 1330 published by JN Hillgarth and B. Narkiss, "A list of Hebrew books 1330) and contract to illuminate ms 1335 from Majorca" in REJ 120 (1961), p.297-315; Two exceptional contracts written in Latin and relating to the production of or the right to copy Hebrew ms. Survived in Chrsitian archives- one drawn up in Majorca in 1335 between a patron who gave specific instruction for the production of 3 illuminated ms. And named a scribe (see Hilgarth and Narkiss "listof Hebrew books", p.317-320.. The other contract made in Marseille in 1316 relates to acquiring copying rights for personal use only of a medical book (se J.Shatzmiller, "Livres medicaux et edition medicale: a propos d'un centrat de Marseille in 1316" in Medieval Studies 42, 1980, p. 463-470..

[329] Gutwirth, E and MA Moris Dolader, "26 Jewish libraries from 15th century Spain,' The Library: The Transactions of the Bibliographical Society, 6th Series, 18, 1996, p.27-53.

[330] See Bonfil, Robert, "La lettura nelle comunita ebraische dell europa occidentale in eta medieval" in G Cavallo and R. Chariter (eds) Storia della lettura nel mondo occidentale, Rema and Bari, 1995, p. 174-176

[331] Colette Sira and Beit Arie sponsored by the Israel Academy of Sciences and Humanities in collaboration with the NNUL in Jersualem in cooperation with the Institut de Recherche et D'Histoire des Textes (Centre National de la Recherche Scientifique, Paris) carried out this worldwide documentation team effort. The project produced digital images of selected pages of each ms. The SFARDATA database has sophisticated retrieveal system. Thus the statistical analysis of the SFARDATA supplies researchers with evidence for theses as a precise tool for the typological characaterization, historical study, and palaeographical identification of undated ms on the bases of objective criteria of codicological parameters.

332 כתבתי זה הספר של ליקוטין וענינים אחרים של קבלה למי שירצה אזתז לקנזת see Rome Biblioteca Casanatense, MS. 3104 fol 96v cited in Beit Arie, Malachi, Commissioned and Owner-Produed Manuscripts in the Sephardic zone and Italy in the 13th – 15th centuries" in The late medieval Hebrew book in the Western Mediterranean: Hebrew manuscripts and incunabula in context, Leiden: Brill, 2015, p. 19.

333 Beit-Arie, Malachi, Commissioned and Owner-Produed Manuscripts in the Sephardic zone and Italy in the 13th – 15th centuries" in The late medieval Hebrew book in the Western Mediterranean: Hebrew manuscripts and incunabula in context, Leiden: Brill, 2015, p.16; Beit Arie estimates that 60% of the colophons suggest that Hebrew ms. Were self produced. He reasons, "since it is inconceivable that a hired scribe would refrain from mentioning in his colophon the person who commissioned the book and hired him, while it is only natural that someone copying for himself would not necessarily bother to state it" because the great majority of the colophoned ms. Have no indication for whom their were copied they must have been user-produced privately done jobs (19).

334 See http://databases.jewishlibraries.org/node/49232

335 Quoted by Haberman, Toledot ha-Sefer ha-Ivri, p.13

336 Introduction to his book Novelot Hakhmah, quoted by Federbush Hikrei Yahadut, p.14

[337] The term "palace of torah" has many concepts associated with it- some rabbinical, sociological, and historical. In the historical context of the 19th century debate arose among Wissenschaft scholars debate ensued regarding the "essential Jewish library" and the "expansion of the palace of torah." Steinschneider weighed in on the debate of what constitutes a core essential Judaica collection as well (see Professor Moritz Steinschneider," Israelitisches Framilienblatt 10 (Jan. 31, 1907):5; other traces of the debate can be found in: "Einiges zur Lesebuchfrage," Israelitisches Familienblatt 10 (Jan. 3, 1907):9; Rotschild-Esslingen, "Zur Lesebuchfrage," Israelitische Familienblatt 10 (Jan, 10, 1907):9; Julius Spanier-Stolzenau, "Zur Lesebuchfrage," Israelitisches Familienblatt 10 (Jan. 31, 1907):9-10; "Noch einmal die Lesebuchfrage," Israelitisches Familienblatt 10 (Febr. 14, 1907):10.

[338] See Schidorsky, Dov, Sifriyah ve-sefer be-eretz Yisra'el be-shilhe ha-tekufah ha-Otmanit, Yerushalayim: Magnes, 1990, 349-351; For example Haredi declarations in Yerushayim in 1875, 1904, and 1927 warned Haredi visitors to the JNUL for their spiritual health. Such Ultra-Orthodox censorship is also identifiable in an Orthodox Convention where Rabbi Ralbag burned publically the siddur and Pesah Haggadah of Mordechai Kaplan. Kaplan had eliminated in his siddur the torah blessings proclaiming Jewish uniqueness and privlidged status (bahar banu mikol ha-amim ve-natan lanu et torato) before being called in an Aliyah to the torah, the notion of "am segulah." The notion of Am segulah was also challenged by anti-Semites who recently censored a new edition of Rav Yehudah HaLevy's Kuzari at a secular bookstore, as Rabbi Yehudah HaLevi makes many "politically incorrect" statements to the modern sensibilities of multicultural inclusiveness that are easily misinterpreted out of context by those not trained in reading the original Hebrew Judeo Arabic text. For example some misreaders infer that Yehudah HaLevy ascribes genetic "superiority" to the "Jewish race" as a function of chosenness. Rather the true reading is the "uniqueness of the Jewish people, and prophecy of the tribe of Levy for whom the Urim and Thumim will not depart" as according to Zot Habracha in Moshe's blessing at the end of Devarim. Kaplan's pesah haggadah also took out the injunction "to pour out Hashem's wrath upon the nations that know not G-d and have destroyed Hashem's servant Yakov, found Tehillim Ayin Tet, when we open the door for Eliyahu haNavi at the pesah seder:

שְׁפֹךְ חֲמָתְךָ -- אֶל הַגּוֹיִם, אֲשֶׁר לֹא-יְדָעוּךָ:
וְעַל מַמְלָכוֹת -- אֲשֶׁר בְּשִׁמְךָ, לֹא קָרָאוּ.   6 Pour out Thy wrath upon the nations that know Thee not, {N} and upon the kingdoms that call not upon Thy name.
ז כִּי, אָכַל אֶת-יַעֲקֹב; וְאֶת-נָוֵהוּ הֵשַׁמּוּ.   7 For they have devoured Jacob, and laid waste his habitation.

In my power point on "women and responsible use of the internet" I include a slide from Boro Park NY warning all Haredi Jews against "the evils of the Internet." Thus apparently the crusade against "unkosher books" has spilled over into Haredi condemnation of rightly concerns with "unkosher websites" of shmut, pritzus, etc. that constitute not only bitul zeman, but corrupting influences on the neshama. See AJL Proceedings Pasadena, CA.

339 Schmelzer, Menachem, "Building a Great Judaica Library- At what price?", in Tradition Renewed: A History of the Jewith Theological Seminary, NY:JTSA press, 1997, p 681; Schmelzer elaborates, "The recovery, collection, organization, and preservation of knowledge were primary goals of the pioneers of modern Jewish scholarship, but the establishment of complete collections of the written and printed (Jewish related) word was not among those ambitions.

340 These words of Geiger are cited in a report of the Jewish community library in Berlin. See Stern, M. Bibliothek der juedischen Gemeinde zu Berlin. Bericht ueber die Begruendung der Biblioothek und die drei ersten Jahre ihres Bestehens, 3 Februar 1902 bis 31, Marz 1905. Nebst einer Beilage: Benutzungsordnung (Berlin: E. Werheim, 1906), 3.

341 "Berlin," Der Israelit 30 (1889):720; Wilhelm Muenz, "Juedische Schueler Bibliothek", AZJ 53 (1889: 31; "Juedische Schul-Bibliothek," AZJ 53 (1889): 82-84; Bibliothek fuer die judische Jugend," AZJ 53 (1889): 115-17; "Zur Schul Bibliotheks-Frage," AZJ 53 (1889): 141; "Jugend-Bibliothek," AZJ 53 (1889): 209-11; Regina Reisser, "Was sollen unsere Toechter lessen?" AZJ 57 (1893): 451-53; "Eine Juedische Vereinsbiblbliothek," AZJ 59 (1895):88-89 and 103-104; Adolf Kurrein, "Volks-Jugend- ud Gemeindebibliotheken," Judische Chronik 4 (897-98): 36-45.

342 Traubenberg, Bernhard, "Gruendet Gemeindebibliotheken," Allgemeine Zeitung des Judenthums (AZJ) 56 (1892): 302; Loewe, Heinrich, "Wir sollen Gemeindebibliotheken gruenden," AZJ 56 (1892): 357.

[343] Besides the reading Hall library in Berlin, the Jewish community had access to the Bet Medrash Libraries, the Juedische Bibliothek, the library of the Deutsche-Israelitischer Gemeindebund, the library of the Masonic lodges, as well of the library of the Academic Society for Jewish history and Literature. See P. Schwenke and A. Hortzschansky, Berliner Bibliothekenfuhrer (Berlin: Weidmann, 1906), 147-48; Festschrift zum 10. Stiftungsfest desAkademischen Vereins fuer juedische Geschichte und Literatur, 82; Ludwig Geiger, "Die Bibliothek der Juedischen Gemeinde AZJ 66 (1902): 101-3.

[344] See "Breslau," Judische Presse 30 (1899):48-49; "Der Gemeindebote: Beliage zur AZJ 57 (Februar 24, 1893):1; "Berlin," Juedische Presse 31 (1900):55; Juedische Lesehalle und Bibliothek Bericht fuer das Jahr 1906, 5 (Berlin, 1906); Berlin: Juedsiche Gemeinde. Sammlung Benas Levy, CAHJP, KG 2/62;

[345] Schmidt, "Judische Bibliotheken in Frankfurt am Main: Vom Anfang des 19. Jahrhunderts bis 1938," 261 and "Karlsruhe," Der Gemeindebote. Beilage zur AZJ 69 (1905):4

[346] Berghoffer, Christian Wilhelm, Die Freiherrlich Carl v. Rotschild'sche offentliche bibliothek. Ein Grundriß ihrer Organisation. Nebst einen Verzeichnis ihrer Zeitschriften und einem Frankfuerter Bibliothekenfuehrer (Frankfurt A. M.: Baer, 1913); Frankfurt am Main consisted of various donated collections that eoncompassed the libraries of R. Salmon Geiger, orientalist Raphael Kircheim, and duplicates from the library of Abraham Berliner as well ast he library of Freiherrn Wilhelm Karl von Rotschild. (see "Lauchheim (Wuerttenberg)," Gegenwart 1 (1867): 103 and Bibliothek der israelitischen Religionsschule zu Frankfurt am Main: Katalog.)

[347] Scholem, Gerschom, From Berlin to Jerusalem: Memoirs of My Youth, trans. Harry Zohn (NY: Schocken, 1980), 37.

[348] See "Eine Judische Vereinsbibliothek," AZJ 59 (1895): 88-89; also see "Eine Judische Vereinsblibliothek," Mitteilungen aus dem Verband der vereine fuer juedische Geschichte und Literatur in Deutschland (Dec. 1902): 47-56; Lists of history books included in this core collection often included works by Heinrich Graetz, Moritz Guedemann, Leo Herzfeld, Isaac Jost, Abraham Geiger, Jost, Abraham Berliner, etc. History of literature lists recommended works by David Cassel, Gustav Karpeles, Moritz Kayserling, Moritz Steinschneider, Michael Sachs, Abraham Sulzbach, Leopold Zunz, etc. In some sense the Adolf Kohut cultural history of German Jewry series sought to also canononize for a core collection scholarly works in academic Judaica.

[349] Markus Lehmann published historical novels as "Lehmanns judische Hausbucherei." The Gesellschaft zur Foerderung der Wissenschaft des Judentums, advertised their publications as "Buecher fuer die Juedische Hausbibliothek; Schriften herausgegeben von der Gesellschaft zur Foerderung der Wissenschaft des Judentum." Thus the phenomena of the Judische Lehrhaus and the student public it represented made library book collecting a "family affair." This thirst for Jewish culture (Bildung) is described by Leo Strauss, in the introduction to Leo Struass' book, Spinoza's Criitique of Religion.

[350] See Shavit, David, Hunger for the Printed Word: Books and Libraries in the Jewish Ghettos fo Nazi-Occupied Europe (Jefferson, NC: McFarland, 1977, 35-39); The focus of this book is on Jewish libraries in Poland, Lithuania, and the Theriesienstadt camp in Czechoslovakia.

[351] Rose, Jonathan, "Introduction" in The Holocaust and the Book: Destruction and Preservation, p.3; In this book on pages 165-170 Dina Abramowicz gives testimony to the reading habits of patrons of the Vilna Ghetto which constituted 3 types: (1) "society ladies" who frequented the library in the early morning hours whose husbands were at hard labor of work, and came to check out serailzationsof Russian sentimental novels issued by publishing houses in Riga, (b) children who visited the library after 2 pm. after shool who sought out stories such as Childen of Captain Grant, Around the world in 80 Days, The Adventures of Tom Sawyer, The Prince and the Pauper, etc.Abromowitz attributes this to the children's need for youthful imagination to transport itself to the world of fantasy which grew more intense in the lack of freedoms imposed by the ghetto and its environment. Abromowitz writes, "Books were possibly the only vehicle for reaching out to the world from which the Jewish children were cut off, possibly forever" (168). (c) the third type of Ghetto library patrons who visited on Sundays were people who went to work outside the ghetto, mostly young people from the Hechalutz Zionist organizations, many refugees from Warsaw. This group of readers tended to read books for analogies to their own situation. For example Franz Werfel's The 40 Days of Musa Dagh described the episode in WWI of the annihilation by the Turks of an entire Armenian population iving in their country. Abromowitz writes, 'The idea of a total annihilatin of a racial group, the method of destruction, the helplessness of the victims, and the futility of diplomatic rescue efforts- this presented such an astonishing similiarity to our situation that we read the book wth a shudder, perceiving it almost as a prophetic vision, revealing for us our inevitable fate" (168)."

[352] Kruk writes, "Reading at that time, could be interpreted only as a form of withdrawal from the surrounding conditions (192)."Kruk notes in a ghetto library report, "Under ghetto conditions, the Reading Room plays a major and significant role. The consulating of reading matter is not all that takes place here; the space affords an opportunity for both reading and mental relaxation." (see diary entry for 8 May 1942]. Kruk notes the great appreciation with wich the ghetto intelligentsia greeted the reopening of the Ghetto Reading room and their recognition of its role as an important cultural enterprise in the ghetto. Visitors regarded the Ghetto reading room as the "nicest cultural site in the ghetto" thanks to its pleasant atmosphere (Togbukh, 262). Kruk witnessed how books became a kind of nacrotic for ghetto inmates, a means of escape. Kruk comments, "A human being can endure hunger, poverty, pain, and suffering, but he cannot tolerate isolation" (192). Kruk writes, "In the ghetto each individual is allotted scarcely 70 square centimeters (7 sq feet). The house is like a giganctic beehive. Still you lie down doubled up on your meager possessions, and you ingest the narcostic- the book. The new ghetto inhabitant thus clings to the little bit of what remained from before. Books carried him away, over the ghetto walls and into the world. A reader could thus tear himself away from hhis oppressive isolation and in his mind be reunited with life, with his stolen freedom" (192). Kruk describes victims deported for gassing in the varios "Actions" as "borrowed readers" (193). Kruk notes that whlle the majority of borrowers of the ghetto library books were children, the next group were women who did not work as hard as the conscripted men. He writes, "The more complicated that life becomes, the harder it gets for there to be any kind of intellectual exertion. Not only does the act of reading get more difficult for the reader, but so does the ability ot make sense of the artistic details. Readers first and foremost women, normally devour light fiction, mysteries, and semitrashy books- and that is the situation that currently preveals." (193). Thus Kruk classifies these readers as those who read for the purpose of intoxication- that is in order to stop focusing on the horror of the present- or reading in order to ponder to become intereste n comparable fates, to make analogies and reach certain conclusion. (mid march 1943 diary entry (Togbukh 471).

[353] See Israelitische Familien-blatt reprinted in Ulircke Schmidt, "Juedische Bibliotheken in Frankfurt am Main: Vom Anfang des 19. Jahrhunderts bis 1938, "Archiv fuer Geschichte des Buchwesen 29 (1987): 236-67.

[354] See Beth Arie, Malachi, "Gershom Scholem: The man and his work, the bibliophile, Jersualem: Israel Academy of Sciences & Albany: State University of NY Press 1994, p.125; Beth Arie writes, "His (Scholem's) crowning achievement in this respect (furthering Jewish Continuity)was the sacred task he took upon himself of rescuing the collections of Hebrew and Jewish books confiscated by the Nazis. After the war, in the summer of 1946, Scholem set out for Europe as a representative of the Hebrew University. For five long and arduous months he gathered information about the fate of Jewish libraries, located concentrations of books in Germany, Czechoslavakia, and Austria, examined their content, and conducted complicated and sensitive negotiations in order to salvage them, under indescribably difficult conditons. For several years he supervised the rescue and transfer of some half million books and hundreds of manuscripts from Germany, Czechoslavakia, Poland and Austria to the JNUL and other libraries in Eretz Yisrael."

[355] Quoted by Federbush, Hikrei Yahadut, p.23; Bialik in the poem Hamatmid also expresses a similar thought that the Jews found refuge in sefarim when he writes, "And shouldst thou wish to know the source from which thy tortured breather drew/ In evil days their strength of the soul?/ They enter the house of G-d/ The Beit Midrash/ Perhaps they eye may still behold/ the profile of some palid face/ upon an ancient folio bent." Bialik also writes a poem Lifnei Aron ha-Sefarim"[standing before the book case]" which opens, "Receive my greetings/ O ancient tomes/ Accept my kisses ye noble shriveled parchments!";

[356] see Kitvei H.N. Bialik (Tel Aviv, 1939), p.47 13 Kitvei Agnon, vol.3, chap. On "Shas al Bet Zikni"; In Agon's story "In the Heart of the Seas" which I learnt in a class with Gershon Shaked of Hebrew University in Jerusalem, Agnon tells of Rabbi Hananya who went on a hazardous journey by sea to the land of Israel when a storm broke out. The rabbi saw someone sitting on the desck calmly learning a sefer. The rabbis fears vanished for he knew "that no tempest at sea would cause him to sink and no beast of the deep could swallow him up protected by the power of holy meditation on sefarim.".. Agnon commented on this literary work, noting that this section was written to re-emphasize that "the Jewish people will survive the brutal and wild storms of history if only they hold fast to the Jewish book (see L Kupershtein, "Kedushat ha-Sefer ve-had Lashion be-Yetzirat Agnon," Am ve-Sefer 45-46 (1971): 32-37];

[357] Agnon Archives, JNUL, No 5:429. The remark by the Besht is quoted by his grandson R. Moses Hayyim Ephraim of Sadylkow, in his Degel mahane Ephraim, Jerusalem 1963, p. 96 as cited by Malachi Beit Arie.

[358] The topic of quantum physics and string theory related to Jewish notions of the mystical properties of light is very "illuminating." I recall that I heard from the mikubal Rabbi Yitzchak Ginsburgh an attempt to try to correlate current scientific knowledge in physics of light as a wave and or particle paradox, with the truths of Kabbalah (derekh ha-emet) understanding light's hidden nature practiced by what Rav Soloveitchik calls homo mysticus integrated into the soul in tandem with ish halakhah. It is Rabbi Ginsburgh who offers the uncanny coincidence that the gematria of Moshe is 345 which is the sum of ohr (207) plus 138 which can either be the numerical equivalent for Menachem, a name for the final redeemer, or Tzemach meaning "plant." Indeed it is the Tzemach Tzedek who is the Author of Chabad Lubavitch's central text Ohr HaTorah. There is nothing outside of torah the Remak notes, for Israel, Torah, and G-d are one. The light of Moshe's face was radiating light at the burning bush, as was the case with Adam and Eve before the primordial sin. Rav Ginsburgh asks " Is it mere coincidence that light, ohr=207, and skin (ayin vav resh= 276), both multiples of 23, the tenth prime number, which is the gematria of radiance (zayin yod vav). Further coincidence that 207 is 9 times 23 and 276 is 12 times 23, whereby 23 plays a key role in string theory? Rabbi Ginsburgh thinks not, for in string theory the reciprocal of 207 (light)= $1/207$= 0.00[483]0 and further 483 is repeated when we add 207 (ohr) and 276 (skin), which equals 690, the equalivant of the "Moshe, Moshe," G-d's call to Moshe to redeem the Jewish people at the sneh." As is well known Rashbi is a gilgul of Moshe Rabbenu as their gematria are also equivalent. What coincidences, as in Megillat Esther- What if the king had not been sleepless that night, what if Mordechai had not overheard the plot of Judeocide in a time of hester panim, where the "light of hashem's face" appeared hidden until the great light of redemption revealed itself as Mordechai makes a tikkun by not bowing to H-m-n yimach shemo (a descendent through Agag of Esauv) while Yakov was coerced for pikuach nefesh to bow to his brother Esauv.?

359 *https://www.bing.com/images/search?view=detailV2&ccid=UOzu9%2fhi&id=D5E110AC614A354582FFC26FB24879408BDFB9EF&thid=OIP.UOzu9_hi31XPns_mdLfl3QAAAA&mediaurl=https%3a%2f%2fjewishreviewofbooks.com%2fwp-content%2fuploads%2f2013%2f02%2fDubnov.jpg&exph=263&expw=425&q=unpacking+one%27s+books+simon+dubnov&simid=608031728676504152&selectedIndex=0&ajaxhist=0*

360 Gershom Scholem confesses that the extra money that his parents sent him as a student to supplement his vitamin deficient diet (mostly eggs and potatoes) was used by Scholem not to purchase more healthy food for his health and nourishment but set aside for buying more books. Scholem writes, :"In the fall I took the money I had saved to my two second hand book dealers in Berlin and bought kabbalistic writings, among them a French translation of the Zohar which appeared in Paris between 1906 and 1912 in 6 thick volumes. (see Scholem, Gershom, "How I came to the Kabbalah", in Commentary, May 1980: 69, 005, p. 40)

361 1 Nedavah, "Gezerot al Sefarim Ivriyim"

362 2 I Maccabees 1:53-56; ""And they made Israel to hide themselves in every place of refuge which they had ... And they rent in pieces the books of law which they found, and set them on fire"

363 3 Taanit 4:6; see: נשתברו בתמוז עשר בשבעה באב בתשעה וחמשה בתמוז עשר בשבעה אבותינו את אירעו דברים חמשה הלוחות ובטל התמיד והובקעה העיר ושרף אפוסטמוס את התורה והעמיד צלם בהיכל בתשעה באב נגזר על אבותינו שלא יכנסו לארץ וחרב הבית בראשונה ובשניה ונלכדה ביתר ונחרשה העיר משנכנס אב ממעטין בשמחה: [משנה מסכת תענית פרק ד]

364 4 Tractate Avodah Zarah 18a

365 5 See: The Koren Mesorat HaRav Kinot, The Complete Tisha B'Av Service with Commentary by Rabbi Joseph B. Soloveitchik

366 6 See, Roth, Cecil, "Jewish Love of books", p.3-4; While I was in Portugal after having come thither with those expelled from Castile, it came into my mind to compose a commentary on the Five scrolls. That was the time of the Second Expulsion from Portugal of the Jews. I abandoned all my books and fled to Lisbon with only the commentary I had composed on the Pentateuch and the commentary on the Five Scrolls, and a commentary on Pirke Avot, and the work "Hibbur HaKasef" that I had composed earlier. When I arrived in Lisbon, certain Jews told me that a proclamation had been issued that any person in whose possession was a Hebrew book would be put to death. I concealed my books beneath a verdant olive tree but my eyes are bitter as wormwood: and I called it the tree of weeping, for there I had buried all that I held most dear.

367 Ibid.; After I had written three chapters anew, I found one single copy of the printed work in the hands of a non-Jew who had snatched it from the blaze in Marheshvan, and I purchased it at a high price, and I found by the providence of G-d that I had made the second copy more complete than the first.

368 See Rose, Jonathan (ed), The Holocaust and the Book: Destruction and Preservation, Amherst: University of Mass Press, 2001, 1;

369 8 See bibliography on M. Luther at: http://libguides.tourolib.org/c.php?g=114197&p=743238

370 http://www.ushmm.org/exhibition/book-burning/ph_fset.php?title=title_burning.gif&content=2003zya7.jpg,20031zgf.jpg

371 9 The German text reads, "The book burning ceremonies were planned with meticulous attention to detail. This invitation to the book burning in Munich outlines the order of events: invitees "must arrive at the designated area at precisely 11 p.m. At 11 p.m. the torchlight procession of the entire Munich Students Association will be arriving. 1. The united bands will play parade music 2. The festivities will begin at 11 with the song "Brothers, Forward!" 3. Speech by the leader of the German Students Association Kurt Ellersiek 4. Burning of the nation-corrupting books and journals 5. Group sing-along of ... songs"

372 See Kaplan, Chaim, Scroll of Agony, NY: Macmillan, 1965, 57.

373 Kohut, Rebeca, "Alexander Marx,' in Alexander Marx Jubilee volume on the occasion of his 70th birthday, NY: NY 1950, xxi.; Marx and others worked to reprint some of the Kohut academic Jewish studies volumes. For example Professor Solomon Skoss of Dropsie College prepared and edition of the Hebrew-Arabic dictionary of David Alf-fasi, a contemporary of Rav Saadia Gaon in two volumes edited from manuscripts in the State Public Library in Leningrad and in the Bodleian Library at Oxford. The 4rth volume continuing the book of Joshua in Greek by Professor Margolis was pubished post-humously. Salo W. Baron's 1935 celebration of the then 800th anniversary of Maimonides birth with Columbia University Press was financed by Kohut. Further Kohut funding enabled the reprint of Tcherikover's The Jews in Egypt in the Hellenistic Roman Age in the light of the Papyri.

374 See: Gershom Scholem: A Life in Letters, 1914-1982 ed by Anthony David Skinner ; 512pp, Harvard University press; reviewed by David B Levy in AJL Newsletter, 2002

375 See Danzig 1939: Treasures of a Destroyed Community, Catalog for the Jewish Museum exhibit by Vivian B Mann and Joseph Guttman (NY: Jewish Museum, 1980).

376 The library of the reading and learning society in Breslau possessed the collectons of Heinrich Herz, S. Guensburg, and MB. Fiedenthal in addition to books they purchased for the collection.

377 Schmelzer, Menachem, "Building a Great Judaica Collection-At What Price?' in Tradition Renewed, NY: JTSA, 1997, p. 704 footnote 125: Extract from letter of Doctor Israel Schapiro of the Library of Congress to Marx, 15 Feburary 1939

378 11 See: Chtoby ty ostalsia evreem (2003) ; revised based on the Hebrew edition, Le'hisha'eir Yehudi (2008)"; reviewed by David B Levy in AJL Reviews 2011

379 In footnote 126 Schmelzer cites the 16 May 1938 memo of Adler to Marx about the fate of the collection of the Berlin Jewish community. Adler did not see a possibility to intervene with the American ambassador in Berlin. In the minutes of the Board of Directors, 31 May 1939, it is related how Louis Finkelstein met with a Mr. Teterka who stated that he could bring the library of the Breslau seminary to the US for 75,000 marks. The following remakr is added to this report cited by Schmelzer, "It would be understood that the Breslau community would not ask any compensation for this transaction." On 21 Feburary 1939, Marx wrote to Adler, "I heard the other day that the Museum of the Berlin Jewish Community could be ransomed for 25,000 " Stating that he realized it "was absolutely against our policy to send American money to Germany," Marx suggested that perhaps steps could be taken to slavage the "irreplaceable treasures" by individuals.

380 Dicker, The Seminary Library, p.54-58; 107-12

381 Schmelzer, M., "Building a Great Judaica Collection-At what price?", in Tradition renewed, p. 705; Footnote Library committee minutes 6 Oct. 1955, p.1

382 Schmelzer, M., 705; footnote Library Committee Minutes 26 March 1958

[383] Jonathan Rose astutely comments on Heine's remark, "Bet even Heine's premonition as true as it is terrible, threatens to become a platutidue if we pursue it no further. Strikingly most histories of the Holocaust have nothing more to say about books. We see that there must be a connection between the book burnings and the gas chambers, but can we explain specifically how one led to the other? Were those bonfires a necessary prelude for what was to follow, and if so, precisely what role did print play in the Holocaust? Through they differ in method and focus, all essays in this volume confromt that question" (The Holocaust and the Book: Destruction and Preservation, Amhrest: University of Mass press, 2001, p. 1); The essays in this book attest that books, and Jewish readers during the Holocaust, often came to relate to books as tools for human endurance and resistance. Thus the printed word came to be endowed with an essential element as a key to survival and identity. Books came to be indisepensable tools for resistance to the Nazis. In occupied Europe bibliophily was more than a hobby for gentlemen and aesthetes: it became something dangerously political that was an affront to the Nazis rage against anything un-German- un-Aryan i.e. defined as the Jewish spirit. Nazi censorship was a war against the Jewish spriit defined as the opposite of the German spirit.

וֶאֱלִישָׁע רֹאֶה, וְהוּא מְצַעֵק אָבִי אָבִי רֶכֶב יִשְׂרָאֵל וּפָרָשָׁיו, וְלֹא רָאָהוּ [384] עוֹד; וַיַּחֲזֵק, בִּבְגָדָיו, וַיִּקְרָעֵם, לִשְׁנַיִם קְרָעִים The *Abarbanel* comments on this pusek 3x: (1) BaMidbar אברבנאל במדבר פרשת במדבר פרק ג

(א) ואלה תולדות אהרן ומשה עד הקרב את מטה לוי. הנה (שם ג' כ') רש"י פירש באלה תולדות אהרן ומשה שלפי שמשה למד תורה אל בני אהרן קראם הכתוב תולדותיו. יסבור הרב שהפרשה הזאת לא באה אלא על בני אהרן בלבד ושנקראו תולדות משה לפי שהתלמידים קרואים בנים שנאמר (מלכים ב' כ' י"ב) אבי אבי רכב ישראל ופרשיו ומדברי המדרש הוא. ויותר נראה לי לפרש שבעבור שספר למעלה מספר עם בני ישראל שפרו וישרצו וירבו ויעצמו במאד מאד והנשיאים **אברבנאל מלכים ב** (2) *Malachim Perek Bet* שנקבו בשמות למעלתם **פרק ב**

(א) ויהי בהעלות וגומר. ספר הכתוב שכאשר העלה השם יתברך את אליהו לשמים בסערה היה ענינו בזה האופן, והוא כי ראשונה הלכו אליהו ואלישע מן הגלגל, (ב) ואמר אליהו אל אלישע שישאר שמה בגלגל כי השם שלחו עד בית אל, והשיבו אלישע בשבועה שלא יעזבהו, והלך עמו עד בית אל, (ג) ושם יצאו בני הנביאים, שהם התלמידים שהיו מכינים עצמם להתנבא, והיו פרושים ונזירים מיוחדים לעבודת הגבוה, ואמרו בסוד אל אלישע הידעת כי היום הזה ה' לוקח את אדוניך מעל ראשך? רצה לומר שיקח את אדוניו שהיה עטרת ראשו, והוא השיבם גם אני ידעתי החשו, רוצה לומר גם כן ידעתי אני זה שתוקו ואל תדברו עוד בדבר הזה, כי היה מחריש לראות מה יעשה אליהו בלקיחתו, ויהיה לפי זה החשו צווי, או יהיה פירוש החשו שהם שתקו והחשו ולא דברו לו עוד:

(ד) ובהיותם בבית אל אמר אליהו אל אלישע שהשם שלחו אל יריחו ושישאר הוא שם בבית אל, ואלישע השיבו כבראשונה שלא יפרד ממנו והלכו אל יריחו,

(ה) ובני הנביאים אשר שם אמרו גם כן אל אלישע מלקיחת אליהו, והוא השיבם כאשר לראשונה. (ח) והלכו אליהו ואלישע אל הירדן ויקח אליהו את אדרתו ויגלום, רצה לומר שכרך אדרתו והכה בה את המים ויחצו המים ויעברו שניהם בחרבה, (ט) ובעברם אמר אליהו אל אלישע שאל מה אעשה לך בטרם אלקח מעמך, ושאל אלישע ויהי נא פי שנים ברוחך אלי, (י - יא) והוא השיבו הקשית לשאול וגומר, ובהיותם הולכים מדברים בזה, ראה רכב אש וסוסי אש אשר שהפרידו בין שניהם ועלה אליהו בסער' השמים,

[385] With regards to the term and concept, etymologically, *"translation"* is a "carrying across" or "bringing across." Latin "translation" derives from past participle *"translatus"* of *"transferre"* (to transfer)- from *"trans,"* "across" + *"ferre,"* "to carry" or "to bring"). "Traducere" means to bring across or "to lead across." The Greek term *"metaphrasis"* ("a speaking across"), gives English *"metaphrase"*- a literal translation," or "word for word" translation versus "paraphrase" ("a saying in other words," from the Greek *paraphrasis*.

[386] The author on translation in the Wikipedia entry distinguishes between translation and interpretations, a boundary I hope to suggest is not so clear cut with regards Biblical texts and the Rabbinic history of perushim. They write, "Interpreters, by contrast, are trained in precise listening skills under taxing conditions, memory and note-taking techniques for consecutive interpreting (in which the interpreter listens and takes notes while the speaker speaks, and then after several phrases provides the version in the other language, taking turns, not speaking at the same time), and split-attention for simultaneous interpreting (in which the interpreter, usually in a booth with a headset and microphone, listens and speaks at the same time, usually producing the interpreted version only seconds after the speaker provides the original). The industry expects interpreters to be more than 80% accurate; that is to say that interpretation is an approximate version of the original. Translation should be over 90% accurate, by contrast." See http://en.wiipedia.org/wiki/Translation, accessed 6/4/2007 1:17 pm As we will see with Shir HaShirim Rabbinic interpretation of the Song sees itself as the true essence of the text's hidden and secret meanings as mushal and nimshal. With regards to the Targumim, Septuagint, Vulgate, Peshita, Tafsir, Beur, etc. certain liberties were taken when translating particular words which clearly give what Benjamin calls an "afterlife" of the text whereby new meanings are given birth.

[387] See, Benjamin, Walter, *Illuminations: Essays and Reflections*, edited and with an introduction by Hannah Arendt, N.Y.: Schocken book, 1968; In Illuminationen, Benjamin penned these thoughts as an introduction to the translation of Baudelaure's *Tableaux Pariesiens*.; This work should be read also in light of Benjamin's ""The work of Art in the Age of Mechanical Reproduction." Seen thusly, translation strives to transmit some of the unfathomable, the mysterious, and the poetic as opposed to a computer program like "Babelfish" which mechanically renders a dictionary translation inattentive to syntax or more importantly to that spirit of the work that cannot be mechanically generated and reproduced by a machine. Benjamin's distinction is between essential and inessential translation when referring to those done by a person with a soul versus those churned out by a machine. For Benjamin translation is not a mechanical act but a mode of being. "A translation issues from the original- not so much from its life as from its afterlife... translation marks the stage of continued life." Every work of art and its translation across history is an expression of the spirit of its age. Benjamin sees translations as "afterlife" or transformations and renewals of something living- making the original undergo a change. Benjamin writes, "While a poet's words endure in his own language, even the greatest translation is destined to become part of the growth of its own language and eventually to be absorbed by its renewal. Translation is so far removed from being the sterile equation of two dead languages that of all literary forms it is the one charged with the special mission of watching over the maturing process of the original language and the birth pangs of its own" (p. 73). " Benjamin refers to the kindredness of languages that grow until the end of their time, and it is the translations of works of art which 'catches fire on the eternal life of the works and the perpetual renewal of language" (p.74) Thus Benjamin is not only offering an abstract theory of translation but a philosophy of language, philosophy of history, and philosophy of art simultaneously. Benjamin anticipates Derridean Deconstruction by drawing on a biological metaphor when he writes, "The transfer (of a translation) can never be total, but what reaches this region is that element in a translation which goes beyond transmittal of subject matter. This nucleus is best defined as the element that does not lend itself to translation. Even when all the surface content has been extracted and transmitted, the primary concern of the genuine translator remains elusive...(p.75) Benjamin states, "the task of the translator consists in finding that intended effect [Intention] upon the language into which he is translating which produces an *echo of the original* (p.76)." Benjamin reveals that more than just "fidelity and license" are at stake in translations- no mere game of hermeneutics. Rather he writes, "a translation instead of resembling the meaning of the original must lovingly and in detail incorporate the original's mode of signification, thus making both the original and the translation recognizable as fragments of a greater language, just as fragments are part of a vessel... (p.78)... as regards the meaning, the language of a translation can- in fact, must- let itself go, so that it gives voice to the *intention* of the original not as a reproduction but as harmony, as a supplement to the language in which it expresses itself, as its own kind of *intentio* (p.79). Benjamin notes, "A real translation is transparent, it does not cover the original, does not block its light, but allows the pure language, as though reinforced by its own medium, to shine upon the original all the more fully" (p.79). Benjamin further sees the task of the translator to release in his own language that pure language, and vital force, which is under the spell of another, to liberate the language imprisoned in a work in his re-creation of that work in the freedom of linguistic flux. The translator must seek to convey the spirit of the original language by returning to the primal elements of language itself and penetrate to the point where work, image, and tone converge. The translator must deepen their language by drawing on the spirit of the original language of the work of art. Benjamin signs his thoughts on translation with a turn to religious texts by writing, "For to some degree all great texts contain their potential translation between the lines; this is true to the highest degree of sacred writings. The interlinear version of the Scriptures is the prototype or ideal of all translation" (p.82)."

[388] Ber. 3b-4b; "At midnight I will rise to give thanks unto Thee" (Ps. 119.62). חֲצוֹת־לַיְלָה--אָקוּם, לְהוֹדוֹת לָךְ: עַל, מִשְׁפְּטֵי צִדְקֶךָ. A harp was hung above David's couch, across his window. When midnight arrived, the north wind blew upon the harp and made it swing to and fro, so that it played of itself. David would immediately rise and occupy himself with Torah until the break of dawn. And after dawn's break, the sages of Israel would come in to see him and say, "our Lord king, your people Israel require sustenance." He would reply, 'Let them go out and make a living one from the other." They would answer, "a handful cannot satisfy a lion, nor can a cistern be filled by rain failing into its surround." So he said, "Go forth in troops and help yourselves to the enemy's possessions. The sages took counsel with Ahithophel, sought advice from the Sanhedrin, and inquired of *the Urim and Tummim*. After that, they would go forth to wage war. And the proof that David was awakened in such a way and at such an hour? The verse, so said R. Isaac bar adds, "Wake up my royal glory, let he psaltery and harp wake it, and I then wake the dawn" (Ps. 57:9) עוּרָה כְבוֹדִי--עוּרָה, הַנֵּבֶל וְכִנּוֹר;   אָעִירָה שָּׁחַר

The sugya in Berachot is in the context of a discussion of the various watches in the night. The passage about King david arising at midnight when a breeze made music on his harp hung above his bed reads:

דוד סימנא הוה ליה דאמר רב אחא בר ביזנא אמר רבי שמעון חסידא כנור היה תלוי למעלה ממטתו של דוד וכיון שהגיע חצות לילה בא רוח צפונית ונושבת בו ומנגן מאליו מיד היה עומד ועוסק בתורה עד שעלה עמוד השחר כיון שעלה עמוד השחר נכנסו חכמי ישראל אצלו אמרו לו אדוננו המלך עמך ישראל צריכין פרנסה אמר להם לכו והתפרנסו זה מזה אמרו לו אין הקומץ משביע את הארי ואין הבור מתמלא מחוליתו אמר להם לכו ופשטו ידיכם בגדוד

[389] See Heller, Chaim, *Al HaTargumim HaYerushalmi LiTorah* (A Critical Essay on the Palestinian Targum to the Pentateuch), A Reprint from the Hebrew weekly Haibri, N.Y., 1921 [in Hebrew]; Heller looks at passages such as Isaiah 9:31, Gen 13:6 (*ram vs. morah*), Ex 16:33 (take *a jar vs. take a golden jar*), 2 Kgs 8:26 (*and his mother's name was Athaliah the daughter of Ahab vs. the daughter of Omri*), lamed vs. lamed aleph , Gen. 18:17 (*Shall I hide from Abraham vs. Shall I hide from Abraham my servant* [servant added in Septuaginta and Peshitta]

[390] The designation Septuagint, from the Latin *septuaginta* (seventy) is from the greek, *Interpretatio*
septuaginta seniorum (translation of the 70 elders) probably owes its name to a story related in the Letter of Aristeas, according to which 72 scholars summoned from Yerushalayim by Ptolemy II Philadelphus (285-244 BCE), achieved the same Greek translation of the Pentateuch, which was deposited in the Alexandrian library. It was maintained that each had worked independently, their finished versions miraculously identical. According to the *Letter of Aristeas*, according to which 72 elders, six from each tribe, translated the Law into Greek in Alexandria. According to a sugya in the Talmud this was one of the saddest days in Jewish history because it caused the Hellenistic Jews not to learn Hebrew, but to rely on a translation. Philo's brilliant allegorical interpretative works for instance do not draw on Hebrew.

[391] Old Latin Versions (OL) abounded before the Vulgate, and excerpts from them can be found on Jewish catacombs in Rome which bear Bible verses in Latin. By the end of the 4rth century accumulated textual
corruptions and alterations gave rise to a need for a uniform and reliable Latin Bible text. This task was entrusted to Jerome (345-420 CE), secretary of Pope Damasus I. Through his work Jerome became aware of the many instances where the Septuagint diverged from the Hebrew Tanakh, and he thus decided to prepare an entirely fresh Latin translation from "the original truth of the Hebrew text," the *Hebraica veritas*.

392 Mendelssohn's collaborators were Solomon Dubno, Hartwig Wessely, Naphtali Herz Homberg and Aaron Jaroslaw. The translation printed in Hebrew characters, appeared under the title, Netivot ha-Shalom, together with the original Hebrew and a commentary, designated Be'ur (Biur). In contrast to Luther's
Biblia, das ist: die gantze Heilige Schrifft Deudsch (6 vols. Wittenberg, 1534), which used God's name as "der Herr" based on the Greek kyrios of the Septuagint and the Latin dominus of the Vulgate, Mendelssohn wrote "der Ewige" (the Eternal), a term which was accepted by German speaking Jews and influenced Rosenzweig's concept of der Ewige Jueden." Luther's work was intended to wean the Jews off of Yiddish. Yiddish glosses of Biblical texts appear from the 13th century. Prose translations of various biblical books were written from the 14th century onward, and these were designed often for women. Such "Teitsch" versions include a 14th-15th century translation of Proverbs, Job, and Tehillim. Rhymed Yiddish translations also abound. For example the Shemuel Bukh, a rhymed paraphrase of I and II Shmuel appeared before 1400. Three 14th century paraphrases of Esther, one of Shoftim, and paraphrases of the Megillot by Rabbi Abraham b. Elijah of Vilna (15th-16th C.), paraphrases of Shoftim and Isaiah by R. Moses b. Mordecai of Mantua (before 1511), and poetic renderings of the Akedah and the death of Moshe embellished with Aggadata exist. Literary works in the late 15th century known as, Ma'asiyyot (tales), abound on topics such as the Akedah, Yonah, and Shlomo. Yiddish glossaries of the Bible such as Sefer R. Anschel (Cracow, 1584), Moses Saertels' Be'er Moshe (Prague, 1605), Lekah Tov (Prague 1604). A summary of Rashi's commentary in Yiddish appeared in Basle (1583). Elijah Levita did a Yiddish translation of Tehillim (Venice 1545) which followed that of Moses b. Mordecai of Brescia (before 1511) and Joseph Yakar (siddur, Ichenhausen, 1544). Two further Yiddish translations of the 16th century were Shalom b.Abraham's Judith and Susanna (Cracow, 1571) and an edition of Isaiah with extracts from Kimhi's commentary (Cracow, 1586). Toward the end of the
the
17 entury two complete Yiddish Bibles appeared one by Jekuthiel b. Isaac Blitz (Amsterdam, 1678), and antoher by Josef Witzenhausen (Amsterdam, 1679). Rhmyed translation of stories form the Humash and Megillot were done by David b. Menahem ha-Kohen. A version of the Humash, Joshua, and Judges written by Jacob b. Isaac ha-Levy of Roethelsee (Kehillat Ya'akov, 1692) also appears. The Lange Megile (Cracow, 1589) and the *Teutsch-Khumesh* by Isaac b.

Samson ha-Kohen of Prague (Basle 1590), and the *Ze'enah u-Re'enah* (Tsenerene) by Jacob b. Isaac Ashkenazi (Lublin, 1616), a reworking of the Humash filled with edifying and instructive material drawn from the Talmud, the Midrash, and folklore, and the Sefer ha-Maggid by the same author (Lublin, 1623), and adaptation of the *Neviim and Hagiographia* with Rashi's *pirush*. *Ze'enah u-Re'enah*
th
appeared in many editions and served as a second Bible in the 19 century among East European Jews. It was translated into French by A. Kraehhaus in 1846 and a German version with introduction by A. Marmorstein was serialized in 1911. Mendel Lefin (of Satanow), produced a Yiddish version of Mishle (Tarnopol, 1817). I.L. Peretz (the 5 Scrolls, 1925) and Yehoash (Yiddish Bible, 1910) also were made. In 1929 Yehuda Leib (Zlotnick) Avida translated *Koheleth* into Yiddish.
See: Une traduction de la Bible en Yiddish, Baumgarten, Jean ; Bible de tous les temps VII (1986) 237-252; Reception and rejection of Yiddish renderings of the Bible., Turniansky, Chava The Bible in/and Yiddish (2007) 7-20, The Bible in/and Yiddish. Edited by Shlomo Berger. Amsterdam: Menasseh ben Israel Institute, 2007

393 See Levy, David B., The Making of the Jewish Encyclopedia (1901) and the Encyclopedia Judaica (1972), AJL Proceedings, Denver Conference; http://www.jewishlibraries.org/ajlweb/publications/proceedings/proceedi ngs2002/levy.pdf

394 Gersonides writes, "In this art (of rhetoric) one uses generally accepted premises, a characteristic of which in most cases is that one may find demonstrations on their basis for both a thing and its opposite, and it is therefore fitting that the mind of the researcher in it be so settled that it takes from these generally accepted premises true premises only. It is also proper that he not delve as deeply into this as he delves into the other sciences which may be delved into, for it is proper that the way of research in each science accord with the level of confirmation achievable in each. "If she be a wall/We will build upon her a turret of silver/ And if she be a door/ We will enclose her with boards of cedar (8:9)." They said that if she is enclosed with the enclosures fitting for one who wishes to commence the investigation of this science, then we will build upon her the building we are trying to build in the most perfect of ways. And if she be a door, that is, if she is broken open, without a wall, then we will enclose her with boards of cedar, that is, we will strengthen her and seal her breach with boards of cedar. "I am a wall/And my breasts like the towers thereof/Then was I in his eyes/As one that fund peace (8:10)." She said that she is a wall, that is, that she is enclosed, with no breach, and no going forth (Ps.144:14); her breasts, with which she emanates what she emanates, are like the strong towers of a city, which add considerably to its security. The meaning of this is that she will prepare from these premises only that which will guide to that which is correct in this science. (see Levi ben Gershom (Gersonides), *Commmentary on Song of Songs*, translated from the Hebrew by Menachem Kellner, New Haven: Yale University Press, Yale Judaica Series, p.92)

395 The Arabic text of that commentary with Hebrew translation was published by Halkin under the title *Hitgalut ha-Sodot ve-Hofa'at ha-Me'orot*. On ibn Aknin, a contemporary of Rambam, but not the Joseph ben Judah to whom Rambam addressed the Guide, and on his commentary on *Shir HaShirim* see Halkin, "Ibn Aknin's Commentary on the Song of Songs"; "The Character of R. Yosef ben Yehudah ibn Aknin"; and "History of the Forcible Conversion during the Days of the Almohades."

396 Sirat, Collete, History of Jewish Philosophy, 222

[397] This was published in Lyck in 1874 under the title *Perush 'al Shir ha-Shirim*.

[398] On Immanuel, see the introduction to *Mahberot Immanuel ha-Romi*, ed. Yarden, 11-19. Thenonphilosophical portions of Immanuel's commentary were published by Eschwege under the title *Der Kommentar zum Hohen Liede*. Immanuel's philosophical commentary was published and analyzed, and the subject of philosophic commentaries on *Shir HaShirim* summarized, in I. Ravitzky, "R. Immanuel b. Shlomo of Rome."

[399] bn Kaspi's brief comments were published with an English translation by Ginsburg in the Song of Songs, 47-49. Last also published the text in his edition of ibn Kaspi, `*Asarah Klei Kesef*, 183-84. See also Adele Berlin

[400] See Kellner, Menachem (trans.), Commentary on the Song of Songs by Levi ben Gershom (Gersonides), New Haven, Yale Univ. Press, Yale Judaica Series volume xxviii, 1998, p.xxi

[401] Ibid., p. 23.

[402] For rationalist philosophers like Gersonides it refers to the emanation of the material intellect on the other faculties of the soul.

[403] Discussion, 5/21/07, 1 p.m.

[404] see: Aggadata section in http://student.ccbcmd.edu/~dlevy11/kavka.htm

[405] The prayer is translated as, "The Almighty may be your will, my G-d and my father's G-d, that in the merit of *Shir HaShirim* that we have read and studied, that it is the holy of holies. In the merit of its verses, its subsections, letters, vowels, tropes, names, combinations, hints, secrets, holy secrets, purities, awesomeness that comes out before us. That will be this hour of mercy, hour serious pondering and listening, and will call you and you will answer us. Forgive you and you will forgive us. It should come before you the reading and study of *Shir Hashirim* as if merit the wondrous awesome secrets that are signed in it, and we will be able to find where the spirits/hosts that were created and as if we did what we were supposed to do to achieve reincarnations and the next reincarnations and to be able to raise and be meritorious to *olam habah* together with the *Tzadikim* and Hasidim and fulfill all what my heart desires to goodness and whatever we spoke in the time of our thoughts, and with our hands whatever we are enslaved, and He should send blessing and success, and *osher*, in all the doing of our hands, and He will pick us up from the dust, and He will find us and repair us, and he should return our Shekhinah to our holy city (Yerushalayim) soon in our days. Amen.

[406] The Ladino translation of the opening of the Zohar reveals much: *"Comme la roza entre los espinos ainsi mi conpanera entre las duenas."*

[407] See fourth to last paragraph for dbl's translation of the famous letter from Rambam to ibn Tibbon

[408] See: Sokol, Moshe, Rabbinic authority and personal autonomy, Orthodox Forum (1st : 1989: N.Y., N.Y.) Northvale: N.J.: J. Aronson, 1992; also see Rav Saadia Gaon in *Sefer Emunot veDeot* on "reliable tradition."

[409] Stereotyping can do violence to whole groups by homogenizing difference into a classified category that can lead to evils such as racial profiling. The etymology of stereotype as a noun: 1798, "method of printing from a plate," from French stéréotype (adj.) "printed by means of a solid plate of type," from Greek stereos "solid" (see stereo-) + French type "type" (see type (n.)). Meaning "a stereotype plate" is from 1817. Meaning "image perpetuated without change" is first recorded 1850, from the verb in this sense. Meaning "preconceived and oversimplified notion of characteristics typical of a person or group" is recorded from 1922. The etymology of stereotype as an adjective: 1804, "to cast a stereotype plate," from stereotype (n.). From 1819 in the figurative sense "fix firmly or unchangeably." By 1953 as "assign preconceived and oversimplified notion of characteristics typical of a person or group."

[410] McReynolds, Rosalee, "A Heritage Dismissed" in Library Journal 110, Nov. 1985, p. 25.

[411] Cravey, Pamela J., "Focusing on the Librarian: Are Librarians selling themselves?" in Georgia Librarian 27, summer 1990, p.28

[412] See: Barnhart, Linda "The Librarians' Stereotyped Image in Mystery Novels, 1980-1990: Has the Image changed?" Masters thesis Kent state University 1991; Long, Lucille, Eileen, "The Stereotyped Librarian as Portrayed in Modern American Belles-Letters, "Masters Thesis Kent State, 1957; Brewerton, Anthony, "There Be Dragons-And They are in Brown Cars", Librarian Association Record 94, August 1992, p. 514; O'Brien, Ann and Raish, Martin, "the image of the Librarian in Commercial Motion Pictures: An Annotated Filmography", Collection Management 17, 1993, p.61-84; Olen, Sandra, "The Image of Librarians in Modern Fiction", Mousaion 5 (1987), 48-57; Radford, Marie L, "Relational Aspects of Reference Interactions: A Qualitative Investigation f the Perceptions of Users and Librarians in Academic Libraries", PHD diss- Rutgers- The State University of NJ.

413 The idea of a lending library is relatively new. The great Universities such as Harvard, Princeton and Yale in the beginning of their collections did not lend but rather archivally gathered. The first lending public library was in 1890 in Cleveland in America. IT was the first to allow unrestricted access to all persons to al books at all times.

414 Sable, Arnold P., "The Sexuality of the Library Profession: The Male and Female Librarian", in Wilson Library Bulletin 43, April 1969, p.748

415 See Stephen King's The library Policeman, where the library is likened to the loneliness of the crypt. The imagery has some validity in the dark tomb like structures of 19th century libraries. King runs with this atomspheric morbidity and represents the library as the repository of dead discourse with moldering texts lined up and decaying like bodies in old coffins. Ghosts and spirits are encased within and ready to rise up if their silence is disturbed. There is a sign in the library on an easel which reads: SILENCE Like the children's cartoon the Pagemaster, the library is deserted but haunted by ghosts. This emptiness causes suspense and fear. Isaac Asimov's Forward the Freedom, also present the library as one a decay as if in a crypt.

416 Boorstin, Daniel J., Library: The Drama Within, Essay by Boorstin; photographs by Diane Asseo Grilliches, Albuquerque: Univ of New Mexico Press, 1996, p.107.

417 Cole, John Y, and Reed, Henry H, The Library of Congress: The Art and Architecture of the Jefferson Building, NY: Norton, 1997, p. 19

418 The NYPL has magnificent lions guarding its entrance. Donald Davidson notes that the stereotypical image of the libraries has evolved from image sof monumental structures of austere but imposing buildings guarded by lions or eagles or oversized concrete urns. (see Davidson, Donald, "Libraries-Relics or PRecusors? In Beyond Media" edited by Richard Budd and Brent D. Ruben, p. 138-59, New Brunswick: NJ, Transaction, p. 146)

[419] At the initial ALA meeting about 200 years ago only 13 women attended, a minority to their male counterparts. The first women library clerk was hired at the Boston public library in 1852, two years after ALA was established when two-thirds of library workers were female. According to Dee Garison in Apostles of Culture: The Public Librarian and American Society, 1876-1920," (Greenwood, 1986, p.13); Garison writes, "Educated women, while meeting resistance in the more established male professions flooded into library work during the last quarter of the 19th century…. Librarianship was quickly adjusted to fit the narrowly circumscribed sphere of women's activities, for it appeared similar to the work of the home, functioned as cultural activity, required no great skill or physical strength, and brought little contact with the rougher portions of society." Garison may be correct but with regards to "rougher portions of society most public librarians interact with such persons on a daily basis. Garison writers further, "Over time, the number of women continued to grow: by 1910, 78.5 % of library staff were women and by 1920 the number had risen to almost 90%. Due to the 1960s librarianship was transformed according to Garison from a feminized environment to a feminist profession. Norman Stevens notes that this trend is reversed with the recent phasing out of libraries and subsuming them under the auspices of IT departments. Stevens forecasts, "the newly appointed directors of information centers of all kinds were once again predominantly male. By 2050 the percentage of women in information centers had shrunken to just over 40% and had dropped slightly further by 2076" (The Last Librarian: In the Twilight of our Profession, a stereotype dies but her bun lives on", American Libraries, Oct. 2001, p.62). Roma Harris is alarmed by this reversal of a gendered female majority (see Harris, Roma M. Librarianship: The Erosion of a Woman's Profession, Nortwood NJ: Ablex 1992.) Roma notes that the history of the profession of librarianship cannot be understood ignoring that for more than 100 years library work in North America has been women's work (xiii). Abigail van Slyck points out that from the beginning of the 20th century a "highly gendered library hierarchy was in place in which women filled the majority of low-paying, low-prestige positions, and men dominated executive and management positions. (see Van Slyck, Abigai, Free to all : Carnagie Libraries and American Culture 1890-1920, Chicago: Univ of Chicago Press, 1995p. 164)

[420] Libraries are more than inert storehouses of written tradition; they are volatile spaces that actively shaped the meanings and uses of books, reading, and consciousness that evolves. They are spaces where conceptions of knowledge are created and grow. They are the crucibles in which knowledge is shaped
Jennifer Summit, Memory's Library

421 Title of DBL's dissertation thesis at Haverford College

422　See　https://networks.h-net.org/node/28655/reviews/30676/levy-kavka-jewish-messianism-and-history-philosophy

423 Leaves of Grass, Song of Myself, 1892; Interestingly Aaron Lichtenstein who was a literature Professor as well as Rosh Yeshivah authored a work, "Leaves of Faith" (Jersey City, NJ : KTAV Pub. House, c2003) which is a clear allusion to Whitman's Leaves of Grass, for anyone with a literature background.

424 In Jewish law it is forbidden to embarrass X in public. For example one may not recall to a proselyte that they are from idol worshipers:

כשם שאונאה במקח וממכר כך אונאה בדברים לא יאמר לו בכמה
חפץ זה והוא אינו רוצה ליקח אם היה בעל תשובה לא יאמר לו זכור
מעשיך הראשונים אם הוא בן גרים לא יאמר לו זכור
מעשה אבותיך שנאמר
(שמות כב)
וגר לא תונה ולא
תלחצנו

425 A Tanna taught the following Baraisa in the presence of Rav Nachman bar Yitzchak: if anyone makes his friend's face turn white from shame in public, it is as if he spilled blood ie. Murdered his friend. He Rav Nachman bar Yitzchak said to the Tanna-What you are saying is right-because I have seen how the red coloring leaves the face of an embarrassed person and his face turns white.

426 אמר דוד לפני הקדוש ברוך הוא: רבונו של עולם, גלוי וידוע לפניך
שאם היו מקרעים בשרי לא היה דמי שותת לארץ. ולא עוד, אלא אפילו
בשעה שעוסקין בנגעים ואהלות אומרים לי: דוד, הבא על אשת איש
מיתתו במה? - ואני אומר להם: מיתתו בחנק, ויש לו חלק לעולם
הבא, אבל המלבין את פני חבירו ברבים - אין לו חלק לעולם הבא.
(ואמר) +מסורת הש"ס: [אמר]+ מר זוטרא בר טוביה אמר רב, ואמרי
לה אמר רב חנא בר ביזנא אמר ...

427 Baba Metzia 59a notes with regards to the merit of Tamar: And Mar Zutrabar Toviyah said in the name of
Rav-and others say, it was Rav Chana bar Biznawho said in the name of R. Shimon Chasida; and others say it was R. Yochananwho said in the name of R. Shimon ben Yochai-It is better that a person cast himself into a fiery furnace-than that he should shame his fellow in public. From where do we know this? From TAMAR. For it is written: Asshe was taken out (to be executed) she sent to her father-in-law, Judah the pledges he had left with her, but she refused to shame him in public by naming him as the father of her child; See אמר מר זוטרא בר טוביה +[אמר] רב, ואמרי לה אמר רב חנא בר ביזנא אמר רבי שמעון חסידא, ואמרי לה אמר רבי יוחנן משום רבי שמעון בן יוחאי: נוח לו לאדם שיפיל עצמו לכבשן האש ואל ילבין פני חבירו ברבים. מנא לן - מתמר, דכתיב בהיא מוצאת והיא שלחה אל חמיה. אמר רב חננא בריה דרב אידי: מאי דכתיב גולא תונו איש את עמיתו - עם שאתך בתורה ובמצוות אל תוניהו. אמר רב: לעולם יהא אדם זהיר באונאת ...

428 They that have power to hurt and will do none,
That do not do the thing they most do show,
Who, moving others, are themselves as stone,
Unmoved, cold, and to temptation slow,
They rightly do inherit heaven's graces
And husband nature's riches from expense;
They are the lords and owners of their faces,
Others but stewards of their excellence.
The summer's flower is to the summer sweet,
Though to itself it only live and die,
But if that flower with base infection meet,
The basest weed outbraves his dignity:
For sweetest things turn sourest by their deeds;
Lilies that fester smell far worse than weeds.

[429] In the film UHF features Conan the Librarian who resorts to violence against his library patrons in humiliating them. In one scene a patron asks Conan "Can you tell me where I can find a book on astronomy?". Conan graps the patron by the scruff of the neck and in an Arnold Schwarzenegger like voice Conan says, "Don't you know the Dewey Decimal System!. When a book is late with returning a library book, the patron timidly says, "Sorry these books are a little overdue." Conan promptly resorts to slicing the boy in two.

[430] Van Slyck, Abigail A., Free to All: Canegie Libraries and American Culture, 1890-1920, Chicago: Chicago Univ Press, 1995, p.210.

[431] Dickson, Paul, The Library in America: A Celebration in Words and Pictures, NY: Facts on File, 1986, p.1

[432] Mumby, Dennis K., "Feminism and the Critique of Organizational Communication Studies", In Communciation yearbook 16, edited by Stanley Deetz, Newbury Park, Calif: Sage, 1993, p. p.157

[433] Ivy, Barbara A, "Identity, Power, and Hiring in a Feminized Profession," Library Trends 34, Fall 1985, p. 292.

[434] Hawkesworth, M. E. Beyond Oppression: Feminist Theory and Political Strategy, NY: Continuum Press, 1990.

[435] See Hunter, Mary, isualizing Medical Masculinities In Late Nineteenth-Century Paris, Manchester,
Manchester University Press, 2016; Review by David B Levy in Journal of the History of Medicine and Allied Sciences, Volume 73, Issue 2, 1 April 2018, Pages 227–229, https://doi.org/10.1093/jhmas/jrx009

[436] Hannigan, Jane Anne, and Crew, Hillary, "A Femiist Paradigm for Library and Info science", Wilson Library Bulletin 67, Oct 1992, p. 31

[437] See Garrett, Jeffrey, "Missing Eco: On Reading The Name of the Rose as Library Criticism," Library Quarterly 61, Oct 1991, p. 373-88

[438] On the nature of the monastery library as a holy space see Bede: Cunctum vite tempus in ejusdem Monaster ii habit atione peragens^ omnem meditandis Scripturis operam dedi ; atque inter observantiam disciplinse regularis et quotidianam cantandi in ec- clesia curam, semper aut discere, aut docere, aut scribere dulce habui." — ' All my life I spent in that same Monastery, giving my whole attention to the study of the Holy Scriptures, and in the intervals between the hours of regular discipline and the duties of singing in the church, I took pleasure in learning, or teaching, or writing something."
Bede Historia ecclesiastica v. 2

[439] Eco, Umberto, The Name of the Rose, trans. By William Weaver, NY: Warner, 1983, p. 75-76.

[440] Eco, Umberto, The Name of the Rose, translated by William Weaver, NY: Warner, 1983, p 35-36.

[441] Consider Paulus of Nola's remark, Si quem sancta tenet meditandi in lege voluntas Hic poterit residens sacris intendere libris. [Here he whose thoughts are on the laws of God May sit and ponder over holy books.]

442 Consider the letter of Lupus Servati : Amor litterarum ab ipso fere initio pueritiae mihi est innatus, nec earum, ut nunc a plerisque uocantur, superstitiosa uel [superuacua] otia fastidiui; et nisi intercessisset inopia praeceptorum et longo situ collapsa priorum studia pene interissent, largiente deo meae auiditati satisfacere forsitan potuissem; siquidem uestra memoria per famosissimum imperatorem K[arolum], cui litterae eo usque deferre debent ut aeternam ei parent memoriam, coepta reuocari, aliquantum quidem extulere caput satisque constitit ueritate subnixum praeclarum Cic[eronis] dictum: honos alit artes et accenduntur omnes ad studia gloria. Nunc oneri sunt qui aliquid discere affectant; et uelut in editio sitos loco studiosos quosque imperiti uulgo aspectantes, si quid in eis culpae deprehenderunt, id non humano uitio, sed qualitati disciplinarum assignant. Ita, dum alii dignam sapientiae palmam non capiunt, alii famam uerentur indignam, a tam praeclaro opere destiterunt. Mihi satis apparent propter se ipsam appetenda sapientia (Lupus Servati Lupi epistulae [SLE] 1).

443 The libraries association with a discourse of fear is also found in novels besides Umberto Eco such as (1) Isaac Asimov's *Forward the Foundation*, (2) William Styron's *Sophie's Choice*, (3) Stephen King's *The Library Policeman*, and motion pictures such as (1) Part Girl, (2) UHF, (3) *The Pagemaster*, (4) Seinfeld etc.; In the animated children's film *The Pagemaster* the image of the library is foreboding. Richie Tyler rides his bike to pick up nails from a hardware store and crashes his bike into a tree. Looking up, he sees a large and imposing granite building with arches guarded by lions that appear to roar at him in the thunder of rain storm. The library is described as a "mysterious place." The library exists in another dimension from Richie's world signified by the passage through a tunnel. The library has the aura of a religious mystery of a high ceilinged cathedral, marble staircases, and rows of statues, shrouded in "huge eerie shadows." Richie is afraid of getting lost in the labyrinth.;

444 Eco, Umberto, The Name of the Rose, translated by William Weaver, NY: Warner, 1983, p..36

[445] Eco, Umberto, The Name of the Rose, trans. By William Weaver, NY: Warner, 1983, p.73; The image of the librarian as stern potentate is a motif in literature and film.Stephen King in the Library Policeman presents an image of an "ill-natured librarian... swooping out of the main room to see who had dared profane the silence." This is in conformity with Newark Star Ledger's which depicts librarians "who prowl the stacks shushing noisy readers or confisgating snacks." (see Kunkie, Frederick, and Sara Treflinger, "Good to the Last Page: Libraries try cafes to Lure Readers," NJ Start Ledger, June 12, 1998, p. 1)

[446] Eco, Umberto, The Name of the Rose, trans. By William Weaver, NY: Warner, 1983, p.89; The description fo the monk who went mad at night in the library seeing things, resonates lihavdil, to the arba sheniknasu biPardes, where Ben Zoma ate too much honey as is reported to say upon emerging "the distance between the 1st rakiah and 2nd rakia is a dove's wings beating...." Ben Azzai cut the shoots and went mad. Aher became a Greek philosopher. See: (*Chagiga* 14b, *Zohar* I, 26b and *Tikunei Zohar*, Tikun 40: The Rabbis taught: Four [Sages] entered the *Pardes* [literally "the orchard."]. Rashi explains that they ascended to heaven by utilizing the [Divine] Name [i.e., they achieved a spiritual elevation through intense meditation on Gd's Name] (*Tosafot, ad loc*). They were Ben Azzai, Ben Zoma, Acher [Elisha ben Avuya, called Acher— the other one — because of what happened to him after he entered the *Pardes*] and Rabbi Akiva. Rabbi Akiva said to them [prior to their ascension]: "When you come to the place of pure marble stones, do not say, 'Water! Water!' for it is said, 'He who speaks untruths shall not stand before My eyes' (*Psalms* 101:7)." Ben Azzai gazed [at the Divine Presence - *Rashi*] and died. Regarding him the verse states, "Precious in the eyes of Gd is the death of His pious ones" (*Psalms* 116:15). Ben Zoma gazed and was harmed [he lost his sanity — *Rashi*]. Regarding him the verse states, "Did you find honey? Eat only as much as you need, lest you be overfilled and vomit it up" (*Proverbs* 25:16). Aher cut down the plantings [he became a heretic]. Only Rabbi Akiva entered in peace and left in peace. ; Thus perhaps we can see the library as a bastion or refuge of order giving sanity to the chaos of multivocal and diverse opinions in a state of uncrontrolable nature where Hobbes holds life is nasty brutish and short. The library is a fortress that wards off chaos or insanity. The ordered stacks hold at bay the mad chaos of uncontrollable discourse. This Foucaultian paradigm can tend to lead to the stereotype of the 1) library as refuge, fortress, and cathedral (see Name of the Rose), (2) the humiliation of the patron (see Sophie's Choice episode), and (3) the library policeman (see Seinfeld episode)

447 Consider Alcuin's remark, O quam dulcis vita fuit dum sedebamus in quieti ... inter librorum copias."
'Oh how sweet life was when we sat quietly ... midst all these books.'
Alcuin Ep. Xxii

448 DeCandido, GraceAnne, "Bibliographic Good vs. Evil", in Media section of American Libraries, Sept 1999, p. 46

449 Styron, William, Sohpie's Choice, New York : Random House, 1979, p. 103

450 Swope, Mary Jo, and Katzer Jeffrey, "The Silent Majority: Why Don't they ask Questions?, RQ 12 , 1972, p. 161-66.

451 King, Stephen, "The Library Policeman" In Four Past Midnight, by Stephen King, p. 405-604, NY: Viking 1990 p.386.

452 Ibid, p. 386.

453 King, Stephen- "The Library Policeman" In Four Past Midnight by SK, NY: Viking, 1990, 428.

454 King, Stephen, "The Library Policeman" in Four Past Midnight, by SK, NY: Viking, 1990, 488-89.

455 https://www.bing.com/images/search?view=detailV2&ccid=2aRQw5L9&id=105E8983404A17B6B116FDE0C68255ED0AB859D5&thid=OIP.2aRQw5L9_Wbgf4ERM7gXZgAAAA&mediaurl=https%3a%2f%2fcdn.shopify.com%2fs%2ffiles%2f1%2f0615%2f0537%2fproducts%2fstatues-librarian-man-made-out-of-books-portrait-of-wolfgang-lazius-by-arcimboldo-6h-ar04-3_large.jpeg%3fv%3d1509909119&exph=480&expw=356&q=image+man+made+out+of+books&simid=607989483399613247&selectedIndex=4&ajaxhist=0

456 Edmund Lester Pearson, The Librararian (Scarecrow, 1976) p. 25-26

457 Stevens, Norman D., "The Last Librarian: In the Twilight of our Profession, a Stereotype dies but her Bun lives on", in American Libraries, Oct 2001, p. 62

458 In reality Foucault does not understand that fact that patrons have a right to a quiet study area to concentrate and do their research and studying. Some people cannot concentrate if loud discussions abound. Thus the library has a duty to provide a quiet study area out of respect so that students can focus and do their work. What Foucault seems to be advocating for in place of the quiet monastery like sanctum silencio is a kind of Beit Midrash alive with the buz, hum, and loud arguments of buckrim in Talmudic debate fighting the wars of Hashem which are the makloket in the Talmud with the swords of pilpul. Focualt's theory of the library as suppressing such lively discussion is not necessarily true, as librarians owe it to their patrons to have a quiet contemplative atmosphere out of basic respect for fellow students who may require silence to focus in the silent zone of the library. However the popular wrong stereotype of the librarian as merely shushing patrons with no more important duties is comically portrayed in the Saturn car commercial which the ALA took upon itself as a crusade to deconstruct as leading to the bad image of librarians.

459 Manley, Will, "On Facing the Public." Wilson Library Bulletin 34, 1984, p.630

460 Crowell, Penny, "Not All in the Mind: The Virile Profession." Library Review 29, Autumn 1980, p.167-75

[461] Stevens, Norman D., "The Last Librarian: In the Twilight of our Profession, a Stereotype dies but her Bun lives on", in American Libraries, Oct 2001, p. 62; Stevens article speaks to the librarian in the past tense. His concluding "eulogy" is: Librarians have offered a great deal to the development of American society over the past 200 years. Their contributions should not be forgotten. During the time they flourished they helped shape the collection, organization, dissemination, use and preservation of information resources in a period that saw both the incredible and at times exponential growth of those resources as well as- especially in the second hundred years- a total transformation of information formats. Indeed with out the continuing guidance of librarians the information structure of society might well have collapsed (p.63).

[462] Morrisey, Locke J, and Case, Donald O, "There Goes MY Image: The Perception of Male Librarians by Colleague, Student, and Self", College & Research Libraries 49, 1988, 453-64; Carmichael, James V, "The Male Librarian and the Feminine Image: A Survey of Stereotypes, Status, and Gender Perceptions", Library and Information Science Research 14, Oct-Dec 1992, 411-46

[463] Agada, John, "Studies of the Personality of Librarians," Drexel Library Quarterly 20, Spring 1984, 25-45; Paul, Meg and Evans, Jennifer, "The Librarians Self Starter: 100s of Questions to Challenge Your Thinking about Your Image, The Profession's Image, Your Job, and Your Future- A Manual for Concerned Librarians, Camberwell, Australia: Freelance Library and Information Services 1988 (Bethesda MD: ERIC Document, Reproduction Service).

[464] Wallace, Linda, "The Image- And What You Can do About it in the Year of the Librarian", American Libraries 20 (Jan 1989, p. 22-25.

[465] See Wiegand, Wayne, "Tunnel Vision and Blind Spots: What the past tells us about the present- Reflections on the 20th century history of American Librarianship", in The Library Quarterly: Information, Community, Policy, vol 69, no. 1 Jan. 199, p.1-32; Wayne writes, " Absent from the discourse driving this field however are the kinds of questions critical theorists such as Michel Foucault, Antonio Gramsci, and Jurgen Habermas, and philosophers of science such as Helen Longino, Margaret Jacob, and Sandra Harding ask about connections between power and knowledge, which all agree is never totally objective and never disinterested (p. 23).

[466] Foucault, Michel, "The Discourse on Language," trans. By Rupert Swyer, in The Archaeology of Knowledge, by M. Foucault, trans. By A.M Sheridan Smith: NY Pantheon, 1972

[467] Sawicki, Jana, "Foucault, Feminism, and Questions of Identity", in the Cambridge Companion to Foucault, edited by Gary Gutting, NY : Cambridge University, 1994, 310.

[468] Some of the goals of feminist philosophy are (1) to cognize why women are suppressed, repressed, and or oppressed in ways that men are not, and (2) suggest morally desirable and politically feasible ways to give woment he same justice, freedom, and equality men have. See Audi, Robert, ed, The Cambridge Dictionary of Philosophy, Cambridge: Cambridge Univ Press, 1995

[469] Diamond, Irene, and Quinby Lee, eds. Feminism and Foucault: Reflections on Resistance, Boston: Northeastern University Press, 1988, p.x

[470] Harris, Roma M, Librarianship: The Erosion of a Woman's Profession. Norwood NJ: Ablex, 1992.

[471] Foucault, Michel, "The Discourse on language" trans. Rupert Swyer, in Michel Foucault, And Archaeology of knowledge , NY: Pantheon, p. 228

[472] De Beauvoir, Simone, Le Deuxieme Sex, New York : Alfred A. Knopf, 1993

[473] Marshall, Judi, "Viewing Organizational Communication from a Feminist Perspectice: A Critique and Some Offerings", in Communication Yearbook 16, edited by Stanley Deetz, Newbury Park: California: Sage, 1993, p130.

[474] See Gilligin, Carol, In a Different Voice, In a different voice : psychological theory and women's development, Cambridge: Harvard Univ Press, 1982

[475] Harris, Michael, "The Purpose of the American Public Library"'" in Library Journal 98, Sept. 1973, p.2509.

[476] Walsh, D P, "On Fire, On Ice" Prefatory Remarks on the library in literature, Reference Librarian 18, 1987, p. 211-38; Castillo DebraA The Translated World: A Post-modern Tour of Libraries in Literature, Tallahasee: Florida State Univ Press, 1984

[477] Consider for instance Vor Dem Gesetz, where an authoritative Tuhrhuter or gatekeeper prevents K. from proceeding further to the palace hierarchical structure. Perhaps the gatekeeper would be seen by Foucault as the representative of controlling logocentric discursive hegemonic control. We read: "Vor dem Gesetz steht ein Turhuter. Zu diesem Turhuter kommt ein Mann vom Lande und bittet um Eintritt in das Gesetz. Aber der Turhuter sagt, dass er ihm jetzt den Eintritt nicht gewahren konne. Der Mann uberlegt und fragt dann, ob er also spatter werde eintreten durfen. `Es ist moeglich, sagt der Turhuter, jetzt aber nicht. Da das Tor zum Gesetz offensteht wie immer und der Turhuter beiseite tritt, buckt sich der Mann, um durch das Tor in das Innere zu sehen. Als der Turhuter das merkt, lacht er und sagt: `Wenn es dich so lockt, versuche es doch trotz meines Verbotes hineinzugehen. Merke aber: Ich bin machtig. Und ich bin nur der unterste Turhuter. Von Saal zu Saal stehen aber Turhuter, einer machtiger als der andere. Schon den Anblick des dritten kann nicht einmal ich mehr ertragen.' Solche Schwierigkeiten hat der Mann vom Lande nicht erwartet; das Gesetz soll doch jedem und immer zuganglich sein, denkt er, aber als er jetzt den Turhuter in seinem Pelzmantel genauer ansieht, seine grosse Spitznase, den langen, dunnen, schwarzen tatarischen Bart, entschliesst er sich, doch lieber zu warten, bis er die Erlaubnis zum Eintritt bekommt. Der Turhuter gibt ihm einen Schemel und lasst ihn seitwarts von der Tur sich niedersetzen. Dort sitzt er Tage und Jahre. Er macht viele Versuche, eingelassen zu werden, und ermudet den Turhuter durch seine Bitten. Der Turhuter stellt ofters kleine Verhore mit ihm an, fragt ihn uber seine Heimat aus und nach vielem anderen, es sind aber teilnahmslose Fragen, wie sie grosse Herren stellen, und zum Schlusse sagt er ihm immer wieder, dass er ihn noch nicht einlassen konne. See Jacques Derrida, "Devant la Loi," in Kafka and the Contemporary Critical Performance (Bloomington and Indianapolis: Indiana Univeristy Press, 1987), pp. 128-150. When Morgan notes that Scholem treats Kafka as a neo-Kabbalist, giving new readings of revelation" (p. 67) we cannot help asking if Scholem would view the gatekeeper of "Vor Dem Gesetz" as analogous to mystical descriptions of various angels as archons of differing rank, who guard the heavenly halls of the seven heavens?

[478] See Pawel, Ernst, The Nightmare of reason, New York : Farrar, Straus, Giroux, 1984

[479] Adorno, Theodor, The authoritarian Personality, New York : Norton, 1982

[480] Ophir, Adi, "A Place of knowledge Re-created: The Library of Michel de Montaigne", Science in Context 4, 1991, p.164

[481] Castillo, Debra A, The translated World: A Postmodern tour of libraries in Literature, Tallahasse Florida State Univ. Press, 1984.

[482] See Foucault, Michel, "Fantasia of the Library" in Language, Counter Memory, Practice: Selected Essays and Interview, edited by Donald F Bouchard, trans. By Donald Bouchard and Sherry Simon, Ithaca: NY, Cornell Univ. Press, 1977

[483] Foucault, Michel, "The Discourse on Language, " Translated by Rupert Swyer. In the Archaeology of Knwoledge, trans by A.M. Sheridan Smith, NY: Pantheon, 1972

[484] Radford, Gary P & Maie L Radford, "Libraries, Librarians, and the Discourse of Fear", in The Library Quarterly, vol 71, no. 3, July 2001, p.299.

[485] Garrett, Jeffrey, "Missing Eco: On Reading the Name of the Rose as Library Criticism," Library Quarterly 61, Oct. 1991, p. 373-88

[486] Foucault, Michel, Power/Knowledge: Selected Interview and Other Writings, 1972-1977, Edited by Colin Gordon, NY:Pantheon, 1980

[487] Radford, Gary P and Marie L Radford, "Libraries, Librarians, and the Discourse of Fear," The Library Quarterly: Information, Community, Policy vol 71, no. 3, Jul 2001, p.304

[488] See: Kuhn, Thomas, The Structure of Scientific Revolutions, Chicago: Univ. of Chicago, 1970

[489] Nietzsche, Friederick, On the Genealogy of Morals: a polemic : by way of clarification and supplement to my last book, Beyond good and evil, Oxford: Oxford University Press, 2008

[490] Foucault, Michel, Discipline and Punish: The Birth of the Prison, trans by A. Sheridan, NY: Vintage Books, 1979

[491] Foucault, Michel, The History of Sexuality, vol 1: An Introduction, trans. By Robert Hurley, NY: Vintage Books, 1980

492 Heidegger, Martin, *Sein und Zeit herausgegeben von Thomas Rentsch*. Klassiker auslegen Bd 25, 2001

493 The doctrine of sabbatical worlds and the "grand Yovel" was developed extensively in the writings of the Kabbalists of Gerona, specifically R. Ezra and Nachmanides. According to the Ramban each world is destined like the one we presently live in, to exist for 7 millennia. There are ultimately seven worlds, paralleling the years of Yovel. In addition each world with it seven millennia parallels the Kabbalistic idea of 7 lower sefirot, from Hesed to Malchut, which represent the natural world and it is the natural world and Ecotheology that is the subject of S's book. The Jubilee year in Kabbalistic terms parallels the sefirah of binah, called the 50th gate (see Bar Yochai hymn below), which ist he beginning fo the hidden sefirot and represents the idea of ultiamate redemption (also found in DSS). This is what Ramban means when he writes, "and possibly this is what our rabbis hinted at when they said 50 gates of intelligence were created". there are 49 thousand years which comprise these 7 worlds and are then followed by supernal Yovel. All this is based on the gemarah interpreting the pusek in Tehillim, "a thousand years in your sight O Hashem, as as but yesterday etc." Thereby the gemarah likens each creation day to 1000 years. Rabbi Isaac of Acre a talmid of the Ramban adds clarity to Ramban's hints of the secret of 50, or the Doctrine of the sabbatical worlds. Rabbi Isaac writes:
You should know that as the Jubilee in one generation is 50 years, in thousand generations you have fifty thousand years. This what King David said, "The promise he gave for a 1000 generations" (Ps 105:8) [and wa also read] "who keeps his covenant faithfully to the 1000s generation (Deut. 7:9). And this is the ORDER of the Sabbatical and Jubilee years about which it says, "and each man shall return to his lot (Lev. 25:12), that all shall return to the Jubilee which is the foundation (yesod) and the believer shall keep silent. And the scholar said, "all was from the Siva Rishona and all will return to Siva Rishona, and this secret now explains the meaning of Shemita and the Yovel years.
Rabbi Isaac of Acre goes on to explain that "one millennia laid waste" means there will be an absence of human and animal life, but then be reinstated and during the 7th cycle o the 7th world of world(s) then the "time of life" will be "remembered" (by Hashem) for renewal etc. That is with Rabbi Issac of Acre the phrase "it will lie destroyed" refers tot he 7th millennia of the 7th millennial cycle. This does not contradict Koheleth' remark "Dor holekh ve dor halakh ve Haretz laOlam omedet." The world as Koheleth asserts will remain and this is in conformity with Rambam's agreement in this case with Aristotle's cosmology.The Mikubalim of 16th C Safed interpret dor holekh ve dor bah ve haaretz olam omadet as a remez to gilgulim. However the earlier 13th century Mikubal Rabbi Menachem Recanti writes:
One millennium it will be destroyed does not mean that the world will return to the tohu vavohu of the beginning of beginings as in the year of the Jubilee. Rather the meaning of destroyed (haruv) is without man animal and other creatures. And all things composed of the 4 elements will return to their fundamental state.
Recanti explains that is only during the "GRAND Yovel" (after the existence of the 7 successive worlds), and not at the endof every Sabbatical (after the 7 millennia of each world), that all of creation returns to the primordial state of being qua Being
The 13th century Rabbi Bahya ben Asher, a student of the Rashba commenting on Shemita in Vayikra interprets "sod" along the lines of Ramban and again affirms that the pusek does not contradict the doctrine of Sabbatical years writing:
They all hint to the length of the world's existence as it indicates in the beginning of Koheleth "ve ha-aretz olam omadet"(Eccl 1:4) which is the secret hint to the GRAND YOVEL. The world "forever (le-olam) refers to the GRAND YOVEL which is also called OLAM related to Olmayah and Olamut. There is the secret of the 50 gates of binah through which the world was created, and all of them were revealed to Moses save one (gate)... This means that Moseh was taught of every millennium which parallels each gate of intelligence, and that he was told of all of Eksistence (yeshmut, il y a , es gibt, SHAM) from beginning to the end (telos) except for the Holy GRANd Final Yovel which is the 50th gate, the innermost gate of total binah etc.
Rabbi Bahya is suggesting the plan of Hashem who sees past,present, future, and even transcends modalities of time, to a "time" of total Shabbos and eternal perpetual rest. This is the world to come (that will become manifest) after the tiyhayat hameytim. according to Rav Baycha the 7th millennia of each of the 7 words, has its own resspetive messianic era, tichayat maytim, and olam-ha ba. Since in this world to come the spiritual (non corporeal, agreement with Rambam - ayn lo Demuth haguf ve-eino guf) dominates the material and soul dominates the body, the material is considered as if "destroyed" or at least totally subjected to ruchanit.
Rabbi Judah Hayyat (1450-1510) citing Ramban and Recanti explains that one millennium of destruction does not imply a total destruction of the earth (ha-aretz). the 7th millennium is necessary because of the Talmud's insistence that" the son of David shall not come until all the souls have merged from their Abode (and have been brought into physical existence, as according to Hazal's teachings of the souls at Har Sinai). Al the souls must emerge before the 7th millennium. The 7th mlllenium is not a physical state in agreement with the rationalist the Rambam. Then only existing souls continue for its duration and go from one spiritual state to another. Recanti explains that each new world is better than the previous one as developed in Ma'arekhet Ha-Elohut from te 14th c and ascribed to REbbenu Peretz.
Each of the 7 worlds exist for 1000 years because each world has a sevenfold cycle, that is the seven worlds that parallel the seven upper celestial worlds for each sefirah is called "a world" and there are 49 years of the Yovel which are the 49 thousand (years of all the 7 worlds). If each world corresponds to one of the sefirot from hesed to malchut, the question arise which cycle are we in now? The author of Sefer ha-Temunah claims that we are in the 2nd world corresponding to gevurah, a world in whih the attributes of stern judgment-truth-din is dominant in the emanation from the distant gardens of the sefirot according to rav Isaac of Acre in hs work Sefer Yezirah.
The complexity of Shemitah and yovel in halakhah and Jewish mysticism is very difficult. Its reception history is even more complex in the works of Rav Don Isaac Abarbanel, R. Judah Hayyat and later mikubalim of 15th C. safed including the Mehaber Rav Karo who touches on the subject in Maggid Mesharim, the mystical dream diary where the Mishnah personified as the shekhinah gave over sod-torah. Rabbi Moses Cordovero (Ramak) mentions the doctrine of sabbatical years alied with Yovel in his Shiur Komah as well as in Eilima Rabbati. As late as 1842 Rabbi Lipschutz in Or ha-hayim discusses the concept of Sabbatical secreds and Grand Yovel relating to the afterlife in Talmudic sources. To prove and demonstrate from tradition the existence of these past worlds he introduces further interpretation on the doctrine of sabbatical worlds we find in the Gerona circle moving forward and later weighed into with discussion by Rabbi Elijah Benamozegh, Rav Shimshon Raphael Hirsch, Rabbi Shem Tov Gefen, and Rav Kook.
Thus the topic of Shemita and Yovel are inextricably bound in halakhah and al pi kabbalah as the blue print not only for the 49 days of counting (sefirat ha-omer) but indeed the paradigm of the history of the world(S). I say worlds because the 7 worlds of the Mikubalim are intricately related to such a radically concise formulation in the hymn of the Rashbi song on Lag b'omer in reference to the secret of 7 weeks which lead to the secret of the 5th gate of understanding (bina).

494 Consider Francis Bacon's remark, Libraries are as the shrines where all the reliques of the ancient saints, full of true virtue, and that without delusion or imposture, are preserved, and reposed."

[495] The Tashbaz writes in his intro to Zohar HaRakia, "However when the wise man lies down [in death] with his fathers, he leaves behind him a treasured and organized blessing: books that enlighten like the brilliance of the firmament (Daniel 12:3) and that extend peace like a river (Isa. 66:12)"

[496] Foucault, Michel, "What is an Author?" Trans by Donal F Bouchard and Sherry Simon. In Language, Counter-Memory, Practice: Selected essays and Interviews, ed. Donald Bouchard, Cornell Univ Press, 1977

497 In Xanadu did Kubla Khan
A stately pleasure-dome decree:
Where Alph, the sacred river, ran
Through caverns measureless to man
   Down to a sunless sea.
So twice five miles of fertile ground
With walls and towers were girdled round;
And there were gardens bright with sinuous rills,
Where blossomed many an incense-bearing tree;
And here were forests ancient as the hills,
Enfolding sunny spots of greenery.
But oh! that deep romantic chasm which slanted
Down the green hill athwart a cedarn cover!
A savage place! as holy and enchanted
As e'er beneath a waning moon was haunted
By woman wailing for her demon-lover!
And from this chasm, with ceaseless turmoil seething,
As if this earth in fast thick pants were breathing,
A mighty fountain momently was forced:
Amid whose swift half-intermitted burst
Huge fragments vaulted like rebounding hail,
Or chaffy grain beneath the thresher's flail:
And mid these dancing rocks at once and ever
It flung up momently the sacred river.
Five miles meandering with a mazy motion
Through wood and dale the sacred river ran,
Then reached the caverns measureless to man,
And sank in tumult to a lifeless ocean;
And 'mid this tumult Kubla heard from far
Ancestral voices prophesying war!
  The shadow of the dome of pleasure
  Floated midway on the waves;
  Where was heard the mingled measure
  From the fountain and the caves.
It was a miracle of rare device,
A sunny pleasure-dome with caves of ice!

498 Borges, Jorge Luis, "The Library of Babel," trans by James E Irby in Labyrinths: Selected stories and other writings, edited by Donald Yates and James Irby Norfolk Conn.: New Directions Books 1962, p.54-55.

499 Hall, Alison, "Batgirl was a Librarian", Canadian Library Journal 49, 1992, p. 345

500 Borges, Jorge Luis, "The Library of Babel," trans by James E Irby in Labyrinths: Selected stories and other writings, edited by Donald Yates and James Irby Norfolk Conn.: New Directions Books 1962, p..56

501 https://secure.server101.com/gnosisny/Tree_of_Life_Diagram_with_names.jpg

[502] Rambam's negation of the corporeality of the Deity as the first criticism in the following list of attacks Rambam faced from anti-Maimonidists: (1) le'enseignement de Mainonide sur l'absolue incorporalite de Dieu; (2) ses theories sur la prophetic ramenee a une vision; (3) sa tendance a restreindre le champ du miracle; (4) sa negation des demons; (5) sa reduction des anges au role de monteurs des Spheres celestes; (6) les interpretations spiritualistes qu'il avait donnees du Paradis et L'enfer; (7) les motifs qu'il avait ass ignes aux precepts religieux (mitsvot); (8) l'alegorization des recites bibliques a laquelle se livraient ses disciples; (9) le dedain qu'ils auraient affiche a l'egard des Sages du Talmud; (9) le relachement de la pratique religieuses qu'on croyait constater chez eux et don't on imputait la responsibilite a l'etude de la philosophie. . see Touati, *"les Deux Conflicts Autour de Maimonide et des Etudes Philosophiques"*. In <u>Juifs et Judaisme de Languedoc</u>. Edouard Privat editeur, Cahiers de Fanjeaux, 174 ;

The rabbinic community objected to *Sefer HaMadah*, for Maimonides placed among the five categories of heretics. Those who believed that the creator was corporeal. [10] The *Midrashim* give accounts of great banquets in *Olam HaBah*, where the righteous will partake of the most delicious foods and wines, while the wicked gaze on with their hands tied, forbidden to partake. Rambam in *Hilkot Teshuvah* and elsewhere proclaims that there is no eating, drinking, or anything corporeal in *Olam HaBah* but the righteous sit with crowns on the heads enjoying the light of the *Shechinah*. The crowns represent the wisdom, understanding, and knowledge gained in this world, including for the Rambam scientific learning such as philosophy and medicine. Rambam rejects a corporeal Creator espoused in works such as *Shi'ur Qomah*[12], as encapsulatred by *Yigdal's* proclamation, *"Ain Lo Demut HaGuf VeAino Guf"*

503 Only the Kohen Gadol was allowed to pronounce the name of G-d in the holy of holies in the Temple only on one day of Yom Kippur. It is said that Moses killed the task master according to Rashi by utterance of the secret name of God and likewise David killed Goliath by knowledge of this name. David evokes the name of the God of the hosts of Israel when saying to Goliath: וַיֹּאמֶר דָּוִד, אֶל-הַפְּלִשְׁתִּי, אַתָּה בָּא אֵלַי, בְּחֶרֶב וּבַחֲנִית וּבְכִידוֹן; וְאָנֹכִי בָא-אֵלֶיךָ, בְּשֵׁם יְהוָה צְבָאוֹת, אֱלֹהֵי מַעַרְכוֹת יִשְׂרָאֵל, אֲשֶׁר חֵרַפְתָּ. So too the concept of name is evoked in the Kail malei Rachamim prayer where the souls in Gan Eden are referred to as "shining names in heaven".

504 Merkavah is also found in Mishneh: Megillah 4:10; Toseftta: Meg 3(4):28, 34, BT: Ber. 21b, Shabb 80b, Sukk 28a (BB134a), Meg 24b, 31a.

505 It is a matter of debate whether the Rabbinic tradition (see TB Hagigah13a) may link ma'aseh merkavah and ma'aseh bereishit together based on the following passage from seder Olam Rabbah (ed Milkovsky p. 445) where we read, "He reveals the deep and secret things (Dan 2:22) deep that is the depths of the merkavah and secret that is the secrets of ma'aseh bereishit.

506 Although religious authorities feared that "la philosophie est responsible du retachement de la pratique religieuse" ; see Touati, "*les Deux Conflicts Autour de Maimonide et des Etudes Philosophiques*". In Juifs et Judaisme de Languedoc. Edouard Privat editeur, Cahiers de Fanjeaux, 174

[507] אין דורשין בעריות בשלשה ולא במעשה בראשית בשנים ולא במרכבה ביחיד אלא אם כן היה חכם ומבין מדעתו כל המסתכל בארבעה דברים ראוי לו כאילו לא בא לעולם מה למעלה מה למטה מה לפנים ומה לאחור וכל שלא חס על כבד קונו ראוי לו שלא בא לעולם: " The subject of the merkavah found in M. Hag. 2:1 is found futher in Tosefta (T. Hag. 2:1-7) and in the gemara to this mishneh in Yerushalmi (Hag. 77a-d) and in Bavli (Hag. 1 1b-16a). These texts presume the dangers of this esoteric subject, for according to M. Hag. 2:1 merkavah may not be expounded (**en doresin bammerkavah**) except under special circumstances, and according to Megillah 4:10 it may not be used a derasha in the synagogue (**en maftirin hammerkavah**)."

[508] the main fear of Jewish religious authorities appears to be direct revelation of secrets. Teaching in writing, to be differentiated from oral teaching, the secrets of the Tanakh (i.e. *ma'aseh merkavah16, ma;aseh bereshit17, prophetology18, angelology19, Sitre Torah* as contradictions of th Torah 2, etc)21 is forbidden by orah law. For example, Mishneh Hagigah 2: 1 reads, *"En doresin ba'arayot biselosah welo bema'aseh beresit bisenayim welo bammerkabah beyahid ella im ken haya hakham wehebin midda 'ato. Kol hammistakkel be'arba'ah debarim ratuy 10 ke'illu lo ba la olam mah lema'lan umah lemattan mah lefanim umah le'ahor. Kol sello has al kebod qono ratuy 10 ke'illu lo ba la'olam."* The subject of the merkavah found in M.Hag 2:1 is found further in the corresponding section of the Tosefta (T.Hag.2:1-7), and in the *gemara* to this to this Mishneh in *Yerushalmz* (hag.77a-d) and *Bavli* (Hag. 1 1 b-16a),22 These texts presume the dangers of this esoteric subject, for according to M. Hagigah 2: 1Merkavah may not be expounded (*en doresin bammerkabah*) except under special circumstantces, and according to Megilla 4: 10, it may not be used as a prophetic lection in the synagogue *(en maftirin hammerkabah).* Special knowledge of esoteric subjects, is reserved for a small group of initiates. Rabbinic anecdotes stress its secret and wondrous nature, and hazard for the pre-mature.

[509] Gitten 60b reads, "Devarim shebal'peh e atah rashaey lekatvatan mekan atah lemad shehatalmud lo netan lektov eleh mepeneai shehatorah meshtakchat.

[510] Rambam recalls a tradition in the Talmud attributed to Rabbi Simeon ben Lakish that the Merkavah are the *Avoi7* and which is recaitilated in *Zohar* 262b *Vaethhanan* where we read. *"Only HaShem had a delight in thy fathers (Devarim 15). Commenting on this, R. Simeon said that the patriarchs are the holy chariot above. As there is a holy chariot below, so there is a holy chariot above. And what is this? As we have said, the holy chariot is the name given to the Whole, all being linked together and made one. But the fathers are only three, and the chariot has four wheels. Who is the fourth? It says, 'And chose their seed after them', this includes David HaMelech, who is the fourth to complete the holy chariot, as we learnt, 'The patriarchs are the consummation of the whole, and the Body was completed through them that made one. Then David HaMelech came and perfected the whole and made firm the body and perfected it. Rabbi Yitzak said, 'As the patriarchs merited to be crowned with the holy chariot, so did David merit to be adorned with the fourth support of the chariot."* Philosophy is comprehension of the whole.

[511] Dubnov comments on these three rabbis placing a ban on Maimonides philosophical work when he writes, "Das dreigliedrige Rabbinerkollegium entschloß sich nun zu einem folgenschweren Schritt: es Verhangte den cherum ueber alle diejenigen, die sich mit Philosophie und mit profanen Wissenschaften ueberhaupt, insbesondere aber mit den philosophischen Werken des Maimonides (More Nevuchim und Sefer HaMada) befaBten, wie auch ueber solche, Die Ueberlieferungen der Bibel und des Talmud in rationalistischem Geiste auszulegen wagten (zu Beginn des Jahres 1232 See Dubnov, Simon, "Die Maimonisten und Ihre Gegner," Weltsges Des Judischen Volkes, 109; Touati puts it this way, "Vers 1230, un eminent rabbin de Montpellier, Solomon ben Abraham et ses deux eleves Rabbi Yonah Geronid and Rabbi David ben Saul, se decident a passer a l'action et a barrer la route a la speculation philosophique en interdisant sous peine d'excommunication, l'etude de Sefer Ha-Mada, l'introduction philosophique au code de Maimonides, celle du Guide et des sciences generals (175). ; These anti-Maimondeans sought th support of the Dominicans to enforce the Cencorship od Main on ides work. Graetz, employing a technique of the Thucydides, reconstructs a possible dialog between R. Solomon ben Abraham and R. Gerondi and the Dominicans by writing, "Ihr Verbrennt eure Ketzer, verflogt auch unsere." See: Graetz, Heinrich, "Maimuni's Schriften und die Inquisition", Geschichte Des Juden vol 7, 66 ; As to the rabbis appealing to the Dominicans, Dubnov gives the following lelengthier reconstruction of the dialog that may have taken place, "Wir wissen da Bes in unserer Stadt Viele Ketzer und Gottlose gibt, die sich durch die Lehre des Moses Aus Aegypten, des Verfassers ruchlosen philosophischen Buecher, verfuehren lieBen. Verilget ihr eure Ketzer, so vertilget mit ihnen auch die unseren und verbrenner die schaedlichen Buecher. ; see Dubnov, Simon, "Die Maimonisten und Ihre Gegner," Weltgeschichte des Judischen Volkes, 113

512 Chelton, Mary K., The Communicative Production of Institutional Authority: The Example of a library service encounter," Paper presented at annual conference of the Speech, Communication Association, San Diego, Nov. 1996

513 Kuhithau, Carol C. "Perceptions of the Information Search Process in Libraries: A Study of Changes from High School through College." Information Processing and Management 24, 1988, 419-27

514 Hanningan, Jane Anne, and Crew, Hillary, "A Feminist Paradigm for Library and Information Science", in Wilson Library Bulletin 67, Oct. 1993, p.28-32.

515 Hannigan, Jane Anne, and Crew Hillary, " A Feminist Paradigm for Library and Info Science", Wilson Library Bulletin 67, Oct 1993, p 31.

516 McCormick, Edith, "Image: Consulting on Saturn", in American Libraries 26, Oct 1995876.

517 Sapp, Greg, "The Librarian as Main Character: A Professional Sampler." Wilson Library Bulletin, 62, Jan 1987, p.135.

518 Newmyer, Jody, "The Image Problem of the Librarian: Femininity and Social Control" Journal of Library History 11, 1976, p. 47.

519 Sapp, Gregg, "The Librarian as Main Character: A Professional Sampler", Wilson Library Bulletin 61, Jan 1987, p. 29.

520 Seinfeld, "The Library", directed by Joshua White, 30 min, National broadcasting Company, tv broadcast, Oct. 16, 1991.

521 Seinfeld. "The Library" Directed by Joshua White, 30 min. National broadcasting Company, tv broadcast, Oct. 16, 1991

522 See http://databases.jewishlibraries.org/node/51186

523 Grafton, Anthony, The footnote : a curious history, Cambridge, Mass. : Harvard University Press, 1997

[524] See http://databases.jewishlibraries.org/node/51676

[525] Lyotard, Jean François, The postmodern condition, Minneapolis : University of Minnesota Press, 1984
Post-script: Libraries and Archives and the Technological Revolution: Ethical Disseratum
[this section appeared in the TC library blog posting at-
See https://tclibraryblog.wordpress.com/2018/01/24/libraries-archives-and-technology-in-post-modern-times/

My interest in the moral and ethical use of technology has led me to publish papers such as Moral and Ethical Concerns of the Online Environment, Halakhah and Netiquette, and Women and Responsible Use of the Online Environment, as to remain silent puts society at great risk.

On one hand, biotechnology has promoted the longevity and quality of life. For example, organ transplants and pain elimination enhance the value provided by the medical profession. Soon, advances in stem cell research and cloning may allow engineered biological enhancements (such as eye implants to enable night vision) and end diseases through reverse genetic engineering. Thus, we understand Friedrich Hölderlin's poetic verse in "Patmos": "Where the danger is, there is the saving power too." Of course, these new scientific advances raise many important ethical and moral questions in the rapid advance of biotechnology. See, for instance, our LibGuides on:
Humanistic Medicine, Jewish Ethics, Jews in Medicine, Internet and Online Ethics, and Philosophy of Science.
Yet, technology may be a two-edged sword. Technology exploited by sinister elements for nefarious ends could lead to nuclear Armageddon if the one-dimensional Marcusian Buberian I-IT relationship triumphs above all. What Nietzsche described as the "will to power" and Heidegger refers to as the essence of technology being Control (*Gestell*) means we must look thoughtfully and critically into this "two-edged sword" which has the power for both immense good and immense evil.